International and Development Education

The *International and Development Education Series* focuses on the complementary areas of comparative, international, and development education. Books emphasize a number of topics ranging from key international education issues, trends, and reforms to examinations of national education systems, social theories, and development education initiatives. Local, national, regional, and global volumes (single authored and edited collections) constitute the breadth of the series and offer potential contributors a great deal of latitude based on interests and cutting edge research. The series is supported by a strong network of international scholars and development professionals who serve on the International and Development Education Advisory Board and participate in the selection and review process for manuscript development.

SERIES EDITORS
John N. Hawkins
Professor Emeritus, University of California, Los Angeles
Senior Consultant, IFE 2020 East West Center

W. James Jacob
Assistant Professor, University of Pittsburgh
Director, Institute for International Studies in Education

PRODUCTION EDITOR
Heejin Park
Project Associate, Institute for International Studies in Education

INTERNATIONAL EDITORIAL ADVISORY BOARD
Clementina Acedo, *UNESCO's International Bureau of Education, Switzerland*
Philip G. Altbach, *Boston University, USA*
Carlos E. Blanco, *Universidad Central de Venezuela*
Sheng Yao Cheng, *National Chung Cheng University, Taiwan*
Ruth Hayhoe, *University of Toronto, Canada*
Wanhua Ma, *Peking University, China*
Ka-Ho Mok, *University of Hong Kong, China*
Christine Musselin, *Sciences Po, France*
Yusuf K. Nsubuga, *Ministry of Education and Sports, Uganda*
Namgi Park, *Gwangju National University of Education, Republic of Korea*
Val D. Rust, *University of California, Los Angeles, USA*
Suparno, *State University of Malang, Indonesia*
John C. Weidman, *University of Pittsburgh, USA*
Husam Zaman, *Taibah University, Saudi Arabia*

Institute for International Studies in Education
School of Education, University of Pittsburgh
5714 Wesley W. Posvar Hall, Pittsburgh, PA 15260 USA

Center for International and Development Education
Graduate School of Education & Information Studies, University of California, Los Angeles
Box 951521, Moore Hall, Los Angeles, CA 90095 USA

Titles:

Higher Education in Asia/Pacific: Quality and the Public Good
Edited by Terance W. Bigalke and Deane E. Neubauer

Affirmative Action in China and the U.S.: A Dialogue on Inequality and Minority Education
Edited by Minglang Zhou and Ann Maxwell Hill

Critical Approaches to Comparative Education: Vertical Case Studies from Africa, Europe, the Middle East, and the Americas
Edited by Frances Vavrus and Lesley Bartlett

Curriculum Studies in South Africa: Intellectual Histories & Present Circumstances
Edited by William F. Pinar

Higher Education, Policy, and the Global Competition Phenomenon
Edited by Laura M. Portnoi, Val D. Rust, and Sylvia S. Bagley

The Search for New Governance of Higher Education in Asia
Edited by Ka-Ho Mok

International Students and Global Mobility in Higher Education: National Trends and New Directions
Edited by Rajika Bhandari and Peggy Blumenthal

Curriculum Studies in Brazil: Intellectual Histories, Present Circumstances
Edited by William F. Pinar

Access, Equity, and Capacity in Asia Pacific Higher Education
Edited by Deane Neubauer and Yoshiro Tanaka

Policy Debates in Comparative, International, and Development Education
Edited by John N. Hawkins and W. James Jacob

Increasing Effectiveness of the Community College Financial Model: A Global Perspective for the Global Economy
Edited by Stewart E. Sutin, Daniel Derrico, Rosalind Latiner Raby, and Edward J. Valeau

Curriculum Studies in Mexico: Intellectual Histories, Present Circumstances
William F. Pinar

Internationalization of East Asian Higher Education: Globalization's Impact
Edited by John D. Palmer, Amy Roberts, Young Ha Cho, and Gregory S. Ching

Taiwan Education at the Crossroad: When Globalization Meets Localization
Chuing Prudence Chou and Gregory S. Ching

Mobility and Migration in Asian Pacific Higher Education
Edited by Deane E. Neubauer and Kazuo Kuroda

University Governance and Reform: Policy, Fads, and Experience in International Perspective
Edited by Hans G. Schuetze, William Bruneau, and Garnet Grosjean

Higher Education Regionalization in Asia Pacific: Implications for Governance, Citizenship, and University Transformation
Edited by John N. Hawkins, Ka Ho Mok, and Deane E. Neubauer

Post-Secondary Education and Technology: A Global Perspective on Opportunities and Obstacles to Development
Edited by Rebecca A. Clothey, Stacy Austin-Li, and John C. Weidman

Higher Education Regionalization in Asia Pacific

Implications for Governance, Citizenship, and University Transformation

Edited by
John N. Hawkins, Ka Ho Mok, and
Deane E. Neubauer

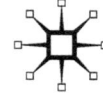

HIGHER EDUCATION REGIONALIZATION IN ASIA PACIFIC
Copyright © John N. Hawkins, Ka Ho Mok, and Deane E. Neubauer, 2012.

All rights reserved.

First published in 2012 by
PALGRAVE MACMILLAN®
in the United States—a division of St. Martin's Press LLC,
175 Fifth Avenue, New York, NY 10010.

Where this book is distributed in the UK, Europe and the rest of the world, this is by Palgrave Macmillan, a division of Macmillan Publishers Limited, registered in England, company number 785998, of Houndmills, Basingstoke, Hampshire RG21 6XS.

Palgrave Macmillan is the global academic imprint of the above companies and has companies and representatives throughout the world.

Palgrave® and Macmillan® are registered trademarks in the United States, the United Kingdom, Europe and other countries.

ISBN: 978–1–137–00287–7

Library of Congress Cataloging-in-Publication Data

    Higher education regionalization in Asia Pacific : implications for governance, citizenship and university transformation / John N. Hawkins, Ka Ho Mok and Deane E. Neubauer, editors.
       pages cm.—(International & development education)
   Includes bibliographical references.
   ISBN 978–1–137–00287–7
     1. Education, Higher—Asia. 2. Education, Higher—Pacific Area.
  I. Hawkins, John N. II. Mok, Ka-Ho, 1964– III. Neubauer, Deane E.

LA1058.H55 20121
378.0095—dc23   2012017752

A catalogue record of the book is available from the British Library.

Design by Newgen Imaging Systems (P) Ltd., Chennai, India.

First edition: November 2012

10 9 8 7 6 5 4 3 2 1

Transferred to Digital Printing in 2013

Contents

List of Figures and Tables   vii
Series Editors' Preface   ix
Acknowledgments   xi
List of Contributors   xiii

Part I   Conceptual Issues

1   Introduction: Some Dynamics of Regionalization in Asia-Pacific Higher Education   3
Deane E. Neubauer

2   A Conceptual Framework for the Regionalization of Higher Education: Application to Asia   17
Jane Knight

3   Regional Cooperation in Higher Education in Asia and the Pacific   37
Molly N. N. Lee

4   The Function of Regional Networks in East Asian Higher Education   45
Miki Sugimura

Part II   Country Studies

5   Japanese Higher Education and Multilateral Initiatives in East Asia   67
Akiyoshi Yonezawa and Arthur Meerman

6   China in the Emerging Reality of Asia Regional Higher Education   79
Wen Wen

7 Locating Indonesia within the Emergent Regionalism of
   Southeast Asian Higher Education   91
   Anthony R. Welch

8 The Philippines and the Global Labor Market: An
   Emergent Form of Trans-regional Influence on
   Philippine Higher Education   117
   Regina M. Ordonez

Part III Regulatory and Governance Dimensions

9 Cooperation and Competition in Tango: Transnationalization
   of Higher Education and the Emergence of Regulatory
   Regionalism in Asia   137
   Ka Ho Mok

10 Institutional Autonomy in the Restructuring of University
   Governance   161
   Molly Nyet Ngo Lee

11 The Challenges of Regionalism and Harmonization for
   Higher Education in Asia   177
   John N. Hawkins

12 The Dynamics of Regionalization in Contemporary
   Asia-Pacific Higher Education   191
   John N. Hawkins, Ka Ho Mok, and Deane E. Neubauer

Index   207

Figures and Tables

Figures

2.1	Conceptual mapping of higher education regionalization terms	26
2.2	Factors characterizing the HE regionalization process	28
2.3	Relationship among three approaches	29
2.4	Regionalization of higher education in Asia	31
2.5	Percentage choosing Asian identity in addition to national identity	33
6.1	Growth of international students in China (2000–2008)	82
6.2	Percentage of international students according to world regions	83
6.3	Origin countries of international students in China (2000–2008)	83
6.4	Origin regions/countries of international students in China (2000–2008)	84
6.5	Percentage of international students in degree and nondegree programs	85
6.6	Percentage of international students by field	86
8.1	Nine-month deployment	120
8.2	Nine-month deployment by type of work	120
8.3	Types of HEIs	123

Tables

7.1	Top ten source countries, Malaysian higher education, public and private, 2010	101
8.1	Growth of HEIs over 18 years, from 1992 to 2010	123
8.2	Criteria for determining the level of HEI	125
8.3	HEIs with accredited programs	126
8.4	Public and private HEIs by program accreditation level	126

Series Editors' Preface

One of the increasingly important trends in higher education in this era of global interdependence is the role of regionalization. Asia has been at the forefront of this trend as regions that historically emerged in human consciousness through the facts of geographic proximity and economic advantage are, through the dynamics of contemporary globalization, themselves being transformed as virtual portals to the increasingly relevant global commons and marketplace. This process of "new regionalization" is given form and substance for traditional regions within these global dynamics that have both push and pull factors. We are very pleased to be able to add to our series with the East West Center, this new volume on regionalization in Asia Pacific higher education offering both theoretical and applied studies of this phenomenon. From issues related to governance and citizenship to case studies of specific organizations, this volume offers new insights to both the potential and limits of regionalization and regionalism. Regionalization will continue to play a critical and at times controversial role in higher education development in the Asia Pacific region for both the public and private sectors.

JOHN N. HAWKINS
University of California,
Los Angeles

W. JAMES JACOB
University of Pittsburgh

Acknowledgments

The 2011 Senior Seminar held in Hong Kong in May of that year was in every respect a joint event in which the Hong Kong Institute for Education joined with the East–West Center of Honolulu to gather this distinguished group of scholars for a three-day meeting. The editors would like to give special thanks to Dr Anthony Chun, President of Hong Kong Institute for Education (HKIEd) for the support provided throughout the visit and for his intellectual contributions to the overall seminar. A similar expression of gratitude is due to Dr Terance Bigalke, Director of the Education Program at the East–West Center, for his support throughout this process and for his intellectual contributions as well. Two additional colleagues, Dr Krissanapong Kirtikara of Thailand and Professor Muhammad Mukhta provided presentations to the seminar that for various reasons did not make it into this volume.

We owe a special and continuing debt of gratitude to our Palgrave Macmillan editor, Kaylan Connally, and our senior editor Burke Gerstenschlager for their continuing support to the series in which this volume appears, along with Professor William James Jacobs who edits the series along with John N. Hawkins.

Finally, but hardly least, our continuing thanks to the staffs at both HKIEd and the East–West Center for their support in this endeavor. Whereas singling out a few individuals necessarily overlooks the contributions of others, we would like to note the efforts of So Lan Cathy Lau at HKIEd and Cheryl Hidano, Sandy Osaki, and Cynthia Yamane of the East–West Center. George E. Neubauer assisted with citation review and Larina Hawkins's last-minute help with graphs was a "day saver."

Contributors

John N. Hawkins is Professor Emeritus and Director of the Center for International and Development Studies at the Graduate School of Education and Information Studies at the University of California, Los Angeles (UCLA). He is also a consultant at the East West Center in Honolulu, Hawaii. He was Dean of International Studies at UCLA, has served as a Director of the UCLA Foundation Board, and as a Director of the East West Center Foundation Board. He is Chief Editor of the new Comparative Education Series of Palgrave MacMillan Press. He has served as President of the Comparative and International Education Society, and Editor of the Comparative Education Review. He is a specialist on higher education reform in the United States and Asia and the author of several books and research articles on education and development in Asia. His latest coedited book (with W. James Jacob) is *Policy Debates in Comparative, International and Development Education* published by Palgrave MacMillan Press (2011) and his latest journal article is: "Regionalization and Harmonization of Higher Education in Asia: Easier Said than Done," *Asian Education and Development Studies* (2012). He has conducted research throughout Asia since 1966 when he first visited the People's Republic of China and Japan.

Jane Knight, Ontario Institute for Studies in Education, University of Toronto, focuses her research and professional interests on the international dimension of higher education at the institutional, national, regional, and international levels. Her work in over 65 countries with universities, governments, UN agencies, and foundations helps to bring a comparative, development, and international perspective to her research, teaching, and policy work. She is the author of numerous articles and publications on higher education, a Fulbright New Century Scholar 2007–2008, received an honorary LLD from Exeter University in 2010, and sits on the advisory boards of many international organizations and journals.

Molly N. N. Lee is the recently retired (December 2011) Coordinator of the Asia-Pacific Programme of Educational Programme for Development

(APEID) and Program Specialist in Higher Education at UNESCO Asia and the Pacific Regional Bureau for Education in Bangkok. As the Coordinator of APEID, she ran programs on higher education, technical and vocational education, education for sustainable development, and Information and Computing Technology (ICT) in education. Prior to joining UNESCO Bangkok, she was a Professor of Education at the University of Science, Penang, Malaysia. Dr Lee has a PhD in International Development Education, a Master's degree in Sociology from Stanford University, and a Master's degree in Education Planning and Development from University of London Institute of Education. Her research interests are higher education, teacher education, ICT in education, and education for sustainable development. Her publications include: *Restructuring Higher Education in Malaysia*; *Private Higher Education in Malaysia*; *Malaysian Universities: Towards Equality, Accessibility, Quality*; *The Corporatisation of a Public University: Influence of Market Forces and State Control*; and *Global Trends, National Policies and Institutional Responses: Restructuring Higher Education*.

Arthur Meerman, has been working with Japanese learners of English in a wide variety of settings and capacities since arriving to Japan from Canada in 1994. His research has focused on administrative leadership in education and the administration of English-language education at Japanese public junior and senior high schools. He has also taken part in collaborative studies on selected psycholinguistic aspects of second-language acquisition among Japanese students of English at university level. He is currently Associate Professor at the Department of Intercultural Studies, Faculty of Literature, Kurume University.

Ka Ho Mok is Associate Dean and Professor at the Faculty of Social Sciences, University of Hong Kong. Before he joined the University of Hong Kong, he was a Chair Professor in East Asian Studies and the Founding Director of the Centre for East Asian Studies at the University of Bristol. His primary area of research is comparative education policy, with particular reference to development and education governance change in East Asia. Other research interests include social developments and social policy in contemporary China. His most recent books are *Changing Governance and Public Policy in East Asia* (2008); *Education Reform and Education Policy in East Asia* (2006); *Globalization and Higher Education in East Asia* (2005); *Globalization and Marketization: A Comparative Analysis of Hong Kong and Singapore* (2004); *Globalization and Educational Restructuring in the Asia and Pacific Region* (2003); and *Centralization and Decentralization: Educational Reforms and Changing Governance in Chinese Societies* (2003). He is currently Editor of the internationally refereed *Journal of Asian Public*

Policy and involved in editing special issues for international journals such as *Pacific Review, Globalization, Societies & Education, Asia Pacific Journal of Education, International Journal of Educational Management*, and *Policy Futures in Education*. He has also published extensively in the fields of comparative education policy, governance and public administration, and social development in contemporary China and East Asia.

Deane E. Neubauer is Emeritus Professor of Political Science at the University of Hawaii, Manoa (UHM), Senior Research Scholar at the Globalization Research Center (UHM), and Senior Advisor to the International Forum for Education 2020 of the East–West Center. He holds degrees in political science from the University of California, Riverside (BA, 1962) and Yale University (MA, PhD, 1965). His interests lie in the analysis of public affairs ranging from policy processes, health care, food security, education, and more recently the development and conduct of globalization. His current work examines the varieties of national policy expressions in health care, food security, and education within the contemporary dynamics of globalization with particular attention to nations in the Asia/Pacific region. He has served as Dean of Social Sciences and Interim Chancellor at UHM, and as Interim Vice President for the ten-campus University of Hawaii system. He has also been active in higher education accreditation since 1985 having served on the Western Association for Schools and Colleges Senior Commission from 1995 to 2001.

Regina (Gina) M. Ordonez is a management and education consultant and researcher whose professional work has focused on socioeconomic development projects in the Philippines. As head of the firm, Quantum Learning Institute, she has designed and facilitated training programs and planning workshops for corporations and nongovernmental organizations (NGOs) in the fields of strategic management and human resource development. She has assisted educational institutions and teachers in developing curricula and culturally appropriate teaching materials in both basic and higher education. She taught Human Behavior and Organizational Development in the master-level programs of the Asian Institute of Management and De La Salle University—Manila in the Philippines. She holds a Master's degree in Educational Psychology and in Business Administration from US universities, and has pursued a doctoral degree in Governance.

Miki Sugimura, is Associate Professor, Department of Education, Faculty of Human Sciences, Sophia University. She worked for National Institute for Education Policy Research in Japan and Center for the Study of International Cooperation in Education, Hiroshima University, as a research fellow. She started to work for Sophia University from 2002. She has been involving in (1) international research project on *Comparative Education Research on International Human Mobility and Change of Multicultural Societies* by JSPS Scientific Research Grant (2011–2014) and (2) international research project on *Higher Education and Human Resource Development for Peace Building and Sustainable Development in Post-Conflict Sri Lanka: International Collaborative Research on Comparative Study with the Case of Malaysia* by Toyota Foundation Research Grant (2011–2013) as a project leader.

Anthony R. Welch is Professor of Education, University of Sydney. A policy specialist, with extensive publications in numerous languages, he has consulted to state, national, and international governments and agencies, and US institutions and foundations, particularly in higher education. Substantial project experience includes East and Southeast Asia. A Fulbright *New Century Scholar* on higher education (2007–2008), he has also been Visiting Professor in the United States, the United Kingdom, Germany, France, Japan, and Hong Kong (China). His most recent books are *The Professoriate: Profile of a Profession* (2005); *Education, Change and Society* (2007, 2010); *ASEAN Industries and the Challenge from China* (2011); and *Higher Education in Southeast Asia* (2011). Professor Welch also directs the national research project, *The Chinese Knowledge Diaspora*.

Wen Wen has the Bachelor's and Master's degree in liberal arts and education, respectively, from Tsinghua University, Beijing. After receiving the Dphil degree in Education from Oxford in 2010, Dr Wen Wen has been working at the Institute of Educational Research, Tsinghua University, China, as a lecturer. Her research interest is mainly in education policy, sociology of education, and critical discourse analysis.

Akiyoshi Yonezawa is Associate Professor at the Graduate School of International Development (GSID), Nagoya University. With a sociological background, he is mainly researching comparative higher education policies, especially focusing on world-class universities, quality assurance in higher education, and the relationship between the public and private spheres of higher education. Before moving to Nagoya University in October 2010, he worked at Tohoku University, the National Institution for Academic Degrees and University Evaluation (NIAD-UE), Hiroshima University, Organization for Economic Co-operation and Development (OECD), and Tokyo University.

Part I

Conceptual Issues

Chapter 1

Introduction: Some Dynamics of Regionalization in Asia-Pacific Higher Education

Deane E. Neubauer

As the past three decades in particular have demonstrated, the phenomenon we conventionally term contemporary globalization is complexly constituted out of a series of dynamics that interact to produce outcomes that are themselves complex, intensely interactive, and in many instances productive of unexpected (and some would suggest unpredictable) outcomes (Hershock 2011). It is increasingly difficult to identify areas of contemporary society that are not profoundly affected by these dynamics; so it is unsurprising to include education in general and higher education in specific within generalization. The essays that constitute this volume are part of a continuing effort on the part of the East–West Center to focus on various aspects of these higher education changes through a series of annual scholarly meetings organized through a program called the International Forum for Education 2020 (IFE 2020).[1] The problematic of this effort is both simple and profound: It is asserted that many aspects of the world—as a direct consequence of the changes being wrought by contemporary globalization—are changing more rapidly than higher education. The purpose of these scholarly activities is to assist in the mapping and articulation of these changes with the focus of this particular collection being the emergent form that regionalization is taking throughout Asia and the Pacific and its relevance to higher education. Across the many dimensions of regional transformation that are touched upon, those affecting governance issues and elements of institutional change are emphasized.

The host of factors associated with this stage of globalization, to name just a few including production, consumption, resource acquisition and movement, transportation, human resource development and education, communication, knowledge production, and finance, have forced a recalibration of what regionalization means in this current and dynamic context. Perhaps foremost among the macro factors that continue to define this particular age are emergent trends in population movements (between and within countries) and the progressive distribution and redistribution of service-based economic activities across the world. Cross-cutting these trends has been the rise and fall over time of various concepts of *regionalism*, the normative and sometimes ideological articulation of how regional entities *should* be conceptualized or drawn together in presumptive common purposes.

In contrast, the concerns of this chapter (and this volume) focus primarily on past, present, and emergent dynamics of *regionalization*, a distinction focused on the presumption that it (in contrast to regionalism) can be supported more usefully by the identification and engagement of various empirical dimensions of interaction among the units presumed to constitute the regional focus. (For an extended discussion of this distinction, see Jane Knight's contribution to this volume, Chapter 2, and John Hawkins, Chapter 11.) Critical vectors within these patterns of movement and activity associated with the regionalization of higher education have been the aggregation and social expression of the whole range of activities that we find convenient to bundle together under the label of "the knowledge society" and the social activities that have led to broad patterns of migration and mobility as delineated patterns of contemporary society (Kuroda and Neubauer 2012). As an activity, higher education within the Asia-Pacific region has exhibited distinctive new forms as it is aggregated along multiple dimensions.

Transformations within Regionalization

Like most such explorations, this one can profitably begin with an exercise in concept clarification.

Regionalization has traditionally been viewed within the dual frames of proximity and patterns of exchange, dimensions that in turn have been conceptualized and actualized along prevailing norms of time and space. Historically, as an organizational form within Asia, the Association of South East Asian Nations (ASEAN) has been an exemplar. These frames have been useful for capturing various differentiated senses of both regionalism and regionalization historically within countries or nation states, as well as to identify and demark multinational aggregations characteristic of regionalization, particularized either by relative geographical affinity or by a specific pattern of exchange (e.g., currency, trade in goods, among others). One might also generalize and see exchange in many aspects as synonymous with "interactions" or patterns of interaction, thereby following the original work several decades ago of Karl Deutsch, which proved so useful in tracking and empirically examining the process toward European nationalism and subsequent regionalization and integration (Deutsch 1966). In a sense, we might refer to this as the "old notion" of regionalization, by which we would mean commonly proffered and accepted references to both proximity and patterns of exchange, with geographic locations and nation-state centralities predominating.

The dramatic reordering of time and space wrought by contemporary globalization over the past five decades has recast many of these more familiar ideas of regionalization and brought novel forms into play. For example, if notions of proximity are linked to those of time, as Harvey would argue (Harvey 1989), it is clear that important aspects of the world have entered a stage of simultaneity wherein for vast numbers of discrete exchanges and engagements across time and space, all are equally proximate. (To take just one example, the software development world is now termed the 24-hour digital workshop, representing the ways by which a code can be developed in one geographic part of the world during portions of the day and debugged and refined in another during other hours. This phenomenon represents as well the growth of a "singular language" of software development, marking yet another transformation in customary notions of regionalization [Jalote and Jain 2006].) Within this revised frame, the notion of geographic proximity as the primary marker for regionalism lessens in relative importance. Something similar begins to happen with concepts of exchange, both large and small. "Old" regionalization, demarked by geographic determination within and among nations, tended to focus on exchange in part as a result of the historical relevance and limitation of transportation and communication systems (including language).

In contemporary regionalization—"new regionalization" if you will—much exchange operates almost irrespective of older separation entities and their physical, social, and national borders. Rather, exchange enables nation states to expand, contract, and change direction as economic entities as a result of interactions that are initiated from afar and often effectuated within national settings in novel ways. Within policy discourse, for example, it has been an accepted proposition for well over three decades that important elements of a national policy agenda would be established and provided their particular dynamics by the placement of that nation with these various networks of economic, social, technical, communicative engagement, what Sakia Sassen has featured in her analyses as circuits of exchange (Sassen 2004). The essential point in this observation is that what is regional in many areas of the lived life of a national society and economy may owe more to its placement within the circuits of exchange than its historical placement in some geographically based scheme of classification.

Viewed from this perspective, "old regionalization" and the things that may have characterized it persist as a form of legacy association, continuing to link former dominant patterns of proximity and exchange as one "fraction" of the current overall pattern of interaction with which given "locales" are associated (or as Castells would have it, they are situated along many multiple dimensions through a vast variety of nodes within the networks they both constitute and share. See Castells 2009). These are supplemented in multiple ways, some more obvious and observable than others, by more novel patterns of association and interaction. It is in this sense that we are asserting the emergence of new forms of regionalization. But as the foregoing suggests, it would be a mistake to view these "new" forms as somehow totally replacing former ones. Rather, the newer forms grow and emerge out of the legacy forms, carrying forward some aspects while leaving others behind.

One dramatic illustration of this process in contemporary Asia can be found in the underlying dynamics of the political economies of those countries and societies located in this historical geographic space. In the period of the 1970s and through to the mid-1990s, several countries of the geographic region of Southeast Asia and surroundings had emerged as early suppliers to the global technology and electronics industries (including health care, communications, etc.). In several notable instances, they had become prime examples of an increasing ability to combine offshore direct investment with technology, bundled with relatively low labor costs and novel production designs—in other words, early adopters of what would become the dominant pattern of offshoring for more developed economies. In many instances, several of these countries—Singapore, Thailand, Indonesia, and Taiwan, to name four in particular—had managed to develop specific market niches for finished products for export, thereby leveraging themselves to a most desirable place in the overall profit structure. Within ten years however of the opening of China to the global economy, China had largely replaced these economies as end-use producers and relegated them primarily to the status of prominent part producers, thereby reducing their relative status on the profit ladder of production (a condition from which Singapore and Taiwan have in large part successfully recovered). China has of course come to dominate the whole of the regional political economy, thereby significantly changing what "it is" within any regional frame (Weiss 2005).

In general, we can suggest that old regionalization (and in this case, regionalism as well, e.g., ASEAN) was most clearly characterized by "similar" countries banding together in familiar forms, most of these of governmental origin. In contrast, new regionalization tends to link legacy structures with newer interregional forms (e.g., Asia Pacific Economic Cooperation, APEC). As suggested, largely as a result of the overall dynamics of globalization itself, this new regionalization has been given its rationale and supplied many of its mechanisms (e.g., World Trade Organization [WTO] and its various trade agreements, particularly the General Agreement on Trade and Services [GATS]) by subscribing to the tenets of neoliberalism while supplementing these widely by other mechanisms and agreements more characteristic of legacy forms, such as bilateral trade agreements, in which Asia now leads the world (Naya and Plummer 2005; Steger and Roy 2010). Elements of this form of regionalization are already in effect in an institutionalized form in such instances as the Asia-Europe Meeting (ASEM), the Asia Cooperation Dialogue (ACD), and ASEAN + 3. Indeed, we might see these and other similar developments, such as the evolving Greater China Region, elements of East Asia cooperation with the four Asian tigers, along with ASEAN + 3 as a new form of subregionalism(s) that is emerging within the new regionalization. (For an extended analysis of this argument and other related points, see Ka Ho Mok's Chapter 9 in this volume that focuses on the regulatory and governance dimensions of these transformations.)

Regionalization and Higher Education

When one turns to the emergent process of higher education regionalization within the Asia-Pacific region, it is clear that European examples have considerable appeal as discrete efforts to promote regional cooperation and more often are explicitly based on the features of both the Erasmus and Bologna processes. The South East Asian Ministers of Education Organization (SEAMEO) was an early manifestation of a regionally focused educational endeavor (albeit with strong legacy ties to older regionalization). Increasingly, it has evolved into a newer regional focus with an explicit emphasis on tying its member countries and their higher education institutions (HEIs) to a globalized problematic. In another quite different form, the current emphasis within China to realize the idea of "the Greater China" may also represent a newer form of regionalization, albeit with strong elements of older forms (i.e., ASEAN), but now with a strong cultural overlay.

This globalization problematic in turn gives rise to various ideas of governance that may emerge from this "new" regionalization.

Regulatory Frames

The examples given immediately above suggest new and emerging modes of governance within a regulatory frame. It is a truism that all HEIs situated within the state admit to various forms of regulation. Conceptually, these can be viewed on a continuum of strong to weak, wherein strong regulation refers to a model (and practices) in which the state controls authorization of HEIs, owns them, finances them, and appoints regulators for them who exercise the administrative functions of the institutions. This form was both familiar and once dominant for public institutions in China, Japan, Korea, Indonesia, Thailand, and other parts of Asia as higher education emerged in the modern period. Even within strong forms of governance, however, private institutions often were permitted, albeit only within the writ and strictures of state authorization. With the advent of liberalization as the policy form for neoliberal restructuring, many regimes moved to a weaker and mixed-mode form of regulation in which both the domestic private sector and external entities are permitted into what becomes reconceptualized as a higher education "market," the explicit purposes of which are to link higher education to the employment, technologic, and knowledge needs of the economy, and as an explicit item of trade (Tilak 2012). This pattern has developed in some form or another throughout the Asia Pacific, albeit with significant local–national variation, and has radically affected the overall dimensions through which higher education is financed and placed within public policy as a market commodity.

With this movement toward relatively weaker national regulatory regimes has emerged an effort to develop regional processes of regulation, initially at the weaker end of the continuum. One example of this development focuses on issues of quality within higher education with emphases on accreditation and quality assurance, inasmuch as notions of *standards* are key to any pattern—proposed or actual—of regulatory practice. Within the region, stimulated by multiple efforts on the part of the United Nations Education, Scientific, and Cultural Organization (UNESCO) to promote a version of both global and regional higher education *engagement*, the Asia-Pacific Quality Network (APQN) was established in 2003 with 51 members from across Asia and the Pacific, and has grown rapidly to its current cohort of 61 members representing 26 countries. It has recently been a recipient of a grant to create a Global Initiative on Quality Assurance Capacity (GIQAC), sponsored by the World Bank through UNESCO (APQN 2012), and appears to be following a path that will take it forward from its formative stages as an associational structure with a relatively strong focus on information sharing and value-adding activities for members (e.g., joint meetings, scholarly and policy papers, and the creation of a library of good practices) and a strong focus on capacity building among members. This, incidentally, is close to the model that historically produced the American regional accrediting associations, which were member organizations operating within the private-not-for-profit policy space, even though this higher educational activity is rarely viewed as a demonstration of a successful model of regionalization of an essential element of higher education. The fact that the United States has never had the equivalent of a Ministry of Education, but nevertheless was faced with very similar issues of how to promote higher education coherence within a universe of 50 separate and quite different state government cultures and policy structures, renders this a case of more than casual interest within a world increasingly characterized by very similar structural elements for higher education. In the case of the resulting six regional higher education accrediting bodies, association members were HEIs, not as in the case of APQN, primarily quality assurance agencies (Eaton 2005). As Wen Wen argues in her contribution to this volume (Chapter 6), this "soft" regulatory impulse can be seen throughout the region as HEIs continue to seek new vehicles for development, responding to global signals and pressures to be competitive, and to meet emergent quality standards in the global cross-border education market.

A more recent example of an entity with greater substantive cross-border/regional regulatory pretenses is the series of talks and meetings among Japan, China, and Korea, fashioned as "Campus Asia," aimed in the direction of promoting more effective higher education student exchanges based in part on some common articulation framework (Ministry of Education, Culture, Sports, Science and Technology 2010). This, of course, is one of the central features of the Bologna Process and arises out of the many aspects of increased interdependency promoted by contemporary globalization and increasing levels of exchanges that result. In a manner that almost exactly parallels the policy "problem" of other large, complex, and differentiated HEIs, to be capable of facilitating and ultimately to *maximize* the whole of a system's institutional capacity requires a common system of value and exchange—a common currency as it were. Within higher education, this process takes the form of articulation and mutual recognition agreements, which in reality are complex interactions between elements of a system to discover signifiers of value and then work to hold their use value and applications constant throughout that system. The most recent example of this is the somewhat controversial decision by the University of Tokyo to revise its academic calendar to align with that of most HEIs in the United States and Europe, as well as some in Asia (a process motivated in large part by Japan's desire to recruit larger numbers of international students from both of these markets). This will likely cause a shift in the entire higher education system in Japan. When such pretenses are at the core of a higher education system of value and exchange, the regulatory *politics* can be strong or weak, just as the structures themselves can be strong or weak.

Affinities and Common Purposes

SEAMEO, initially founded in 1965, describes itself as "a chartered international organisation (sic) whose purpose is to promote cooperation in education, science and culture in the Southeast Asian region" (SEAMEO 2012a, 2012b). Within the frame we are developing here, the primary purpose of the organization can be viewed as capacity building within an overall structure of value-added activities for its members. This type of regionalization situated well toward the weak-regulation end of the regulatory continuum and seeking to provide the means to greater economic and social development becomes inextricably bound up with other processes of integration, such as exchanges of technology, knowledge specialists, and efforts to promote student mobility, all of which are increasingly the common fare of higher education throughout the region as amply detailed in the chapters that follow.

Structural

Regulatory endeavors such as those mentioned above are significant (one might even argue crucial!) to the development of more tangible forms of regionalization in which the focus shifts away from the regulatory function and toward the "delivery" function. Within this frame, we would point to instances of regional structures that have been developed and are either operating for the performance of the traditional functions of higher education (teaching, research, and knowledge conservation), but with an explicit regional purpose, or have been established to develop novel educational activities (such as joint public sector–private sector research, innovation, and production). Examples of the former may be ongoing efforts in Hong Kong, Singapore, and Malaysia to constitute themselves as de facto knowledge "entities" (hubs) that not only take a discrete form, but also constitute the basis for novel regimes of regulation and governance (Mok and Ong 2011; Tan 2011).

Governance

As the Hong Kong, Singapore, and Malaysia examples make clear, at some point in the process of movement from strong to weak on the regulatory and/or affiliation continua, the two, much like a double helix, move across each other, only because in both concept and practice, regulation and governance are never far from each other as means for promoting desired outcomes.

The phenomena that we are seeking to embrace with these concepts require continuous elaboration and experimentation. The following lines of inquiry are critical:

1. What are various ways to describe regionalization such that they capture the full range of activities being undertaken within the higher education community? Can a useful typology of regionalization be constructed that may (in a best-case scenario) become a *default* frame of reference for discussion and research? Like any good typology, this should be linked to conceptual elements (theoretical soundness) as well as yield empirical veracity, and (ideally) surprising and perhaps unexpected implications. (See, for example, Tomblin and Colgan's efforts to extend the empirical referents of regionalism in a global context with particular emphases on implications for the policy process [Tomblin and Colgan 2004].)
2. In what ways throughout the region is this impression toward the regionalization of higher education producing or stimulating new and demonstrable examples of governance? Within this frame, how is governance conceived of and executed? Is there, for example, palpable evidence of convergence in structures, policies, and activities? Are governance constituencies affected bringing new players into governance relationships? (And if so, is their participation authentic or largely symbolic—a critical question when such new constituents may be faculty, students, families of students, employers, consumers of higher education research, etc.) If new constituents are brought into the governance process, how are roles and functions apportioned among them? What are the kinds of structures that are/may be emerging of which these governance activities are themselves a part?
3. What is the relationship of these emerging governance "activities" to established forms of governance, that is, the state and formal international and multinational associations (e.g., ASEAN)? Are they on a trajectory to clash with these more familiar forms? To supplement them? To supplant them? Or are interactions of such a form such that mergers might occur? In other forms of regionalization, as elements of governance move outward to include more elements of traditional authorization (such as licensing and recognition of rights to participate in ranges of practice), issues of balancing these new writs of authority

with existing structures often prove contentious—a dynamic we have witnessed in a number of cases—for example, in the emergence of nation states out of regional elements, and which we find repeated across broad ranges of multinational organizational forms. Given that higher education as a form of authorization activity has historically stood so close to the state for its legitimacy, and given that as a policy and political sector activity, it is relatively weak in terms of other competitors for governance authority (such as the military and forces of finance for example), it seems prudent to ask how higher levels of presumptive regional integration may evoke new governance calculi that may affront the traditional balance of political forces.

4. How do these forms appear to migrate? Easily or with difficulty? For example, might a Bologna-type accord be a possibility for some quantum of new regional governance activity for a few countries, but not for others? What might be the critical determinants of such relative ease of migration? Might, for example, such activities be a source of new subregionalism, or new "currencies of exchange" such as that represented by the Programme for International Student Assessment (PISA) process? Might not this be a critical arena in which international accreditation, especially for professional programs, comes into play? At the institutional level, does developing regionalism account for a migration and emulation of institutional forms for both governance *and* academic endeavors? If so, what might be the characteristic forms of such emulation, especially with respect to governance modalities? Will there be a distinctive regionalism "with Asian characteristics"?

Within the range of these constructs of regulation, governance, and restructuralizing of higher education, it would, however, be an error to overdetermine the role that regionalization, as I have framed it, accounts for the vast changes occurring within the sector. Indeed, reflecting back on the earlier argument of the chapter, the vast and in many ways still unchartered dynamics of globalization that have become inseparable (a la Harvey's collapse of time and space) with transnationalization, digitization, the growth of the "global university," and more, have affected the "status" of higher education throughout the world and contributed a largely new and far-reaching discourse about quality, global rankings, and "substance" within higher education that has implications for all of these regional related activities. (See in this regard Marginson 2007; Liu 2011; Robertson and Olds 2011.)

5. Historically, within the frame of the nation state over the past two or more centuries, the conjunction of regional affinity, exchange

propensity, and a common regulatory regime has occurred inseparably from the phenomenon of citizenship. To be a citizen has meant to have rights and responsibilities linked to a specific governing entity, always associated with territoriality. (Although again, as with federated nation states and now with the European Union, such territoriality can itself be viewed as a strong to a weak constraint on activity and movement. The American experience with the dual origination of citizenship with state and federal constitutions is instructive in this regard.) Will the emerging governance activities of *regionalism* bring forth identifications that make de facto citizenship rights and responsibilities a possibility? With higher education as the focus, what might be some of the elements of such a possibility? And how far within this frame can regionalization proceed across variations of outcomes arising from normatively and often ideologically propelled regionalisms?

6. How have individual nations/HEIs coped with this evolving regionalization? How have the HEIs themselves responded to these push–pull factors, either with constructive engagement or resistance? It is important to remember that there continue to exist powerful national, cultural, and historical forces of resistance to meaningful regionalization in the region suggesting that it will likely occur in a series of "small steps" rather than the establishment of dramatically new meta-organizations (see John Hawkins's Chapter 11 in this volume). How, we need to ask, have specific regional organizations of either the old or the new type impacted HEIs particularly with respect to their governance strategies? Efforts are multiplying within the Asian region to promote examples and instances of best practice that assist in answering these questions. What we are seeing is a culture of evidence emerging with respect to the playing out of these dynamics of regionalization in higher education from which, with continuing research, we will be able to begin a systematic comparison of these Asian processes of regionalization with those in other places and on other dimensions.

Conclusion

These views of the new and evolving regionalization enveloping higher education in the Asia region have developed out of what has essentially been a regional totality marked by complex regional demographics, but with key nations providing steadily increasing populations and expanding economies that demand better-educated workforces and a global economy that has itself been transforming in the direction of privileging knowledge skills and innovation as it continually expands. These have been central elements of the centripetal forces that have brought nations and subregions in closer contact to seek increased regional cooperation. However, as much of the world outside of Asia enters what appears to be a period of decided uncertainty in terms of both economic development and governance coherence, this "external environment" may do much to energize the centrifugal forces that move nation states away from further cooperation and regional association. At least historically, this has been the dynamic in past periods of economic distress, when economies are likely to emphasize competition over cooperation. The critical questions may be lodged, yet once again, in what already over the past three or four decades has proved to be recurring issues of how increased global interdependence simultaneously creates and articulates these forces of contraction and expansion in both national and regional economies. It is probably not so bold to suggest that in terms of the next decade or so, the economic and demographic forces within Asia that have already done so much to transform higher education in the region will only gain momentum and provide inputs to the global system that become in some respect singular. This has already been the case as Asia presents to other regions of the world in such areas as cross-border education (Lewin 2012). One can predict with some confidence that such effects will also be observed along other dimensions of higher education impacts both within the symbolic regions created by global circuits of exchange and the legacy constructs of historical regionalization. Collectively, our research and inquiries into these dynamics—so critical for an understanding of the courses that higher education is taking in Asia—are indeed in early stages of development.

NOTE

1. Papers from the first three seminars have been published in Peter D. Hershock, Mark Mason, and John N. Hawkins, eds, *Changing Education: Leadership, Innovation and Development in a Globalizing Asia Pacific*. Hong Kong: Springer, 2007. Those from the fourth seminar have been published as a special issue of *The Journal of Asian Public Policy* 1 (2), 2008. Papers from the fifth seminar have been published in Terance W. Bigalke and Deane E. Neubauer, *Higher Education in Asia/Pacific: Quality and the Public Good*. New York: Palgrave Macmillan, 2009. Papers from the sixth seminar were published in Deane E. Neubauer and Yoshiro Tanaka, *Access, Equity and Capacity in Asia Pacific Higher Education*. New York: Palgrave Macmillan, 2011. Those from the seventh

seminar were published as Deane E. Neubauer, *The Emergent Knowledge Society and the Future of Higher Education: Asian Perspectives*. London and New York: Routledge, 2011. A selection from the eighth seminar has been published as a special edition of *Asian Education and Development Studies* 1 (1), 2011.

References

Asia Pacific Quality Network. 2012. Global Initiative on Quality Assurance Capacity (GIQAC), sponsored by the World Bank through UNESCO. Available at: www.apqn.org/about/giqac/. Accessed February 8, 2012.

Bigalke, Terance W., and Deane E. Neubauer, eds. 2009. *Higher Education in Asia Pacific: Quality and the Public Good*. New York: Palgrave Macmillan.

Castells, Manuel. 2009. *Communication Power*. Oxford: Oxford University Press.

Deutsch, Karl. 1966. *Nationalism and Social Communication: An Inquiry into the Foundations of Nationality*. 2nd ed. Cambridge: MIT Press.

Eaton, Judith. 2005. "An Overview of US Accreditation." Council for Higher Education Accreditation. Available at: www.chea.org/. Accessed November 15, 2010.

Harvey, David. 1989. *The Condition of Postmodernity*. Oxford: Oxford University Press.

Hershock, Peter. 2011. "Information and Innovation in a Global Knowledge Society." In *The Emergent Knowledge Society and the Future of Higher Education: Asian Perspective*, ed. Deane E. Neubauer. London and New York: Routledge, 2011.

Jalote, Pankaj, and Gourav Jain. 2006. "Assigning Tasks in a 24-hour Software Development Model." *Journal of Systems and Software*, 79 (7), July: 904–911.

Lewin, Tamar. 2012. "Taking More Seats on Campus, Foreigners Also Pay the Freight." *New York Times*, February 5, 2012. Available at: www.nytimes.com/2012/02/05/education/international-students-pay-top-dollar-at-us-colleges.html?_r=1&emc=eta1. Accessed February 9, 2012.

Liu, Nian Cai. 2011. "The Phenomenon of Academic Ranking of World Universities Model: Future Directions." Paper presented to the APEC Conference on Quality in Higher Education: Identifying, Developing and Sustaining Best Practices in the APEC Region, Honolulu, Hawaii, August 4–6, 2011.

Marginson, Simon. 2007. "Global University Rankings." In *Prospects of Higher Education: Globalization, Market Competition, Public Goods and the Future of the University*, ed. S. Marginson. Rotterdam: Sense Publications.

Ministry of Education, Culture, Sports, Science and Technology-Japan. 2010. "CAMPUS Asia" Launched as First Japan-China-Korea Committee for Promoting www.mext.go.jp/english/koutou/1292773.htm. Accessed November 28, 2010.

Mok, Ka Ho, and Kok Chung Ong. 2011. "Asserting Brain Power and Expanding Education Services: Searching for New Governance and Regulatory Regimes in Singapore and Hong Kong, " in *The Emergent Knowledge Society and the*

Future of Higher Education: Asian Perspectives, ed. Deane E. Neubauer. New York: Routledge.
Naya, Seiji F., and Michael G. Plummer. 2005. *The Economics of the Enterprise for ASEAN Initiative*. Singapore: Institute for South East Asia Studies.
Neubauer, Deane E., and Kazuo Kuroda, eds. 2012. *Migration and Mobility in Asia-Pacific Higher Education*. New York: Palgrave Macmillan.
Neubauer, Deane E., and Yoshiro Tanaka, eds. 2011. *Access, Equity and Capacity in Asia Pacific Higher Education*. New York: Palgrave Macmillan.
Robertson, Susan, and Kris Olds. 2011. "Global Higher Ed: Surveying the Construction of Global Knowledge/Spaces for the 'Knowledge Economy,' " Blog Editors of *AboutHigherEd*. Available at: http://globalhighered.wordpress.com/about/. Accessed February 13, 2012.
Sassen, Saskia. 2004. "Economic Globalization and World Migration as Factors in the Mapping of Today's Advanced Urban Economy." Paper commissioned for the Globalization Research Network, www.global.grn.org. Available at: http://globalgrn.files.wordpress.com/2009/08/sassen.pdf. Accessed June 12, 2010.
SEAMEO. 2012a. "What is SEAMEO?" Available at: www.seameo.org/index.php?option=com_content&task=view&id=25&Itemid=31. Accessed February 8, 2010.
SEAMEO. 2012b. "Strategic Goals." Available at: www.seameo.org/index.php?option=com_content&task=view&id=25&Itemid=31. Accessed February 8, 2012.
Steger, Manfred, and Ravi K. Roy. 2010. *Neoliberalism—A Very Brief Introduction*. Oxford: Oxford University Press.
Tan, Eng Chye. 2011. "The National University of Singapore's (NUS) Mission to be a Leading Global University." Paper presented to the Quality in Higher Education: Identifying, Developing, and Sustaining Best Practices in the APEC Region Conference, Honolulu, August 2011. Available at: http://publications.apec.org/publication-detail.php?pub_id=1204. Accessed February 8, 2012.
Tilak, Jandhyala B. G. 2012. *Trade in Higher Education: The Role of the General Agreement in Trade and Services (GATS)*. Paris: International Institute for Educational Planning, UNESCO.
Tomblin Stephen G., and Charles S. Colgan. 2004. *Regionalism in a Global Society: Persistence and Change in Atlantic Canada*. Toronto: University of Toronto Press.
Weiss, John. 2005. "China and Its Neighbors: Evolving Patterns of Trade and Investment." Asian Development Bank. Available at: www.brad.ac.uk/acad/bcid/research/**China/WeissChina**ppt.pdf. Accessed October 13, 2011.

Chapter 2

A Conceptual Framework for the Regionalization of Higher Education: Application to Asia

Jane Knight

Introduction

Increasing Emphasis on Intra-regional Cooperation

There is no question that the international dimension of higher education has transformed the higher education landscape in the last two decades. The more globalized and interconnected world in which we live has stimulated higher education institutions (HEIs), organizations, and national governments to pay more attention to academic relations and opportunities with partners in other countries (Knight 2008). A more recent development has been an increased focus on higher education collaboration and exchange within a region. In Asia for example, the expansion in the number of regional research and university networks, the growth in intra-regional student mobility and institutional agreements, the new emphasis on regional quality assurance frameworks, and the rise in joint education programs are testimony to the growing importance of Asian regionalization of higher education (Yavaprabhas 2010; Kuroda et al. 2011). In fact, the movement to increased intra-regional cooperation and harmonization of national systems is occurring in all regions of the world. The well-known Bologna Process, which aims to create a common higher education space in Europe, has stimulated more attention being given to the importance of both intra-regional and interregional cooperation in higher education.

Four Lines of Inquiry

A review of academic articles and gray literature, such as policy documents, working papers, and conference reports, reveals a vibrant debate on the topic of regions and their importance, formation, and function. It is interesting to note the different interpretations and permutations of the concept of region. Frequently used terms include regionalism, regionalness, regionality, regionalization, regional integration, interregional cooperation, and so on, to name a few. It is clear that region constitutes the root concept and the suffixes introduce subtle and nuanced differences in meaning. For example, the suffix "ism" relates more to an ideology or set of beliefs, "ization" focuses on the process of becoming, and "tion" reflects a condition. An examination of these terms and how they relate to the higher education sector leads to four lines of inquiry. These different lines of inquiry are: (1) the impact of regionalism on higher education; (2) higher education regionalization; (3) higher education as an instrument for regional integration; and (4) interregional cooperation in higher education.

The "impact of *regionalism* on higher education" focuses on how the changing notion and increasing importance of a region is affecting higher education. It can lead to a type of trend analysis where higher education is seen in more of a reactive position to the increasingly significant influence of regionalism. *Higher education regionalization* introduces the process of intentionally building connections and relationships among higher education actors and systems in a region. Regionalization attributes more of a proactive role and "agency" to higher education. *Higher education as a tool for regional integration* takes a more tactical approach to how higher education can be used to achieve regional integration. Given the importance of the knowledge economy, higher education is perceived as a tool for the overall goal of regional economic integration. The question of "agency" is again central to the discussion as the higher education sector itself may have limited influence over what role it plays to enhance regional integration. Higher education can be seen as a means to an end where the end is political and/or economic integration. *Interregional cooperation in higher education* introduces yet another direction of inquiry that involves interactions between two regions. It often means two world regions, such as Asia and Europe, although it could also be regions of smaller scale. Interregional cooperation is clearly different from intra-regional cooperation, with the pivotal point being how a region is defined.

All lines of inquiry merit further examination, but this chapter focuses on the second line of inquiry: the "higher education regionalization." For the purposes of this discussion, regionalization of higher education refers to the "process of building closer collaboration and alignment among higher education actors and systems within a defined area or framework called a region." There are three key points. The first is the idea that it is an ongoing and evolutionary process, the second is the notion of intentional region building based on existing and new relationships and activities by a diversity of actors, and the third is the view that region is defined by the players involved and can be interpreted as a specific area or an organizational/programmatic/political framework.

Purpose, Scope, and Terminology

Given the mounting complexity and importance of regionalization, the purpose of this chapter is to explore the development of a conceptual framework to better understand and analyze the regionalization process as it applies to higher education. A constructivist approach, building on current realities and developments in all major world regions, is used as it is essential to create a framework that has relevance and value to different parts of the world and diverse cultural, political, and economic contexts. The framework is a work in progress. It needs to be sufficiently generic to encompass different approaches but specific enough to be useful for empirical analysis and comparison. Higher education is the main focus, but the discussion has relevance to the broader tertiary education sector. The framework concentrates on the process of facilitating closer collaboration and alignment among HEIs, actors, networks, and systems within a designated area or framework. Furthermore, the model builds on the multitude of activities, networks, and bilateral/multilateral relationships that are already functioning and improving higher education and its contribution to society. A key assumption is that the regionalization and internationalization processes of higher education coexist and are compatible and complementary processes. In fact, both processes include similar activities, actors, and outcomes, but regionalization emphasizes intra-regional initiatives.

The terminology related to the concept of region is like Pandora's box. As regions evolve and change, so does the interpretation and use of key terms. The diversity of disciplines examining the topic of regionality brings different lenses to the discourse and vividly illustrates that the concept of region is both complex and elusive. A myriad of definitions and interpretations exists. Traditionally, region has been defined in geographic terms and primarily as a collection of nation states in a particular geographically designated area (Vayrynen 2003). In the more interconnected and interdependent world in which we live, the idea of region is becoming increasingly elastic and porous. In both theory and practice, regions can be overlapping, multilayered, multi-actor, and multifaceted. Regions can be politically, socially, functionally, and culturally defined (Hettne 2005). Regions can be subnational and supranational. The supranational level is the focus of this chapter, but this level is also layered as it can include subregional, regional, and pan-regional levels. The nation state is no longer always at the core of a region, especially for culturally based regions. Regions do not need to be based on boundaries any more; the connections and interactions among key actors are of greater importance than the defining perimeter. In the proposed framework, the concept of region is fundamental, but not defined. Instead, the focus is on the dynamic processes of building a region. Thus, the framework is intended to be applicable to any region; however, it is delineated by the user. It could be in geographic terms, such as the major world regions Africa, Europe, Latin America, or smaller regions, such as Southeast Asia, Eastern Europe, Sub-Saharan Africa; or in cultural/linguistic terms, such as Francophone Africa or Arab States; or in political/economic terms, such as Asia Pacific Economic Community or Mercosur.

Outline of the Chapter

The first section provides examples of higher education regionalization initiatives from different parts of the world. This illustrates the diversity of activities and players as well as the commonalities across world regions. An analysis of terms used to describe regionalization follows. The key concepts are mapped on a continuum that is anchored by the notions of cooperation and collaboration at one end, moving to a more formalized and intentional concept of integration and interdependence at the other end. The next section introduces the framework of three approaches to the regionalization of higher education; a functional approach, an organizational approach, and a political approach. These three approaches are interrelated; they are not independent silos of activities. The framework is generic in substance and purpose so that it can apply to the evolving processes of higher education regionalization in different parts of the world. To elucidate the framework and illustrate the relationship among the three approaches, examples from the higher education landscape in Asia are used. Finally, the relationship between regionalization of higher education and the development of regional identity in Asia is explored.

Higher Education Regionalization Initiatives from around the World

Supporters and critics of the Bologna Process, both internal and external to Europe, agree that it continues to be the boldest and largest planned effort to enhance regionalization of higher education in the world (Tauch 2005). Opinions differ on the driving rationales, long-term outcomes, unintended consequences, and subsequent steps; but, there is no question that the Bologna Process has propelled other regions and subregions around the world to look more seriously at the significance and modality of building closer collaboration and alignment of their higher education systems.

For example, in 2007, the African Union released a major report "Harmonization of Higher Education Programmes in Africa: A Strategy for the African Union" that focused on building closer links among HEIs, networks, national systems, regional university associations, and other key higher education actors (African Union 2007). An interesting feature of creating a pan-African higher education and research space is the emphasis on strengthening the capacity and role of regional university associations. Examples of African higher education regionalization initiatives that already exist or are planned include the African Quality Rating Mechanism, the Nyerere African Scholarship scheme, AfriQAN network of quality assurance agencies, regional centers of excellence, updated Regional United Nations Education, Scientific, and Cultural Organization (UNESCO) Arusha Convention on the Recognition of Qualifications, a Pan-African University, and the new Open Education Africa project. At the regional level, there are varying levels of progress in initiatives to facilitate the establishment and alignment of quality assurance and accreditation systems, student mobility schemes, common degree levels, a research and education Information and Computing Technology (ICT) backbone, and research networks. These initiatives illustrate the intention and commitment of Africa to establish stronger intra-regional collaboration and harmonization of systems while still recognizing the importance of interregional bilateral and multilateral internationalization efforts (Hoosen et al. 2009).

The situation in Asia is complex and evolving. To date, most efforts toward enhancing higher education regionalization have been within Southeast Asia, but not exclusively. For instance, the Asia Pacific Quality

Assurance Network (APQN) was established in 2004 and covers 53 countries in Asia. Among its goals is capacity building within nations to establish national quality assurance systems and greater mutual recognition and collaboration among member countries. The University Mobility in Asia Pacific (UMAP) is a student mobility project, which was established over 15 years ago. The Association of South East Asian Nations (ASEAN) decided in 2003 to embark on a program of strengthening relations and activities among HEIs through the establishment of the ASEAN University Network (AUN), which is comprised of 26 leading universities in Southeast Asia. The AUN in turn has developed a series of thematic networks and projects that primarily involve member institutions; but, it is gradually yielding to pressure to include other universities in its regional conferences and projects.

Another key player in the Asia higher education scene is the South East Asia Ministers of Education Organization (SEAMEO). It has established a series of 22 centers throughout the region that deal with specific aspects of education. The Regional Institute for Higher Education Development (RIHED) has undertaken an impressive number and diversity of projects to create a stronger frame of collaboration among the 11 member countries of Southeast Asia. Examples of initiatives undertaken include the ASEAN Quality Assurance Network, the ASEAN Regional Research Citation Index, the ASEAN Regional Credit Transfer System, and the ASEAN Higher Education Clusters (Aphijanyathan 2010). Many of these schemes are in early stages of development and will take time to mature and be sustainable. Interestingly, countries outside Southeast Asia are starting to be included in these projects. For instance, Japan has recently joined the MIT (Malaysia, Indonesia, Thailand) Student Mobility Scheme organized by RIHED.

Campus Asia, a program created in 2010, is the most recent project to build closer ties among Korea, Japan, and China through student mobility and quality assurance. Campus Asia is a result of the second Tri-lateral Summit held in 2009. This program is still working out the complexities of quality assurance mechanisms, credit systems, and the controversial but central issue of language for the mobility scheme. Although it is currently focused on mobility for students in Korea, China, and Japan, it hopes to expand and include students from other East Asian nations.

These examples illustrate that Pan-Asia (usually interpreted to cover six Asian regions) initiatives are not as numerous as individual regional efforts such as those in Southeast Asia. ASEAN figures as the key player in the different configurations of regional groupings such as ASEAN + 3 (Japan, Korea, and China) or ASEAN + 6 (Japan, Korea, China, Australia, New Zealand, and India) and even ASEAN + 8 (six plus United States and

Russia). These configurations are primarily politically driven, but do have implications for higher education and show the elasticity of the concept of region.

In Latin America and the Caribbean (LAC), a major new initiative for the regionalization of higher education has been established as a result of a region-wide UNESCO conference held in 2008. The name of the initiative is ENLACES, which, in English, means the Latin America and the Caribbean Area for Higher Education. This project is hosted by and is a part of the IESALC—the UNESCO Institute for Higher Education in Latin America and the Caribbean. ENLACES is a regional platform formally created for the mobilization of projects and studies that support academic cooperation and knowledge sharing in the region. Membership in this initiative is open to individuals, institutions, government bodies, organizations, and networks in all LAC countries. The ultimate goal is to promote improved quality and relevance of higher education so that it can better serve society.

A major activity is the development of a Map of Higher Education in LAC that brings together data on national higher education systems in order to facilitate academic mobility and the development/alignment of national and institution policies. In terms of quality assurance and accreditation, there is a commitment to strengthen the convergence of national and subregional assessment and accreditation systems. Two other priorities are the mutual recognition of studies, titles, and diplomas founded on quality assurance, as well as the establishment of common academic credit systems accepted throughout the region. Fostering the intra-regional mobility of students, researchers, faculty, and administrative staff through the implementation of funded programs is another area of activity. The establishment of multi-university and multidisciplinary teaching and research networks is part of the work plan, as is developing shared distance education programs within the region. Finally, strengthening of the learning of languages of the region in order to foster the kind of regional integration that incorporates cultural diversity and multilingualism is a primary concern and modality for building the common higher education area in LAC.

An interesting part of the ENLACES program is the establishment of regional-level observatories which gather studies, publications, initiatives, events, news, and discussions on specific topics. The four observatories established to date are as follows: (1) Cultural Diversity and Interculturality; (2) Academic and Scientific Mobility; (3) University Social Responsibility; and (4) Latin America University Thinking. In principle, ENLACES serves as a portal to strengthen intra-regional collaboration and understanding in LAC by supporting and coordinating the multitude of higher education initiatives at institutional, national, and subregional levels.

These brief descriptions illustrate the diversity of actors and projects that is contributing to the regionalization of higher education in three regions of the world. While some activities are well-established programs, others have only been introduced in the last few years showing the increased interest in intra-regional cooperation. At the same time, interregional cooperation is expanding as well. In fact, Europe is investing considerable efforts and funds into promoting its reforms from the Bologna Process to other parts of the world. It is establishing interregional mobility programs, policy dialogues, and networks. Interestingly, a number of these efforts are in fact bilateral initiatives, that is, between Europe as a region and a single country or subregion. This is due to the fact that pan-regional higher education agencies or frameworks do not exist in all regions. There is no doubt that Europe is a stimulus and model for regionalization initiatives. Other regions are benefiting from the Bologna Process but they are giving careful consideration about how to adapt the European experiences to their own stage of development; their own cultural, historical, and political contexts; and most importantly, their own reasons for promoting regionalization.

Conceptual Mapping

Conceptual Mapping of Regionalization Terms

The analysis of the "process of higher education regionalization" involves a multitude of terms such as collaboration, harmonization, and integration. At times, the terms are used interchangeably and at other times, they have very different meanings. While this confusion of terms is not unusual with new developments or trends, it does lead to misunderstandings and muddles. The terms and concepts that are most commonly linked to regionalization include the following: cooperation, integration, harmonization, convergence, collaboration, community, coherence, partnership, and alignment. Worth noting is the number of words that start with "co" indicating the notion of "togetherness." The similarity among these terms is striking but when studied more closely, it becomes clear that there are subtle and important differences. The next section focuses on the conceptual mapping of these terms, their meaning, and their relation to one another.

It is both challenging and enlightening to discern the differences and similarities among these terms and then try to group and map them. This could be criticized as a rather subjective and normative exercise, but the purpose is to stimulate reflection and raise questions. The categorization of terms is highly influenced by the language of analysis. What these terms mean in English will probably differ from how they are used in Japanese, Spanish, or Arabic. Thus, it is important to ask what is the principal factor or criterion for the grouping of terms, and secondly, what does movement along the continuum or scale represent. In short, the groups include terms of similar levels of intensity of activity and the continuum represents the degree of intended "togetherness" or what is often labelled "regionalness" (Terada 2003). The continuum is anchored by the concepts of cooperation at one end and integration at the other. Cooperation represents a fairly loose and open kind of relationship, while integration denotes a much stronger cohesion and collective type of arrangement often referred to as a community or "common area." The risk of placing these terms on a continuum is that regionalization is understood to be a linear progression along this scale. This is definitely not the case as change rarely happens in such a systematic way. Most importantly, the objectives and anticipated outcomes of regionalization differ among regions and for various regionalization strategies. One region may be working toward alignment and collaboration rather than harmonization and convergence, while other regions may make integration the ultimate goal. An effective way to look at this continuum is through a musical metaphor. The collaboration and partnership group can be likened to an informal jazz concert where musicians gather to play the same composition with individual interpretations, while the harmonization and integration end can be compared to a professional orchestral performance where different musicians are playing the same musical composition under a single conductor and common interpretation of the music (Yavaprabhas 2010).

Figure 2.1 presents a schematic diagram of the conceptual mapping. The first group includes cooperation, collaboration, and partnership. Networking could be added to this list. These terms denote an open, voluntary, and perhaps informal type of relationship among actors. In practical terms, it describes the multitude of bilateral and multilateral collaborative activities by universities and other higher education actors.

The second group of terms—coordination, coherence, and alignment—introduces an element of organization and most likely some adaptation to ensure that the interactions among higher education actors in the region are complementary, productive. and bring added value. In practice, this would include the organized networks, joint education programs, or research partnerships among HEIs and systems.

The third group of terms—harmonization and convergence—involves stronger and more strategic links and can involve systemic changes both at institutional and national levels. This can include the development of regional quality assurance schemes; an academic credit system with a common currency for determination of credit or work load; similar

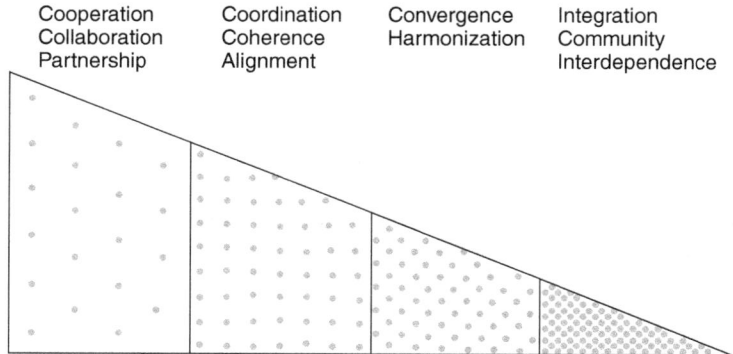

Figure 2.1 Conceptual mapping of higher education regionalization terms.

interpretation of degree levels such as BA, MA, and PhD; regional citation index; or compatible academic calendars.

The fourth group of terms—integration, community, and interdependence—represents more formalized, institutionalized, and comprehensive levels of connection and relationships. In practice, this would involve regional-level agreements and bodies that aim to facilitate a more robust and sustainable type of regional work and influence such as "a common higher education and research space."

It is equally interesting to look at concepts that are intentionally not included in this conceptual mapping, but which are in use and appear in the literature. Terms such as standardization, conformity, uniformity, compliance, and homogenization are omitted because they do not acknowledge the important differences among systems and actors within a region. This underlines a fundamental value or tenet of higher education regionalization, which is respect for and recognition of differences and diversity among key actors, systems, and stakeholders within the region. Failure to recognize this diversity can lead to the "zipper effect," whereby being completely interlocked neglects differences, stifles innovation, and leads to standardization.

Characteristics of the Process of Higher Education Regionalization

Regionalization is not a straightforward or uniform process. Progress evolves according to the specific goals and activities plus cultural and political contexts. Thus, it is necessary to pay attention to factors that influence and characterize the evolution of the regionalization. For example, when and why is the regionalization process characterized as being informal or formal, bottom up or top down, ad hoc or intentional, gradual or quantum leap, internally or externally driven, and finally whether it is reactive, proactive, or strategic?

These factors characterize the development and governance of any change process and are central to the analysis of the stages of the regionalization process as illustrated in Figure 2.2. The informal end of the spectrum could be represented by bilateral and multilateral activities initiated and managed by HEIs and organizations within the region. A more formal approach would involve policy making or regulating bodies which apply a more organized or harmonized dimension to the regionalization process.

Bottom up or top down is another key variable. For instance, initiatives coming from the HEIs are most often seen as representing a bottom-up approach, while regional (and in many cases national)-level bodies or legally binding or regulatory agreements characterize a top-down approach. Another critical factor is whether the higher education sector itself is driving regionalization or whether the process is being promoted and managed by external actors with their own agenda. This factor is directly linked to key rationales and expected outcomes. For example, if higher education regionalization is being used as a tool for political or economic integration, activities and results might differ than if the process was managed by the education sector for purposes of improving the quality and relevance of the education programs, research, knowledge, and service to society. The role of education services in regional trade agreements could be an example of an external sector regulating the higher education regionalization process.

Progression along the continuum is another important dimension to consider. A gradual incremental approach is evolutionary with critical mass and change gradually being built over time. A quantum leap approach is different and could be described as more of a revolutionary approach and involve a major break through often catalyzed by a top-down intervention or formalized declaration.

It is recognized that change is seldom linear as illustrated in Figure 2.2. It likely involves several steps forward followed by some steps backward and so on. Finally, it is interesting to reflect on whether the higher education actors (institutions, organizations, national government agencies, regional or interregional bodies) are (1) reacting to external factors and mandates to promote regionalization; (2) whether they are proactive in seeing the benefits of increased collaboration and alignment for higher education research and education; or (3) whether their efforts are indeed strategic and based on a vision for how to enhance higher education and its contributions to society through regionalization efforts.

```
Informal .......................................................... Formal
Ad hoc.......................................................... Intentional
Bottom up .....................................................Top Down
Internal ......................................................External
Incremental progression ....................................Quantum Leap
Reactive .........................Proactive ..................... Strategic
```

Figure 2.2 Factors characterizing the HE regionalization process.

In the next section, the discussion moves from a look at the characteristics of the process to the three approaches or three key elements of higher education regionalization.

Three Approaches to the Regionalization of Higher Education

Building and Strengthening Current Connections and Activities

Regionalization can be understood as an intentional process, a desire to build on what is already happening within the region and move beyond an ad hoc situation of cooperation to a more planned approach. For several regions of the world, this is seen as a logical and essential next step toward formalizing intra-regional cooperation. It can often emerge from a belief that it is important to know and interact with your neighbours while at the same time maintaining involvement with distant relations. It is understood, therefore, that regionalization occurs in concert with internationalization of higher education activities. International cooperation, whether it is intra-regional or interregional is not a zero-sum situation.

The current reality is that regional cooperation and alignment of systems is becoming increasingly important but not to the exclusion of other international relationships. History will likely show that regionalization and internationalization have a symbiotic relationship. They coexist, can be complementary or competitive, and each will have prominence at different stages of international cooperation.

Functional, Organizational, and Political Approaches

Three interrelated approaches—the functional approach, the organizational approach, and the political approach—constitute the core of the proposed framework. These approaches are not mutually exclusive. They are not like three separate silos of change; they work in unison complementing and reinforcing each other. While this is the optimal situation, it does not always happen in practice for there could be tension among the three approaches because of conflicting priorities or politics. At any one time, one of the approaches could be more dominant than another; but, ultimately, progress needs to occur on all three to ensure sustainability. Current realities and priorities will dictate the emphasis attributed to one approach over the other. Figure 2.3 illustrates the relationship and intersection of these three approaches.

The first approach takes a *functional* perspective of regionalization and focuses on the practical activities of HEIs and systems. The initiatives making up the functional approach can be put into two distinct groups. The first group relates to policies or strategies that facilitate closer alignment or in some cases harmonization among national/subregional higher

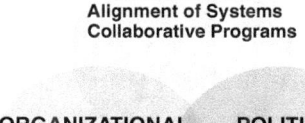

Figure 2.3 Relationship among three approaches.

education systems such as quality assurance schemes, academic credit systems, or qualification frameworks. The second category includes programs like student mobility schemes, cross-border collaborative education programs, pan-regional universities, and centers of excellence. The relationship between these two groups is critical as the systems in group one are needed to facilitate and expedite the programs in group two. For instance, compatibility between quality assurance systems and academic credit systems will help student mobility programs within a region. Generally, it is a more complex and serious undertaking to align national systems within a region than to establish bilateral or multilateral academic activities.

The second approach is called the *organizational* approach and refers to the organizational architecture that evolves to develop and guide the regionalization initiatives in a more systematic (although some might call it bureaucratic) manner. It is labeled the organizational approach because frameworks, structures, or agencies are necessary to help establish and oversee regional-level and intra-regional initiatives. A diversity of networks and organizations is emerging, which include government and nongovernment bodies, professional organizations, foundations, and networks. These entities assume a variety of responsibilities such as policy making, funding, research, capacity building, regulation, and advocacy among others. Furthermore, noneducation organizations with a regional mandate, such as trade-related bodies, are also making higher education a higher priority

The third approach is labeled the political approach. It refers to political will and strategies that put higher education initiatives on the agenda of decision-making bodies. The political approach helps to launch major programs or funding schemes and to formalize initiatives. Declarations of intent, binding conventions, treaties, agreements, and special meetings like summits or policy dialogues are instruments for generating political support and visibility in order to make regionalization of higher education a priority. This approach can be characterized as having more of a top-down, formal, and intentional orientation.

Application of the Three-Approach Framework to Asia

The purpose of Figure 2.4 is to illustrate the fundamental elements of the "three approaches" framework by using examples from Asia. It is noted that not all regionalization initiatives are included and those that are listed are at different stages of development with various degrees of sustainability.

Approach	Examples from Asian Region
Functional	***Alignment of Higher Education Systems*** ASEAN Credit transfer system ACSAM—Academic Credit System for Asian Mobility ASEAN University Inter-Library Online Quality Assurance—mutual recognition of QAA systems ASEAN Research Citation Index Collaborative Programs Student mobility program among Malaysia, Indonesia, Thailand, and Japan (JMIT) University Mobility in Asia Pacific (UMAP) CAMPUS ASIA—Collective for the Mobility of University Students—Japan, China, and Korea AUN/SEED-NET—South East Asian Engineering Education Dev Network ASEAN Graduate Business Economic Program ASEAN University Human Rights Network
Organizational	***Organizational architecture*** Association of South East Asian Nations—ASEAN South East Asia Ministers of Education Organization—SEAMEO Regional Centre for Higher Education Development—RIHED Asia Pacific Quality Network—APQN ASEAN University Network—AUN Ass of Universities of Asia and the Pacific—AUAP Asia Pacific Rim University Network—APRU Association of Southeast Asian Institutions of Higher Learning—ASAIHL Association of East Asian Research Universities—AEARU Asia Pacific Regional Bureau UNESCO Asian Development Bank—ADB Asian and Europe Meeting—ASEM
Political	***Political will*** Brisbane Communique Chiba Principles Asia Pacific UNESCO Convention on the Recognition of Qualifications South East Asian Ministers of Education Meetings Tri-lateral summit Asia Pacific Economic Community—APEC East Asian Summit ASEAN +3, ASEAN +6, ASEAN +8

Figure 2.4 Regionalization of higher education in Asia.

These examples show that the nations constituting Southeast Asia have made significant progress in all three approaches; while Northeast Asia, consisting of Japan, Korea, and China, is in the initial stages of more formal cooperation through the recent establishment of the Campus Asia initiative. There are almost no examples from South, West, or Central Asia. It is not clear whether there are no current initiatives or that the information is not available at this time. These examples also illustrate that regions are multilayered and overlapping. The different configuration of regions in Asia includes the following scenarios: Pan-Asia (47 nations), Asia Pacific Economic Cooperation (APEC) (21 nations), North East Asia (NEA) (3 nations), South East Asia (SEA)/ASEAN (10 nations), ASEAN + 3 (13 nations), ASEAN + 6 (16 nations), and ASEAN + 8 (18 nations). It is evident that these regional groupings have overlapping memberships, and in the case of APEC and ASEAN + 8, even go beyond the common notion of Asia by including the United States, Russia, and countries on the Pacific Rim. This reality illustrates why the proposed definition of regionalization of higher education emphasizes the process of region building through closer collaboration and alignment of systems and does not try to develop a common understanding of what constitutes Asia or a specific region in Asia.

Implications for Regional Identity

An articulated rationale for regionalization or regional integration is to develop and strengthen a sense of regional identity—shared views and values within a region. The attention being given to regional identity stems from the belief that a strong regional identity is an important foundation for political and security cooperation (Johnston 2010). A fundamental tenet of regional identity is that it exists in addition to a sense of national identity. It does not replace national identity. Thus, it is not a case of either a national or regional identity; rather, they are seen to be complementary perspectives. The Asian Barometer, a research organization situated in Taiwan with adjunct research teams located in 13 Asian countries, conducted a major study in 2006–2007 to determine the percentage of the population (determined by a representative sample) in 13 Asian nations that had a sense of regional identity in addition to their national identity. Figure 2.5 presents the results and raises interesting questions as to why there is such a dramatic spread across the countries.

The question of regional identity is pertinent to the regionalization of higher education as student/scholar mobility, increased partnerships, and

Country	Percentage
Vietnam	87.2
Cambodia	76.6
Laos	61.3
Taiwan	60.6
Philippines	57.5
Thailand	54.9
China	43.5
Malaysia	42.3
Myanmar	42.3
Indonesia	36.8
Singapore	32.0
Korea	32.0
Japan	22.3

Figure 2.5 Percentage choosing Asian identity in addition to national identity. Asian Barometer 2006–2007 taken from Johnston 2010.

exchange of knowledge among academics are potential determinants helping to foster regional identity. For example, in the 2006 Asian Barometer study of the Chinese population sample that reported an Asian identity, 78 percent had traveled abroad. Of those who reported no Asian identity, only 22 percent had traveled abroad (Johnston 2010). It is important not to take these results out of context, but they raise important questions as to how intra-regional academic mobility and collaboration could help contribute to a sense of regional identity. Perhaps, this is why the Asianization of Higher Education is raised as an important element of regionalization of higher education in the same way that Europeanization of Higher Education has been attributed to the Bologna Process and Africanization of Higher Education is being debated.

The issue of regional identity raises further questions when it is juxtaposed to the concept of global citizenship. The concept of global citizenship means different things to different people, but it is often linked to the development of certain competencies such as intercultural awareness and understanding; increased international knowledge and commitment to global issues; ability to function in different cultures; and appreciation of the differences and similarities among cultures and countries. The concept of regional identity, which does not emphasize competencies but shared perspectives and values, seems to be understood in a different way from global citizenship. This is an area that merits further reflection and research. The waters are murky when one discusses the relationships between national identity and regional identity; national citizenship and global citizenship; and the role of regionalization and internationalization of higher education in enhancing identity and citizenship.

The purpose of this chapter is to discuss a proposed conceptual framework for analyzing the complex and evolving phenomenon of higher education regionalization. The model builds on the fact that intra-regional collaboration is already in progress and has substantially increased in the past several years. In other words, the "regionalization" train has already left the station. But questions like where is it headed, which tracks will it use, what passengers or cargo will be on board, how many stops will it make, and what is the final destination are yet to be answered. The journey of higher education regionalization has begun and the objective of this chapter is to offer a search light plus a series of questions to help analyze and guide the journey.

References

African Union. 2007. "Harmonization of Higher Education Programmes in Africa: A Strategy for the African Union: Summary Report." Meeting of the Bureau of the Conference of Ministers of Education of the African Union (COMEDAF II+), Addis Ababa, Ethiopia.

Aphijanyathan, R. 2010. "A Research Report on East Asian Internationalization of Higher Education: A Key to Regional Integration." Program Report 24, Regional Centre for Higher Education and Development, South East Ministers of Education Organization, Bangkok, Thailand.

Hettne, B. 2005. "Beyond the New Regionalism." *New Political Economy* 10 (4): 543–571.

Hoosen, S., N. Butcher, and B. K. Njenga. 2009. "Harmonization of Higher Education Programmes: A Strategy for the African Union." *African Integration Review* 3 (1): 1–36.

Johnston, A. 2010. "Obstacles to Governance in East Asia: The Case of Security Communities." In *Security Cooperation and Regional Integration in Asia Conference Proceedings*, Global Institute for Asian Regional Integration, Waseda University, Tokyo, Japan, pp. 78–92.

Knight, J. 2008. *Higher Education in Turmoil: The Changing World of Internationalization*. Rotterdam, the Netherlands: Sense Publishers.

Kuroda, K., Y. Takako, and K. Kang. 2011. *Cross-border Higher Education for Regional Integration: Analysis of the JICA-RI Survey on Leading Universities in East Asia*. JICA- Research Institution Working Paper, Tokyo, Japan.

RIHED. 2008. Harmonization of Higher Education—Lessons Learned from the Bologna Process Lecture Series #1, Regional Centre for Higher Education Development, South East Asia Ministers of Education., Bangkok, Thailand.

Tauch, C. 2005. "The Bologna Process: State of Implementation and External Dimension." In *Opening Up to the Wider World: The External Dimension of the Bologna Process*, ed. F. Muche. Bonn, Germany: Lemmens, pp. 23–29.

Terada, T. 2003. "Constructing an 'East Asian' Concept and Growing Regional Identity: From EAEC to ASEAN+3." *The Pacific Review* 16 (2): 251–277.

Vayrynen, R. 2003. "Regionalism: Old and New." *International Studies Review* 5 (1): 25–51.

Yavaprabhas, S. 2010. "Regional Harmonization of Higher Education in ASEAN." Presentation at 2010 Global Higher Education Forum, Universiti Sains Malaysia, Penang, Malaysia.

Chapter 3

Regional Cooperation in Higher Education in Asia and the Pacific
Molly N. N. Lee

Introduction

A significant trend in the Asia-Pacific region is the rapid expansion of many higher education systems brought about by ever-increasing social demand due to population growth, democratization of secondary education, and the growing affluence of many countries in the region. As higher education systems expand, there is an urgent need to seek diverse sources of funding and resources. With the advancement of information and communication technologies and increased mobility of students and staff, higher education institutions from different countries are forming and developing strategic cooperation and collaboration to mobilize resources, to facilitate academic exchanges and to offer joint programs. The purpose of this chapter is to examine the different types of university exchanges and to analyze some of the regional cooperation initiatives that are initiated by intergovernmental as well as nongovernmental organizations (NGOs).

Types of University Exchanges

The traditional functions of universities are teaching, research, and service. The various types of university exchanges can also be broadly categorized as academic exchange, research collaboration, and university–community engagement. Academic exchanges can take the forms of movement of people such as students, professors, scholars, or experts; program mobility; and provider or institutional mobility. United Nations Educational, Scientific, and Cultural Organization (UNESCO) estimates that, in 2007, there were more than 2.8 million internationally mobile students, an increase of about 53 percent over the estimated figure of 1.8 million in 2000 (UNESCO-UIS 2009). At the program level, universities collaborate to offer twinning programs, credit transfer programs, and joint degree programs. There are also universities that set up branch campuses in other countries such as Monash University in Malaysia, RMIT University in Vietnam, and Nottingham University in Malaysia and China. Furthermore, academics exchange ideas through journals, seminars, conferences, and social networking on the Internet.

With the ease of communication and travel, academics collaborate in joint research projects, offer joint doctoral degrees, and share resources and facilities. For example, Universitas 21, a global network of 23 research universities from 15 countries, was established in 1997. It has several collaborative groups in which colleagues from similar disciplines meet regularly virtually or physically to discuss topics of mutual interest and collaborate on issues of importance within their field. Some representative collaborative groups include the Career Group, Global Issues Group, Research Leaders Group, Early Career Researcher Workshop, and others (Universitas 21 2011). Malaysia provides an example of another kind of university partnership, wherein a consortium of 11 public universities was established in 1999 to set up a private university named the Open University Malaysia. Although established as a private university, Open University Malaysia leverages on the quality, prestige, and capabilities of its strategic partners to provide distance education to the point where from an initial population of 753 learners in August 2000, it now is able to advertise a cumulative intake over the intervening period of over 100,000 (Open University Malaysia 2011).

Universities are often called upon to be responsive to the needs of their communities and contribute to the development of their surrounding environments. The social responsibility of higher education was stated explicitly in the Final Communique from the 2009 UNESCO World Conference of Higher Education (UNESCO 2009), in which it was held that universities need to be engaged with their communities to promote participatory and sustainable development. Community engagement and participation can be seen as mechanisms through which higher education institutions forge partnerships and linkages with communities, governments, the private sector, business, and NGOs. On September 23, 2010, eight international networks supporting community university engagement across the world gathered to issue a call for increased North–South cooperation in community university research and engagement. In their release, they called for "All higher education institutions to express a strategic commitment to genuine community engagement, societal relevance or research and education and social responsibility as a core principle" (Global Community University Networks 2010). An example of a northern university involved in the capacity development of southern universities and their immediate communities is the "Localized Poverty Reduction in Vietnam Project" and the "Community-based Watershed Management" project, both of which are based at the University of British Columbia, Canada. This kind of north–south university partnership is quite common in Canada where they are mainly funded by the Canadian International Development Agency and the International Development Research Centre (Angeles 2008).

Intergovernmental Initiative

The intergovernmental organizations that are actively involved in higher education activities in the Asia-Pacific region include the UNESCO, the South East Asian Minister of Education Organization (SEAMEO) Regional Institute for Higher Education Development (RIHED), the Association of South East Asian Nations (ASEAN), the Asia–Europe Meeting (ASEM), the East Asian Summit (EAS) – consisting of ASEAN + 6 (Japan, South Korea, China, India, Australia, and New Zealand) and the Asia Pacific Economic Cooperation (APEC). Along the same line of thinking as the Bologna Process, SEAMEO RIHED has developed several initiatives to create a higher education common space in Southeast Asia. One initiative is the ASEAN Quality Assurance Network, formed to promote and share good practices among quality assurance agencies in this subregion. The Malaysia, Indonesia, Thailand (MIT) organization is another initiative to promote student exchanges among universities in these three countries. The ASEAN Citation Index is yet another regional cooperation initiated by SEAMEO RIHED. The regional block ASEAN established the ASEAN University Network (AUN) in 1992 comprising 17 leading universities in 10 ASEAN countries. AUN is very active in facilitating collaborative work on quality assurance, university governance and management, credit transfer, ASEAN studies, and other areas in this network. On the other hand, ASEM is an informal process of dialogue and cooperation bringing together the 27 European Union Member States and the European Commission with the ASEAN + 6 countries (ASEM 2011). In fact, ASEM works very closely with AUN to strengthen collaboration in higher education between Europe and Southeast Asia under the Academic Cooperation Europe South East Asia Support (ACESS) project. The East Asia Summit (EAS) is another forum for dialogue on broad strategic, political, and economic issues of common interest and concern with the aim of promoting peace, stability, and economic prosperity in East Asia (EAS 2011). Although the objectives of EAS are broad in scope, it had organized a regional workshop on recognition of higher education qualifications for its member states in June 2011 (UNESCO 2011a). The APEC is a bigger forum consisting of 21 Pacific Rim countries that seeks to promote free trade and economic cooperation throughout the Asia-Pacific region. As a lead-up to the 2011 APEC Conference, an international conference on Quality in Higher Education was held in August 2011 in Honolulu, Hawaii (APEC 2011).

UNESCO's position is that higher education in a globalized society should assure equity of access, respect cultural diversity, and respect national sovereignty. UNESCO's aim is to establish the conditions under which the globalization of higher education benefits all. To achieve this aim, UNESCO's work on higher education focuses on cross-border higher education, qualification recognition, quality assurance, open and distance learning, analytical work on higher education reforms, networking, and information sharing. Some of UNESCO's initiatives in the region include the University Network and Twinning Programme (UNITWIN)/UNESCO Chairs, the Global University Network for Innovation (GUNI), the Association of Universities in Asia-Pacific (AUAP), and the Asia Pacific Education Research Association (APERA). The UNITWIN/UNESCO Chairs was established in 1992 with the aim of developing interuniversity cooperation, emphasizing the transfer and sharing of knowledge between universities and the promotion of academic solidarity across the world. The projects under this initiative deal with training and research activities and cover all major fields of knowledge within UNESCO's competence such as education, natural sciences, social and human sciences, culture, and communication and information. There are more than 500 established chairs and interuniversity networks, out of which 60 chairs and 8 UNITWIN networks are based in the Asia-Pacific region (UNESCO 2011b). GUNI was one of the outcomes of the UNESCO 1998 World Conference on Higher Education. GUNI holds regular conferences in Barcelona, and it has published several volumes on current issues of higher education such as financing of universities, accreditation for quality assurance, higher education for human and social development, and higher education for sustainability (GUNI 2011). The AUAP was established in 1995 and at present consists of 210 member universities in 19 countries. AUAP facilitates networking through regular conferences and seminars (AUAP 2011).

APERA was launched in 2011 with the aim of promoting collaboration in educational research and to build stronger links among research, policy, and practice in education. It has 17 institutional members from 14 countries and organizes biennial conferences and produces the APERA research journal (APERA 2011).

Nongovernmental Organizations

There are quite a number of higher education networks in the region that are very active in promoting academic exchanges, student exchanges, and research collaboration. One of the oldest organizations is the Association of Southeast Asian Institutions of Higher Learning (ASAIHL) founded in 1956 with the aim of fostering university development and regional identity. It has about 200 members in 16 countries including non–Southeast Asian countries. It runs fellowships and academic exchange programs (ASAIHL 2011). Another active organization is the University Mobility in Asia-Pacific (UMAP) founded in 1993, the main objective of which is to facilitate student exchanges among universities in its 31 member countries, territories, and administrative regions. Currently, the active members are Australia, Japan, South Korea, Thailand, Hong Kong, and Taiwan.

The Association of Pacific Rim Universities (APRU), which was established in 1997, is a consortium of 42 leading research universities in the Pacific Rim that aims to foster cooperation in education, research, and enterprise, thereby contributing to the economic, scientific, and cultural advancement of the Pacific Rim (APRU 2011). Its wide range of activities includes human capital development, research-centric, and student-centric activities. The Asian University Federation (AUF) was founded in 1998 and is linked with the World University Federation. It has 50 member universities from 12 countries with the aim of promoting academic cooperation and student and staff exchanges among its members through international conferences, seminars, and workshops (AUF 2011). The Asian Association of Open Universities (AAOU) founded in 1987 is primarily concerned with education at a distance. It has about 60 member institutions. Its main activity is an annual conference that is a stimulating forum for all those associated with open and distance learning in Asia, including academics, administrators, and students (AAOU 2011). These organizations are just a few of the more prominent higher education institution networks found in the Asia-Pacific region that join many other professional organizations in which the memberships are on an individual rather than institutional basis. For example, the Asia-Pacific Association of International Education (APAIE) is an NGO consisting of individual members. With more than

1,000 international education professionals, its mission is to achieve greater cooperation among those responsible for international education and internationalization in Asia-Pacific institutions (APAIE 2011).

Regional Initiatives

A few other regional initiatives deserve mention. One is the Asia-Pacific Quality Network (APQN), established in 2004 with the support of UNESCO and World Bank. Its mission is "To enhance the quality of higher education in Asia and the Pacific region through strengthening the work of quality assurance agencies and extending the cooperation between them" (APQN 2011). The establishment of this network has been very timely in view of the increasing mobility of students and providers across national borders and the need to establish and develop quality assurance agencies to deal with both public and private providers and with students who cross national borders. APQN is already helping to build alliances among agencies and is assisting countries/territories that do not have a quality assurance agency of their own.

Another significant regional initiative is the UNESCO Regional Convention on the Recognition of Studies, Diplomas and Degrees in Higher Education in Asia and the Pacific, which was adopted in 1983 (UNESCO 2011c). The main objective of the convention has been to promote international cooperation in higher education and reduce obstacles to the mobility of students and teachers. The key ideas embedded in the regional convention are fair recognition of qualifications; developing supporting instruments, guidelines, good practices, and recommendations; and facilitating information sharing as well as networking at the expert level. Under the principles of the convention, applicants have the right to fair assessment of their qualification by a competent authority and recognition is granted if no substantial differences can be demonstrated. If recognition is not granted, then the competent authority has to identify the substantial differences between the applicant's qualification and that of the host country, and the applicant has the right to appeal.

Concluding Remarks

It is easy *to establish* a network, but much more difficult to *sustain* a network. The higher education institution networks that have been described in the above sections are some of the more prominent and well established in the Asia-Pacific region. Many of these are involved in promoting regional cooperation in the areas of student exchanges, collaborative research, capacity building, and joint degree programs. Most are established at the higher education institutional level, initiated by intergovernmental organizations and NGOs. Some of the more important regional initiatives include the establishment of a common higher education area in ASEAN, the development of a regional framework for quality assurance of higher education, and the Asia-Pacific regional convention on the recognition of higher education qualifications. Besides intra-regional cooperation among higher education institutions within the Asia-Pacific region, there are efforts to facilitate interregional cooperation especially between Europe and Asia as well as between Asia and Africa. Within the Asia-Pacific region are also found subregional organizations such as the Pacific Islands Forum (PIF), SEAMEO, South Asian Association for Regional Cooperation (SAARC), and others.

References

AAOU. 2011. "Asian Association of Open Universities." Available at: www.aaou.net. Accessed March 7, 2012.

Angeles, Leonora C. 2008. "The Scholarship of International Service Learning: Implications for Teaching and Learning Participatory Development in Higher Education." In UNESCO (2008), *Reinventing Higher Education: Toward Participatory and Sustainable Development*. Bangkok: UNESCO, pp. 78–87. Available at: http://unesdoc.unesco.org/images/0016/001631/163155e.pdf. Accessed March 6, 2012.

APAIE. 2011. "Asia Pacific Association of International Education." Available at: www.apaie.org. Accessed March 7, 2012.

APEC. 2011. "APEC Conference on Quality in Higher Education: Identifying, Developing and Sustaining Best Practices in the APEC Region." Available at: http://hrd.apec.org/index.php/Quality_in_Higher_Education. Accessed March 7, 2012.

APERA. 2011. "Asia-Pacific Education Research Association." Available at: www.aperahk.org/. Accessed March 7, 2012.

APQN. 2011. "Asia-Pacific Quality Network." Available at: www.apqn.org/about/mission/. Accessed March 7, 2012.

APRU. 2011. "Association of Pacific Rim Universities." Available at: www.apru.org/. Accessed March 7, 2012.

ASAIHL. 2011. "Association of Southeast Asia Institution of Higher Learning." Available at: www.seameo.org/asaihl/. Accessed March 7, 2012.

ASEM. 2011. "ASEM Infoboard." Available at: www.aseminfoboard.org/. Accessed March 7, 2012.

AUAP. 2011. "Association of Universities of Asia and the Pacific." Available at: http://auap.sut.ac.th/. Accessed March 7, 2012.

AUF. 2011. "Asian University Federation." Available at: www.sunmoon.ac.kr/~auf/aboutauf.htm. Accessed March 7, 2012.

EAS. 2011. "East Asia Summit." Available at: www.aseansec.org/aadcp/repsf/abouteastasiasummit.html. Accessed March 7, 2012.

Global Community University Networks. 2010. "Global Community University Networks Call for Increased North-South Cooperation." Available at: http://pascalobservatory.org/pascalnow/pascal-expertise/other-resources/global-community-university-networks-call-increased-north. Accessed March 7, 2012.

GUNI. 2011. "Global University Network for Innovation." Available at: www.guni-rmies.net/. Accessed March 9, 2011.

Open University Malaysia. 2011. Available at: www.oum.edu.my/oum/index.php?c=oum&v=art_view&domid=1&parent_id=25&cat_id=5&art_id=83&lang=eng. Accessed March 7, 2012.

UNESCO-UIS. 2009. *Educational Statistics*. Available at: http://stats.uis.unesco.org/unesco/ReportFolders/ReportFolders.aspx?IF_ActivePath=P,50&IF_Language=eng. Accessed March 7, 2012.

UNESCO 2009. *World Conference on Higher Education Communique*. Available at: www.unesco.org/...2009/FINAL%20COMMUNIQUE%20WCHE%2...www.unesco.org/en/wche2009/. Accessed March 9, 2011.

UNESCO. 2011a. "East Asia Summit Meeting on the Recognition of Higher Education Qualifications in the Asia-Pacific Region." Available at: www.unescobkk.org/education/higher-and-distance-education/guidelines-on-cross-border-higher-education/east-asia-summit-meeting-on-the-recognition-of-higher-education-qualifications-in-the-asia-pacific-region/. Accessed March 7, 2012.

UNESCO. 2011b. *University Twinning and Networking*. Available at: www.unesco.org/en/unitwin/university-twinning-and-networking/. Accessed March 7, 2012.

UNESCO. 2011c. "The Regional Convention on the Recognition of Studies, Diplomas and Degrees in Higher Education in Asia and the Pacific." Available at: http://portal.unesco.org/education/en/ev.php-URL_ID=22140&URL_DO=DO_TOPIC&URL_SECTION=201.html. Accessed March 7, 2012.

Universitas 21. 2011. Available at: www.universitas21.com/collaboration. Accessed March 7, 2012.

Chapter 4

The Function of Regional Networks in East Asian Higher Education

Miki Sugimura

Introduction

This chapter seeks to clarify the function of regional networks and international cooperation of higher education with perspectives of regionalism and regionalization in East Asia. International cooperation in East Asian higher education can be largely categorized into regional cooperation and university cooperation, including cases in which individual universities form agreements and consortia to deploy their programs. Such international cooperation suggests new forms of international higher education through education and research exchanges, and they also bring with them perspectives for regional integration and socioeconomic development in East Asia.

This chapter will first organize the elements that enable international cooperation in Asia and break down the current situation into patterns, for example, international and regional organizations, such as United Nations Educational, Scientific, and Cultural Organization (UNESCO), the Asian Development Bank (ADB), the Association of South East Asian Nations (ASEAN), the South East Asian Minister of Education Organization (SEAMEO), and the Asia Pacific Economic Cooperation (APEC), and those among governments of various countries. The analysis then examines how they unfurl based on their mutually related multilayered structures including the autonomy of individual countries and higher education agencies in the case of quality assurance networks and Chinese-language education. The chapter further discusses the appearance of new regionalism through a regional higher education network in the case of the South Asian Association for Regional Cooperation (SAARC). Finally, I consider the function of international cooperation in Asian higher education, which can be the foundation of both regionalism and regionalization for East Asian integration.

Rationales of Regional Networks and International Cooperation in East Asia

Regional networks and international cooperation in East Asia symbolize an implication of international higher education. Regarding cross-border higher education, Knight (2006) mentions that education had moved across borders for centuries with nothing new about academic mobility, but what is new is that it is no longer just the students, professors, and researchers who are moving across borders with their knowledge, but programs moving across borders as well as providers.[1] The characteristic feature of regional networks and international cooperation is that the linkages are constructed from various rationales and are developing from their respective institutional levels to regional levels through to national government levels, which are closely related with regionalization and regionalism.

National Governments and People in General in the Region as Actors of Networking

The trend for regionalization in East Asia has affected politics and economy as well as sociocultural changes. Katzenstein has pointed out that "the process of Japanization and Americanization have fused to create regionalization that goes beyond any one national model" and "the rise of China and East Asia's 'Sinicization' is reinforcing that trend," which is named "hybrid regionalism." This argument implies that regionalization in East Asia has been driven not only by national governments' policies on security, finance, and trade, but by "a large number of other actors dealing with technology, ecology, consumptions, and lifestyle issues that reflect the emergence of an urban middle class in East Asia's major metropolitan areas" (Katzenstein 2006, 19). Shiraishi analyzes the social foundations of East Asia's hybrid regionalism by focusing on the formation of middle classes in East Asia. Shiraishi pointed out that "these middle classes who are dependent on the economic performance of their respective countries, constitute expanding regional markets for multinational corporations, and "the regional middle-class markets open up the possibility of constructing market-mediated national and regional cultural identities" (Shiraishi 2006, 268–269).

This argument is closely related to Pempel's explanation of *"East Asia's webs of cooperation."* He argues that,

> Clearly many of East Asia's more cooperative ventures have been driven by the national governments of the region. At least equally as often, however, the key spinners of East Asia's webs of cooperation (and occasionally conflict) have been non-state actors, including such diverse players as multinational corporations, NGOs, private citizens engaged in so-called track II processes, and cross-border media, as well as individual workers, students, athletic teams, rock bands, and dance troupes. (p. 12)

This means that regionalization in Asia has been moved by national governments and "people in general." In other words, "regionalism which involves national autonomy and regionalization which develops from the bottom up through societally driven processes" has been in progress in East Asia (Pempel 2005, 12).

Diversification of International Student Policies and Student Mobility

The regional networks and cooperation in higher education on which this chapter focuses can be regarded as one of the phenomena of East Asia's webs. It can be drawn by various student mobilities and by country governments. International student policies and their networking are based on the typical human mobility that is affected by both international student policies and educational needs of people in general.

The critical factors enabling regional cooperation and university cooperation in Asia are the internationalization and privatization of higher education promoted by each country since the mid-1970s and the international student policies that accompanied such changes. The international student policy of each Asian country serves as an important tool of political and economic strategies for national development by nurturing and acquiring human resources, and because of this, interuniversity international cooperation programs generally known as transnational programs or cross-border programs have gained rapid popularity. One characteristic of these programs is that participating students take courses in two or more countries; the executing country/region of the program and the agency conferring the degree do not always match. McBurnie and Zigrus's (2007, 21) analysis suggests that "While the international mobility of students is a well-established and growing feature of higher education, the international mobility of institutions and courses on a large scale is a more novel phenomenon, made possible in part by recent innovations in information and communications technologies." The spread of such transnational programs has given much versatility and many choices to higher education curricula by selecting English as the prevailing language used by professors, resulting in increased student mobility and privately funded international students who seek cheaper and shorter methods of acquiring degrees and qualifications.

The situation of student mobility in Asia is such that although outflow to English-speaking countries is continuing to increase, mutual exchanges among East Asian countries such as Japan, China, and South Korea are booming. Postiglione and Chapman (2010, 381) give evidence that the cross-border linking of Asian with Western universities would continue as the dominant patter of previous collaborations, but Asian-to-Asian collaborations would also increase. In fact, from China to ASEAN or among ASEAN countries' international student flow has become more active than before. Moreover, with shifting within the ASEAN region as well as increased inflow into Asia from the Middle East and African countries, student mobility is becoming truly diverse. As can be seen from the recent rapid increase of students from African countries, the trend to view Asia as a transit point toward obtaining a final degree in Europe or the United States is prominent (Sugimura 2010). As a result, Asia's international education market is beginning to attract much attention from other regions as well, and it is in Asia that various countries engage in the acquisition battle for international students in order to become an international hub of human resource shifting.

Efforts Toward Multi-country Regional Cooperation and Human Resource Development

Aside from such international human resource competition among various countries, the trend to aim for regional cooperation in human resource development is another factor propelling international cooperation. This is a multi-country effort to develop international human resources with broader perspectives and compound-eye thinking abilities, aside from and transcending the conventional human resource development framework employed domestically by each country, in order to counter various border-transcending issues that have emerged through the progress of globalization and internationalization in international society. It is also a movement that seeks a new form of higher education that leads to regional harmony and integration in the future.

Development of International Networks and Cooperation in East Asia

As mentioned above, national governments, regional organizations, regional societies, and individual higher education institutions are actors in international networks and cooperation. The transnational programs of those linkages can be categorized into three types: government cooperation programs, regional organization programs, and institutional-based programs (Sugimura 2011, 54–56), and they are managed by the following organizations in East Asia.

Regional Networks

Amid such international cooperation trends, the following are higher education regional networks set up mainly in Asia: ASEAN, SEAMEO, APEC, UNESCO, ADB, the ASEAN University Network (AUN), the AUN/Southeast Asia Engineering Education Development Network (AUN/SEED-Net), the Association of Pacific Rim Universities (APRU), University Mobility in Asia and the Pacific (UMAP), and the Asia-Pacific Quality Network (APQN). Such networks can be divided into organizations with governments as members (ASEAN, SEAMEO, APEC, UNESCO, and ADB) and organizations with universities, and the like, as members or relative educational organizations of quality assurance, and so on (AUN, AUN/SEED-Net, APRU, and APQN). Furthermore, when divided by target regions, there are those with ASEAN as their axis, such as ASEAN, SEAMEO, AUN, and AUN/SEED-Net, and those targeting Asia-Pacific regions, such as APEC, APRU, UMAP, APQN, and UNESCO. Of these, for UNESCO, the Asia and Pacific Regional Bureau for Education in Bangkok is especially active, with a focus on the region including South Asia and Central Asia. It can be also pointed out that these regional organizations are closely related with member country governments' policies and autonomy issues.

University Cooperation Programs

Another form of international cooperation is the universities cooperation program, conducted through interorganizational agreements among individual higher education agencies in various countries. Such university cooperation programs can be divided into five categories, based on their program content. The first category comprises workshop-style programs aimed at fostering international understanding. This program seeks to promote international mutual understanding in a multifaceted manner not only in university classrooms, but also within and outside the campus, including in overseas locations. When overseas, the program often takes the form of hands-on training, including field studies, internships, volunteer activities, and exchange programs. Many such hands-on programs target undergraduate students, and their content covers a broad area of liberal arts education from humanities and social sciences to natural sciences.

The second category consists of programs for fostering sophisticated professionals and specializing in specific fields, mainly targeting graduate students. For these programs, enhanced cooperation with universities and relative organizations that have strong expertise in the pertinent fields is required. It is characteristic for such programs to focus on specific topics that are usually difficult for research organizations other than universities to take on.

The third category comprises programs connected with global cooperation. The characteristic of global cooperation makes collaborative networks indispensable for this type of program. Similarly, the fourth type, emphasizing the region, also requires collaborative networks to function. Such programs are diverse, from those handling issues and problems of specific subregions of Asia to those promoting regional communication within an international framework of ASEAN + 3 that would eventually lead to the globalization of education.

Finally, by utilizing an educational system that involves university cooperation, there are movements to pioneer new academic fields. This type includes those focusing on the Asian region and pioneering a new academic field to analyze and explain current rapid social changes that are shared across the Asian region, such as declining populations and aging societies, and human resource development of the next generation (Sugimura 2009, 285–288).

Structures of Regional Networks and University Cooperation

The formats of international cooperation are diverse, but what must be noted is that both regional cooperation education networks and university cooperation are deployed in multiple layers and in different phases. These networks and cooperation systems have a function of distribution of Asian higher education as public goods for regionalization. Postiglione and Chapman (2010, 378) classified international collaborations into top-down mechanism and bottom-up mechanism. The top-down mechanism is initiated by government interests, and the bottom-up emerges from individual institutions. The regional network is organized by its member countries' governments; on the contrary, each educational institution makes various kinds of international exchange programs.

Regional Networks

For regional networks, ASEAN, SEAMEO, AUN, and AUN/SEED-Net are good examples, and these are only those with ASEAN as their axis. They are all mutually and closely connected and complementary to each other. ASEAN adopted the ASEAN Vision 2020 in 1998 at the Sixth ASEAN Summit to present the ideal state of regional cooperation in various areas of politics, economy, culture, and others, in order to unite Southeast Asia and realize an ASEAN community. It also confirmed that for regional development, human resource development through intra-regional international cooperation is essential. In response to this, ASEAN began placing emphasis on the field of education, and in 2006, held the First ASEAN Education Ministers Meeting in conjunction with the Forty-first SEAMEO Council Conference where the building of ASEAN social and cultural community awareness and education quality for national development were discussed. Furthermore, the Second ASEAN Education Ministers Meeting (in conjunction with the Forty-second SEAMEO Council Conference) held in 2007 discussed the fostering of ASEAN citizens, the importance of cultivating ASEAN identity and education, the continuance of the ASEAN Student Exchange Programme, the formation of high school networks on science and mathematics, educational cooperation with participating nations of the East Asia Summit, cooperation with SEAMEO, fortification of the AUN, and the promotion of "ASEANness" among students. In the Third ASEAN Education Ministers Meeting (in conjunction with the Forty-third SEAMEO Council Conference) held in 2008, agreement was reached on progressing regional networks in higher education, further strengthening the relationship between ASEAN and SEAMEO. Especially recently, coordinated activities with SEAMEO Regional Institute for Higher Education and Development (RIHED) are being enhanced.

Similarly, ties with AUN are very strong. This intra-regional network of ASEAN countries is conducting activities, for example, student–faculty exchanges, collaborative research, information sharing, and ASEAN research promotion in order to promote mutual understanding. AUN/SEED-Net, another ASEAN network on engineering education, was also established as a subnetwork of AUN in order to improve the educational/research abilities of member universities, enhance intra-regional academic exchanges, and contribute to accompanying socioeconomic developments of Asia. The above indicates that even when we consider ASEAN alone, there are mutually intimate and overlapping networks supporting regional cooperation. As of January 2012, 26 universities from ten ASEAN countries are members of AUN. AUN states that it emphasizes specific fields of cooperation, which include Engineering, Business and Economics, Human Rights Education, Inter-Library Cooperation, Intellectual Property, and University Social Responsibility and Sustainability, as well as cultural programs to build mutual understanding and increase linkage of peoples that would yield regional identity and promote regional mobility in the near future. AUN also extends its cooperation to the active ASEAN Dialogue Partners such as China, Japan, Republic of Korea, the European Union (EU), and the United States.[2]

University Cooperation Programs

The multilayered nature can also be seen in the university cooperation programs conducted by individual universities. With today's increasing need for internationalization, individual universities in Asia are becoming more active in launching coordinated programs. For example, the MBA program titled *S3 Asia MBA* conducted by Korea University Business School (South Korea), the National University of Singapore Business School (Singapore), and the Fudan University School of Management (China) is a double-degree program in which students study for six months in each of the three universities, and after completing the one-and-a-half years receive two MBAs, one from their enrolled university and another from one of the other two universities, chosen by the students. Meanwhile, Fudan University, a member university of this program, also operates another double-degree program with Keio University (Japan) and Yonsei University (South Korea), targeting Master's Program students in order to "foster researchers that lead the governance of the information society."

Furthermore, Yonsei University and Keio University comprise, together with the University of Hong Kong, the 3 Campus Comparative East Asian Studies. In this program, all undergraduate students study one semester at each of Keio, Hong Kong, and Yonsei universities. This shows that one university participates in several networks based on its strategy, seeking for diverse international cooperation schemes. It is an instance of *an East Asia's web* of cooperation as Pempel (2005) has pointed out.

International Cooperation Originating in the Asia-Pacific region

Some of these regional networks and university cooperative activities within the Asian region also involve interregional cooperation outside of Asia, creating another multilayer in this aspect. For example, in addition to the cooperation program within the ASEAN region, out-of-region programs include the ASEAN–EU University Network Programme (AUNP) and ASEAN–India Academic Exchanges.

There are also increasing numbers of interregional cooperation programs based in the Pacific region. In this region are found the APRU, the APRU World Institute (AWI), the Asia-Pacific Association for International Education (APAIE), the International Alliance of Research Universities (IARU), the Association of East Asian Research Universities (AEARU), the East Asia Four Universities Forum (Beijing University, Seoul National University, Vietnam National University, Hanoi, Tokyo University: BESETOHA), the Association of Southeast Asian Institutions of Higher Learning (ASAIHL), and so on. Furthermore, networks transcending the Asia-Pacific framework include the International Association of Universities (IAU), Academic Consortium 21 (AC21), the International Forum of Public Universities (IFPU), and Universitas 21 (U21), showing a multilayered spread of diverse networks: the movement to transcend borders of organizations and countries to enhance higher education functions so as to enable full exploitation of the characteristics of each member in fostering human resources that are truly needed in a globalized society.

Issues in International Cooperation

Requirements in establishing a cooperative structure

Multiple issues attend efforts to promote such regional cooperation, perhaps first and foremost of which is that of the international political and economic situation, and the visa problems that are attributed to this situation. Neubauer (2009) has emphasized how "increasing global interdependence" affects higher education focusing on quality assurance issues and this caveat can be applied to another aspect of international higher education. For example, the Asian economic crisis, often mentioned as the trigger that greatly influenced student mobility within Asia, brought major changes to the economic situations of students, causing some of them to return home without completing their study abroad and some of them to abandon their dreams and plans of studying abroad due to lack of funding. Moreover, the tightened regulations on visa acquisition for the United States in the wake of the 9/11 terrorist attacks forced Asian countries to adopt policies for higher education enhancement in their own countries, where the effects of economic situations are much smaller, accelerating the trend to fortify the system so as to answer the needs for domestic higher education. In any case, each country adjusts its dispatching and receiving of students by managing its immigration control policy, and this is a major factor also when conducting universities cooperation programs where faculty members require flexible mobility across borders.

The next important issue in enabling university cooperation is that of program language. Since cooperative programs are chosen by students from diverse cultural backgrounds, the mainstream program language of convenience is English. However, some humanities projects, while also using English, focus on the languages and cultures of the cooperating countries themselves, and therefore, other languages can also become program languages.

An important issue regarding program operation is credit approval and curriculum adjustment. Determining the mutual approval and compatibility of credits and adjusting curriculum differences between the original institution of enrollment and cooperating universities requires meticulous preparations before launching university cooperation efforts. Of equal or even greater importance is the very complicated issue of coordinating the academic calendars of institutions seeking to cooperate. These issues are sufficiently complicated when only two universities are involved; when three seek such coordination, the result is extreme complexity.

Along with the program content, essential items in terms of the sustainability and development of the program are financial and human resource bases. Especially for international university cooperation, the issue of sustaining the financial base also involves that of the autonomy of participating countries and education agencies, making mutual adjustment difficult. For instance, in the case of ASEAN, the network includes ten countries with significant economic disparities, and one of the major operative issues is how to arrange compensation for these differences. The financial base of international education exchange is, for all programs including international universities cooperation programs, generally directly connected to the program's operating expenses, scholarships, and housing. What is more, the financial base is not something that can be secured once and forgotten; in order to sustain the program, it is a continuing issue that must be constantly considered.

The importance of the human resource base connected with the program also must not be ignored. Many of the cooperation programs are initiated through personal relationships among faculty members, after which the education entities start to make formal contact. In planning and operating the program, an attitude of active involvement in such a cumbersome process, including the logistics aspect, is especially important, and therefore, without a solid human resource base, dealing with the myriad of tasks and procedures required when establishing a network for cooperation programs would be nearly impossible. From another perspective, the operation itself of such cooperation programs may provide opportunities to consciously consider the significance of transnational cooperation and regional networks. The strong leadership and practical abilities of program personnel are key points in conducting cooperation programs, and each university must adopt a proactive and independent stance.

Related to program content is the issue of how to assure the quality of the university cooperative program. This issue is already being faced by many of the transnational programs being conducted in Asia in various forms. The credibility of the program itself cannot be assured unless verification is conducted on points such as the type of human resources the program intends to foster, how the program plans to achieve this goal, and the kinds of abilities, including qualifications and skills, are the objects of the human resources being fostered by the program and their relation to those deemed necessary to be successful in a global society. This is also a major issue from the perspective of program sustainability.

Coordination and Multilayered Nature of the Quality Assurance System

The requirements for constituting collaborative structures of this type are closely related to higher education quality assurance issues. Along with the development of various regional networks and university cooperation programs, the development of an overall quality assurance "system" is also occurring on a multilayered basis in Asia. Outside the region, international quality assurance efforts are already being made, namely the UNESCO/Organization for Economic Development (OECD) guidelines on "Quality provision in cross-border higher education" and the call by UNESCO for cooperation among higher education stakeholders including governments, universities, student organizations, evaluation agencies, and international evaluation organizations/networks. As for the international quality assurance network of third-party evaluation agencies in each country, the International Network for Quality Assurance Agencies in Higher Education, or INQAAHE, was established in 1991, which promotes good practice for quality maintenance and the improvement of higher education; controls quality and encourages practice and research; supports the development of quality assurance agencies and promotes coordination among such agencies; supports the establishment of international standards; disseminates information on quality assurance; develops credit compatibility plans; and promotes international student mobility (INQAAHE 2012).

A regional agreement regarding quality assurance in the Asia-Pacific region is the APQN established in 2003. The purpose of APQN is to enhance coordination and cooperation among quality assurance agencies of higher education in the Asia-Pacific region and to improve the quality of regional higher education. To supplement the UNESCO/OECD guidelines on "Quality provision in cross-border higher education" (aforementioned), the UNESCO-APQN Toolkit: Regulating the Quality of Cross-border Education (2006) was announced, discussing support and methods of support for regulating education quality assurance in providing and receiving cross-border education. The characteristics of this guideline are that it targets policy makers, government employees, quality assurance agencies, education agencies, international organizations, and others, and is specific and practical, based on case studies of regulation frameworks in receiving/providing countries (China, Hong Kong, Malaysia, New Zealand, Australia, the United Kingdom, and the United States).

The activities of APQN accelerated when the Brisbane Communiqué in 2006 identified the trend of international student mobility and the importance of quality assurance in regional education resulting from this trend. This Communiqué dealt with regional quality assurance networks based on international standards, qualification authentication, teaching licenses especially in the fields of science and mathematics education, and authentication of technologies and skills conducive to regional development, and at the same time, suggested the creation of a framework similar to those in Europe, such as the Bologna and the Copenhagen processes. Furthermore, APQN presented a report titled "Quality Assurance Arrangements in Higher Education in the Broader Asia-Pacific Region" (2008) as well as the Constitution that would serve as the foundation of APQN activities, confirming its intent, as a nonprofit global network collaborating with INQAAHE, of supporting and promoting good practice that contributes to the maintenance and improvement of quality assurance in higher education in the Asia-Pacific region. In the same year, the Chiba Principles (2008), with its main pillars of quality assurance, quality assessment, and quality assurance agencies, was adopted. Confirmed through this adoption were the needs for: (1) contribution to the regional cooperation system in dealing with issues and the practice of quality assurance; (2) efforts toward consistency and agreement on a standard in quality assurance; (3) the promotion of regional shifting/exchanges of students and staff; (4) fostering mutual trust and understanding in the higher education system of the Asia-Pacific region; (5) improvement in transparency and accountability in higher education agencies and their practices; and (6) regional cooperation that follows international developments in quality assurance.

Aside from APQN, ASEAN recently devised guidelines on quality assurance. The AUN has been emphasizing quality assurance activities named "AUN-Quality Assurance" since 1998 based on the awareness that quality assurance at regional levels helps improve and maintain the quality of all higher education agencies of ASEAN and devised the AUN-QA Guidelines in 2004 and the AUN-QA Manual for the Implementation of Guidelines in 2006. In 2008, the ASEAN Quality Assurance Network (AQAN) comprising ASEAN member countries was organized, so as to promote collaboration among QA-related agencies in individual ASEAN countries. It is said that AQAN is attempting to realize collaboration with INQAAHE and APQN, which indicates that international cooperation in quality assurance is now taking on a multilayered structure. It is important for ASEAN to raise standards at higher education institutions across 10 member countries to improve the higher education quality to ensure the quality of their graduates, and to train the skilled work force necessary for economic development.

Autonomy of Country Governments and Higher Education Agencies and Networks

On the one hand, such international responses surrounding quality assurance provide an international guarantee of the quality assurance system of higher education necessary for fostering successful global human resources, and also facilitate program selection by students from other countries/regions by determining through international networks the various forms that higher education should take, resulting in an ease of acquiring more human resources. On the other hand, there arises the dilemma of establishing quality assurance based on international standards while maintaining national governance within the country and the autonomy of higher education agencies. Hawkins (2011, 75–86) has reviewed quality assurance systems of various Asian countries on some axes and, as one of the results, pointed out that quality assurance of higher education institutions in some respects is recognized as part of the national system, but in other contexts, it requires a procedure above and beyond standard regulatory measures and ministry of education approval. He has categorized examples of Asian countries where the goal of becoming globally or regionally competitive in higher education appears to be the priority, and there are other cases where more local/national interests prevail. Amid the development of transnational higher education and the intensification of international shifting of and the acquisition battle for students, competing with other countries in promoting the superiority of one's country's higher education has become an urgent issue.

As a result, for example, countries like Malaysia chose to link its accreditation system with those of other Asian countries, and are aiming to fortify the function of domestic quality assurance in this international competition by referring to the standards of the Australian Universities Quality Agency, the New Zealand Qualifications Authority, the office for National Education Standards and Quality Assessment in Thailand, and the University Association Quality Assurance Network in Singapore. Malaysia is also characteristic in its development of an international quality assurance network, collaborating with AQAN; on the one hand, while on the other, it is beginning to actively participate in the Association of Quality Assurance Agencies of the Islamic World (AQAAIW), with Malaysia as an Islamic society choosing to take a leadership role.

Such participation in and collaboration with international networks is a new trend that has emerged from the advancement of globalization in higher education as a national strategy that aims to match Malaysian higher education policy to not only meet domestic needs but also to seek international standards so as to gain more versatility in its international higher education. Amid the transnational movement of international higher education, the issue of quality assurance is an indispensable aspect for human resource development and the establishment of a solid education program for this purpose.

Transnational programs are effective in attracting international students for multiple reasons, including economic reasonableness, efficiency, and ease of degree acquisition, and constitute an effective method for governments to enhance their overall higher education. However, without guarantees for the credibility and validity of the degrees and qualifications gained through the process, the incentives for these programs would soon lose their appeal. In that sense, the transnational movement of higher education reflects the processes of international student mobility, concerns with transnational programs and the political and economic intentions of governments joining these networks as member countries.

The relatively newly developed Confucius Institutes are another case of international networking under the autonomy of an individual country. The Confucius Institutes are a nonprofit public organization aligned with the Chinese government that aim to promote Chinese language and culture by supporting Chinese learning and study internationally, and promoting cultural exchanges. Headquartered in Beijing, the program is controlled by the Office of the Chinese Language Council International (Hanban). The institutes operate in cooperation with local affiliated colleges and universities around the world with financing shared between Hanban and the host institutions. After establishing a pilot institute in Tashkent, Uzbekistan, in 2004, the first Confucius Institute opened in 2004 in Seoul, South Korea, and after that, the number of schools has been increasing rapidly in the United States, Japan, and other major countries. As of November 2011, 350 Confucius Institutes have been established in 105 countries, and the website can be accessed in English, French, German, and others, and it is said that Hanban aims to establish 1,000 Confucius Institutes by 2020.[3]

The networking of Confucius Institutes has expanded beyond Asia and its influence cannot be overlooked as *soft power*. This system consists of the mutual cooperation of local institutions and educational exchanges, but at the same time, it symbolizes the Chinese government's cultural policy and international strategy to expand Chinese political power related with its economic development. Hayhoe and Liu (2010, 89) conclude that the establishment of Confucius Institutes around the world and China's cross-border programs are attracting more international students, and China's universities are moving from the periphery toward the center.

New Regionalism and Regionalization through Regional Networks

Besides the relationship of member countries and regional networks, it should be pointed out that a regional network is organized in order to integrate the region in competition with another region, which leads to a new regionalism. The SAARC and its regional academic network is one of the cases. SAARC consists of eight countries of South Asia: Afghanistan, Bangladesh, Bhutan, India, Maldives, Nepal, Pakistan, and Sri Lanka. Even while these countries have myriad differences across political, economic, and social issues, they have started a cooperation program for human resource development and regional exchange through higher education, namely the South Asian University (SAU hereafter), which was sponsored by the eight member states of SAARC and established in the suburb of New Delhi in 2007.

SAU's vision was first outlined by the Prime Minister of India, Manmohan Singh, at the Thirteenth SAARC Summit in Dhaka in 2005. He proposed the mission as:

> The people of our subcontinent are at the cutting edge of scientific and technological research and in the front ranks of the knowledge society across the world. Wherever an enabling environment and world-class facilities are made available to our talented people, they excel. Let this become a forum where our academicians, scholars, researchers and gifted students can work together in the service of human advancement.[4]

As the speech indicates, SAU aims to achieve human resource development of a knowledge-based society in the South Asian region and focuses on science and technology fields to do so. It also encourages regional leaders to share a common way of thinking and understanding of the multicultural society and different cultures. Based on this mission, SAU's curriculum consists of economics and computer science since August 1010, and law, sociology, international relations, and biotechnology since July 2011 as graduate programs. Besides these SAU courses, SAARC supports distance-learning programs and cooperation among major universities in the region.[5]

Examining the SAARC regional network in higher education demonstrates that South Asian countries are seeking to build regionalism through a regional education system. Prime Minister Singh has said:

> It is important that we assess South Asia Regional Cooperation in the larger Asian context. Today, ASEAN is evolving rapidly into a truly integrated economic community. Parallel to this intra-ASEAN integration is the broader movement towards economic integration in the context of the proposed East Asian Economic Summit. We are clearly witnessing nothing short of an Asian resurgence based upon the rebuilding of the pre-colonial arteries of trade and commerce that created a distinct Asian identity in the first place. My question is, is SAARC prepared to be an integral part of this emerging Asian resurgence or is it content to remain marginalized at its periphery? If our region wishes to be a part of the dynamic Asia, which is emerging in our neighborhood, then we must act and act speedily.[6]

From this point of view, South Asian countries are aware of the ASEAN movement.

This SAARC concern applies to another new movement toward a regional network among China, Japan, and South Korea, called "Campus

Asia: Collective Action for Mobility Program of University Students in Asia." This concept has been initiated by these country governments, and aims at development of human resources in the region as the Asia version of the Erasmus Mundus Program in Europe. Students can take educational programs from the member universities of three countries. The Campus Asia is an instance of government-led networking and also promotes student and faculty mobility among East Asian countries in the "larger Asian context" as well as the AUN. This trend is one of the subjects to be considered by SAARC.

The region of South Asia has become an international education market and, at the same time, it has suffered from brain drain. The SAU and its related regional educational network is a strategic way to integrate and educate young regional leaders to keep up with other regions like ASEAN, Central Asia, the Middle East, and West Asia. South Asian countries have already recognized that they must resolve to become a part of ongoing transformations and there is an imperative need to change and overcome the divisions of history and politics to forge a new architecture of mutually beneficial economic partnership – the regional network structure has important functions to perform in building such a new partnership.

Conclusion: Prospects of Regional Networks and International Cooperation in East Asian Higher Education

The regional networks and other instances of international cooperation in East Asia today are becoming truly expansive and multilayered based on mechanisms initiated by national governments and by non-state actors including individual universities. Such broadening is expected to continue further, along with the diversification of student mobility, with the globalization of higher education, expansion of international student policies, and the development of transnational education structures that support such trends. Although there are still issues that need to be resolved, such as immigration control relating to the shifting of people and programs, program language, financial and personnel affairs, as well as adjustments to be made in accreditation assessment, credit compatibility, and quality assurance including curriculum setting, the regional network structure and the international cooperation urge of various actors to exchange and discuss what is a more appropriate educational system for human resource development in a region are likely to continue.

These have an effect on both regionalism and regionalization. The regional networks in East Asia have been initiated by the national governments or regional communities and they symbolize regionalism that is based on the member countries' political and economic strategies. The AUN, SAU of SAARC, and Campus Asia are examples of international higher education reflected by the member countries' interests and autonomy. However, they are also seeking greater regional unity and identity through the development of common academic programs, which is a common direction of integration by regionalization. On the other hand, there are various kinds of international cooperation programs based on non-state actors developing in East Asia. Many of them are managed by their respective universities and are both driven by and respond to individual education needs. They are reflected by the popularity of people in general at the grassroots level. In this sense, these cooperative efforts lead toward regionalization. However, as the quality assurance network systems show us, it is important for each university program to adhere to and advance quality standards, and every national government is very keen on gaining quality control of transnational programs. This means that regionalization in East Asia is in progress in accordance with regionalism fostered by national governments.

Regional networks and international cooperation in higher education suggest new and enriched forms of international higher education for bettering human resource development in East Asia. Considering the current status of the dynamic and diverse dimensions of student mobility and the development of transnational programs, ample potential exists for the expansion of educational linkages in the near future. The function of regional networks and international cooperation of East Asian higher education is to produce a prospect of regional integration with a multilayered cooperation structure, in which regionalization and regionalism progress simultaneously.

Notes

1. Knight, Jane (2006), Interview on "Commercial Cross border Education: Implications for Financing Higher Education" by Global University Network for Innovation http://web.guni2005.upc.es/interviews/detail.php?chlang=en&id=185 (accessed January 31, 2012).
2. ASEAN University Network-Quality Assurance 2012, http://www.aunsec.org/site/meeting/AUNQATrainingCourse/2012/wp-content/uploads/2011/12/011.jpg (accessed January 30, 2012).

3. China Central Television 2011, "Confucius Chinese school's influence to international cooperation between China and foreign countries," CCTV, December 5, 2011. www.chinese.cn/college/article/2011–12/05/content_391203.htm (accessed January 27, 2012).
4. SAARC, South Asian University 2005, "Speech of Prime Minister of India, Man Mohan Singh" at the 13th SAARC Summit in Dhaka, November 12, 2005, www.southasianuniversity.org/default.html (accessed January 24, 2012).
5. SAARC, South Asian University 2011, http://www.saarc-sec.org/ (accessed November 22, 2011).
6. SAARC, South Asian University 2005, "Speech of Prime Minister of India, Manmohan Singh" at the 13th SAARC Summit in Dhaka, November 12, 2005, www.southasianuniversity.org/default.html (accessed January 24, 2012).

References

Hawkins, John N. 2011. "Higher Education and Quality Assurance: Trends and Tensions in Asia." In *Policy Debates in Comparative, International, and Development Education*, ed. John N. Hawkins and W. James Jacob. New York: Palgrave, Macmillan, pp. 71–88.

Hayhoe, Ruth, and Liu, Jian. 2010. "China's Universities, Cross-Border Education, and Dialogue among Civilization." In *Crossing Borders in East Asian Higher Education*, ed. David W. Chapman, William K. Cummings, and Gerard A. Postiglione. Heidelberg: Springer Dordrecht, pp. 77–100.

INQAAHE. 2012. Available at: www.inqaahe.org/. Accessed March 13, 2012.

Katzenstein, P. J. 2006. "East Asia: Beyond Japan." In *The Dynamics of East Asian Regionalism*, ed. P. J. Katzenstein and Takashi Shiraishi. Ithaca, NY: Cornell University Press, pp. 1–33.

Knight, Jane 2006. Interview on "Commercial Cross border Education: Implications for Financing Higher Education" by Global University Network for Innovation. Available at: http://web.guni2005.upc.es/interviews/detail.php?chlang=en&id=185. Accessed January 31, 2012.

McBurnie, Grant, and Christopher Zigrus. 2007. *Transnational Education: Issues and Trends in Offshore Higher Education*. London and New York: Routledge.

Neubauer, Deane E. 2009. "Doing Quality as Public Policy." In *Higher Education in Asia/Pacific*, ed. Terance W. Bigalke and Deane E. Neubauer. New York: Palgrave Macmillan.

Pempel, T. J. 2005. "Introduction: Emerging Webs of Regional Connectedness." In *Remapping East Asia: The Construction of a Region*, ed. T. J. Pempel. Ithaca: Cornell University Press.

Postiglione, Gerard A., and Chapman, David W. 2010. "East Asia's Experience of Border Crossing: Assessing Future Prospects." *Crossing Borders in East Asian Higher Education*. Hong Kong: Springer, Comparative Education Research Centre, The University of Hong Kong, pp. 377–382.

Shiraishi, Takashi. 2006. "The Third Wave: Southeast Asia and Middle-Class Formation in the Making of a Region," in *The Dynamics of East Asian Regionalism*, ed. P. J. Katzenstein and Takashi Shiraishi. Ithaca, NY: Cornell University Press, pp. 237–271.

Sugimura, Miki, and Kuroda Kazuo, eds. 2009. *Ajia ni okeru Chiiki Renkei Kyôiku Furemuwaku to Daigakukan Renkei Jireino Kensyô* (*Verification of Regional Education Network and Universities Cooperation Cases in Asia*). Research Report Provided in the FY 2008 Support Center Project for Academia's International Development Cooperation by the Ministry of Education, Culture, Sports, Science and Technology. Available at: www.emeraldinsight.com/journals.htm?articleid=17009851 (in Japanese). Accessed March 13, 2012.

Sugimura, Miki. 2010. "kôtô kyôiku no Kokusai-ka to Ryugakusei Idô no Henyô" (Internationalization of Higher Education and Change of International Student Mobility: The Case of Malaysia as a Transit Point). *Journal of Educational Studies*, Sophia University, 44: 37–50 (in Japanese).

Sugimura, Miki. 2011. "Diversification of International Student Mobility and Transnational Programs in Asian Higher Education." *Comparative Education*, Japan Comparative Education Society, 43: 45–61.

Part II

Country Studies

Chapter 5

Japanese Higher Education and Multilateral Initiatives in East Asia

Akiyoshi Yonezawa and
Arthur Meerman

Introduction

In March 2011, eastern Japan was struck by the largest earthquake and tsunami on national record, triggering an ongoing crisis at the Fukushima nuclear power plants. Many of the cities and institutions directly impacted by this triple-faceted event have managed to achieve remarkable recovery in a very short time. However, confidence and trust in those in positions of political, administrative, and intellectual leadership were badly shaken. Preparedness of the nation and the mechanisms in place not only to deal with unforeseen crises, but also with the increased pace of change both at the national and regional levels are now being questioned. Furthermore, ongoing economic stagnation, the various predicted consequences of a rapidly aging population, and challenges posed by the expansion of largely uncoordinated multilateral initiatives in East Asia have placed pressure on Japanese higher education to adapt to changing expectations and evolve with changing realities.

Japan has for about the last 40 years enjoyed a distinguished position in terms of economic strength and soft-power influence. On the world stage, in 2011, Japan maintained the third largest economy in terms of nominal gross domestic product (GDP) (US$5.9 trillion), following the United

States (US$15.2 trillion) and China ($7.0 trillion). Within the Asia-Pacific region, the ten wealthiest countries and economies in terms of nominal GDP were, behind China and Japan, Australia ($1.5 trillion), the Republic of Korea ($1.2 trillion), Indonesia ($834.3 billion), Taiwan ($504.6 billion), Thailand ($339.4 billion), Malaysia ($247.6 billion), Hong Kong ($246.8 billion), and Singapore ($266.5 billion).[1]

However, with regard to higher education as a global service industry in education and research, the visibility of Japan is highly limited (Marginson and van der Wende 2007). Japan's culturally and linguistically isolated labor market acts to further the invisibility of its higher education system. In a nation that has come to be afflicted with "diploma disease" (Dore 1997), Japanese employers have come to rely on the selectivity of higher education institutions as a proxy indicator of applicant trainability, rather than emphasizing the acquisition of skills, knowledge, or competencies of future employees. The direct linkage between the content of higher education and what is expected of higher education graduates in the labor market is weak (Honda 2009; Yoshimoto and Yamada 2007). In Japan, the proportion of students who completed a tertiary program was 89 percent in 2008, highest among Organization for Economic Cooperation and Development (OECD) countries (OECD 2010). On the one hand, these facts may explain long-standing doubts as to the relevance and quality of Japanese higher education (Morita 1966; McVeigh 2002).

On the other hand, the research performance of Japanese universities and governmental investment in research has enabled several Japanese universities to maintain "world-class" rank and recognition. In the 2011 Academic Ranking of World Universities (ARWU), for example, nine Japanese universities were ranked among the top 200 universities worldwide (specifically, the University of Tokyo, 21; Kyoto University, 27; Osaka University, 82; Nagoya University, 94; Tohoku University, 97; Hokkaido University, the Tokyo Institute of Technology, 102–150; and Kyushu University, University of Tsukuba, 151–200). However, a new ranking by *Times Higher Education* employing wider indicators with modification in size, fields, and regions works negatively toward the ranking positions among top Japanese universities (the University of Tokyo, 30; Kyoto University, 52; Tokyo Institute of Technology, 108; Osaka University, 119; Tohoku University, 120 in 2011).[2]

In addition, the latest data on the numbers of international students published by prospective governments show that Japan (138,075 in 2011) is no longer the distinguished destination it previously was for international students compared with China (265,090 in 2010) and Korea (83,842 in 2010). The transnational mobility of Japanese researchers has not improved over the last decade, either, which is not in line with the rapidly increasing "brain circulation" (or flow) among newer industrial economies such as South Korea, China, and India (Sunami 2010).

Most Asian higher education systems have managed to sustain continuous development in a global environment characterized by economic uncertainty, which is also increasingly punctuated with the sudden rise and decline of governments, if not entire nations. However, increasingly complex regional dynamics, involving any combination of changing sociopolitical, demographic, economic, or technology/information-based factors, now present Japanese higher education with the need to reposition its role as a distinguished global leader to one as an active member in supporting multilateral initiatives within the Asia-Pacific region.

With an eye to effecting budgetary constraints, the newly governing Democratic Party of Japan (DPJ) from 2009 has redirected national fiscal priorities toward investment in human resources and the reduction of the financial burden for child-raising families. However, the budget for public services including higher education is now faced with possible reductions again, partly for generating budgetary room for recovery from disasters. At the same time, the DPJ government has also declared its intention to start collaborative action for promoting student exchanges with China and Korea under the scheme "Collective Action for Mobility Program of University Students" (CAMPUS Asia). However, at least at present, countries within the Asia-Pacific region do not enjoy a clear political consensus as to what fostering a "regional higher education arena" entails, while the region has already developed large cross-border flows of students and academics.

This chapter analyzes the recent structural evolution of the policy debate over the internationalization of Japanese higher education in times characterized by particularly strong financial constraints and with reference to trends in the higher education systems of neighboring East Asian countries. The authors describe the de facto formation of the regional but open higher education arena in Asia Pacific through multilateral initiatives, which continue to develop despite the lack of a developed regional policy consensus.

The Changing Context of Higher Education in the Asia-Pacific Region

Debate over the internationalization of Japanese higher education started in the early 1980s, when Japan had established its status as both a regional and global economic leader. At that time, Japanese enterprises faced strong pressure to internationalize themselves, both in an effort to combine the country's advanced technology and highly skilled labor force with less-expensive human resources in Asia, as well as to expand its markets worldwide. Furthermore, pressure for Japan to internationalize and to contribute to international society became a top policy agenda in light of growing anti-Japanese sentiment in the United States, whose automobile industry was then entering a protracted state of crisis. In the field of education, Prime Minister Nakasone started discussion on constructing a comprehensive strategic vision as a world leader based on knowledge and culture, which was followed by the introduction of several landmark policy initiatives. The academic positions of national universities, which had been almost monopolized by Japanese nationals as civil servants, were opened up to foreign nationals in 1982. A plan to invite 100,000 international students to Japan was realized in 2003. Graduate schools for international cooperation and development were established in several national universities, such as Nagoya University, Kobe University, and Hiroshima University, to provide programs in English for international students from primarily developing countries and Japanese students wishing to contribute to the international community. Other universities such as the University of Tokyo and Tokai University (private) actively accepted international students in the science and technology fields under the scheme of Official Development Aid, also offering programs in English. The government also stated its aim to increase investment in the basic sciences to contribute to the international academic community, partly in an effort to avoid criticism that the Japanese economy had enjoyed a "free ride" from the concentration of investment in the applied sciences. Through these schemes, Japan succeeded in attracting elite students and young researchers, especially from the East and Southeast Asia regions, and established a wide human network among academic and governmental leaders.

Over the last two decades, most countries and economies in East and Southeast Asia, with the exception of Japan, have experienced rapid economic development. The internationalization of higher education in this region has also progressed significantly. Initiatives such as the full-cost tuition policies for international students by the United Kingdom and Australia and the Asian economic crisis in 1997 did not change the overall pursuit of internationalization, but rather inspired the formation of transnational education and international student and faculty mobility based on market principles.

The rapid economic development of neighboring countries has resulted in an especially favorable international student market opportunity for Japan. In 2010, Japan attracted 141,774 international students, with 78.7 percent originating from China, South Korea, and Taiwan.[3] About two-thirds of international students are studying in the field of the humanities and social sciences and around 80 percent do not receive government scholarship support. The majority of international students in Japan are studying in undergraduate programs at private higher education institutions. These facts indicate that the international student market has been relying mainly on the tuition fees paid by international students and that demand remains high for programs offered in the Japanese language that allow students to develop skills and knowledge related to the Japanese economy and society. In the early 1980s, most international students were thought to have earned their living and study expenses though part-time employment during work in their study period in Japan. Presently, although the majority are still supporting themselves by such means, the number of students who can expect financial support from their home countries is increasing. In 2011, the number of international students (138,075) dropped slightly (–2.6 percent) especially among the non-university sector (special training colleges: –8.6 percent, preparatory programs: –24.3 percent).[4]

Impetus for Internationalization

In order to foster the internationalization of Japanese higher education, the attraction of international students and the internationalization of home campuses are indispensable. From the beginning of the twenty-first century, the government has redoubled efforts to enhance the international competitiveness of higher education in both these respects.

First, the government has tried to support world-class research through concentrated investment in a limited number of projects. In 2001, the then minister of education, Atsuko Toyama, revealed the "Toyama Plan" for revitalizing Japanese higher education by fostering the achievement of around 30 world-class universities. This policy entailed focused investment into top research units called "21st Century Centers for Excellence (COE21s)," for which leading universities competed (Yonezawa 2003). In 2007, the COE21 scheme was replaced by a further intensified program called Global Centers of Excellence, which reduced the number of selected units but invested more into each selected unit. For further concentration into top research, the government started the World Premier International Research Center Initiative scheme in 2007 (Yonezawa 2007). The government selected only five research units, calling for additional applications in 2010. Adding to this, the government started the Funding Program for World-Leading Innovative R&D on Science and Technology, investing 100 billion Japanese yen in 30 projects over five years starting in 2009.

Trends in neighboring countries, such as South Korea and China, as well as the United Kingdom and the United States, have always served as reference points when planning details.

Second, the government has implemented university governance reforms. Under the strong influence of the new public management policies, all national public universities were incorporated in 2004, with most local public universities having also been incorporated since that time. All national universities set up respective six-year goals and plans, and achievements were assessed by an evaluation committee set within the Ministry of Education, Culture, Sports, Science and Technology (MEXT). Within this evaluation scheme, the performance of education and research activities of each school at national universities (both undergraduate and graduate) were assessed, with results being published in March 2009. The results of the assessment were linked to financial allocation from 2010, while the actual amount of budgetary differentiation was in most cases negligible. However, private universities have been facing severe competition to survive in market conditions characterized by oversupply and a continuous decrease in the youth population. Sudden closures of programs or entire private institutions are not uncommon. The corporatization of public universities and the privatization and "marketization" of higher education are not unique to Japan but have now become general trends in East Asian higher education systems (Mok and James 2005).

Lastly, the government has tried to strengthen international linkages in Japanese higher education. Japanese business tends to emphasize lifetime employment with in-house training, and barriers exist for the international mobility of highly skilled human resources (Kuznetsov 2006). However, regardless of their size, the global economy forces enterprises operating in Japan to become globally minded and therefore both their motivation and capacity to invest in in-house training and lifetime employment have diminished. Together, the Ministry of Economics, Trade and Industry, and MEXT have published reports for fostering "global human resources" through Japanese higher education. From a macro-policy perspective, the internationalization of higher education, both through sending and accepting students, is an urgent goal to be achieved.

Obstacles to Further Development

In principle, the development of the Asian region presents favorable circumstances to the Japanese economy and society by improving the region's global status and furnishing a promising, highly populated consumer market. At the same time, the development of neighboring countries inevitably transforms the Japanese position within the region from being one of a distinguished leader into one of economic and political rivalry and competition. The attention Japan receives both within and from outside of the region as an example of a successful economic upstart and later powerhouse has declined. In around the 1980s, Vogel (1979) and numerous others (e.g., Duke 1986; Stevenson et al. 1986; Stevenson and Stigler 1992) tried to analyze the economic success of Japan in relation to educational practice, and the US Department of Education (1987) launched a joint mission with the Japanese Ministry of Education to similarly investigate the characteristics of Japanese education. Currently, South Korea attracts much more attention in light of its enthusiastic attitude toward public and private investment in education. In terms of political and economic influence, China is definitely a current leader both for developed and developing countries and is sometimes referred to as being a member of the "G2" (the other partner being the United States). The Association of South East Asian Nations (ASEAN) countries are now transforming themselves into a more autonomous region through intra-regional collaboration and integration, and the organization is balancing linkages with Australasia, Northeast Asia (China, Korea, and Japan), North America, and Europe. Widespread academic and professional communication in the English language has doubtlessly improved the status of higher education in Singapore, Hong Kong, and Malaysia as regional hubs.

The development of international university rankings, such as Asia Week in the late 1990s, the Times Higher Education Supplement/QS, and the ARWU by Shanghai Jiao Tong University in the 2000s, has stimulated a race to achieve "world-class" universities throughout East Asia (Altbach and Balán 2007). Japan, however, has continued to struggle with prolonged economic recession and stagnation. Especially, decreased mobility throughout the social strata in a mature society lessened competition for access to higher education due to increased higher education provision combined with a decreasing youth population, and reduced study content in primary and secondary education in an effort to enhance "creativity" and to meet diversified learning needs has damaged the competitiveness and academic readiness of university entrants in this country. On the other hand, the graduation rate is still extremely high (89 percent in 2008; OECD 2010). This represents a structural difficulty for assuring high competency among university graduates. At the same time, a drastic change in the economic and political context of East Asia has forced Japan to conduct an introspective examination, resulting in a shift in the nation's self-identification in terms of higher education. In 2006, the Abe Cabinet had tried to establish an identity for Japan as the "Asian Gateway." In

2008, the Fukuda Cabinet established an official plan to invite 300,000 international students to the country, that is, to double or triple the existing number of international students in Japanese higher education by 2020. This target was based on the intention to bolster Japan's position as one of the largest host countries in terms of numbers of international students. However, this greatly expanded plan lost its impetus soon after having been announced, as a result of both an administration change with the election of Prime Minister Aso in September 2008 and a coinciding global financial crisis. In September 2009, the long-standing political dominance of the Liberal Democratic Party (LDP) ended with the formation of a new government alliance, led by the DPJ.

CAMPUS Asia and Its Consequences

The 2010 CAMPUS Asia initiative appeared to mark a shift in Japan's approach toward Asia, as was reflected in Prime Minister Yukio Hatoyama's vision of an "East Asian Community," which reflected his intention to make Japan's diplomatic position more independent of the strong influence of the United States. In fact, the movement to strengthen the relationship among China, Korea, and Japan had already started under the leadership of the LDP. In December 2008, the first Japan–China–Republic of Korea Trilateral Summit was held as the first official meeting independent of other occasions such as ASEAN + 3 or Asia Pacific Economic Cooperation (APEC) meetings. At the second summit in October 2009, Prime Minister Hatoyama argued for the importance of university exchange among the three countries, with this idea to be further promoted in the "joint statement on the tenth anniversary of trilateral cooperation among the People's Republic of China, Japan and the Republic of Korea." Based on this consensus, "CAMPUS Asia," the first Japan–China–Korea Committee for Promoting Exchange and Cooperation, was held in Tokyo in April 2010.[5] The purpose of this project is to let universities in the three countries serve as a platform for the exchange of academics and students. The immediate agenda of the meetings included the following:

1. Achieving mutual understanding on exchange programs and quality assurance;
2. Elaborating guidelines for exchange programs, including credit transfers and grading policies;
3. Implementing a pilot program and identifying necessary support systems; and

4. Achieving mutual understanding on university evaluation, publishing a common glossary of quality assurance, sharing information on university evaluation, visiting each other to observe the evaluation activities.

This movement parallels the establishment of the regional higher education framework in ASEAN countries. In 2008, the ASEAN Quality Assurance Network (AQAN) was established to allow collaboration and networking in higher education among ASEAN member countries. In 2010, following the general conference of the Asia Pacific Quality Network, an AQAN gathering and a meeting of three northeast Asian countries (Japan, South Korea, and China) were held separately in Bangkok. These varied gatherings illustrate that efforts to define "region" in terms of the Asia Pacific are still in their initial stages. Northeast Asian countries and economies in particular, namely, South Korea, China (including Hong Kong), Japan, and Taiwan, are now closely involved in pursuing effective means to foster the development of the international dimension in higher education based on prospective perspectives.

Hatoyama's political objective in shifting attention to relationships with Asian countries represented a diplomatic disagreement with the United States. Faced with territorial conflicts with Asian neighbors and strong support after the disasters in March 2011, Naoto Kan and Yoshihiko Noda, two prime ministers following Hatoyama, returned to the traditional diplomatic policy that stresses an alliance with the United States. At the same time, almost all Asian countries continued to stress the importance of higher education exchanges with the United States. This also had a significant influence on the practices of the CAMPUS Asia project. The discussion for promoting linkages between universities and industry in the three countries is still in its preliminary stages, with little possibility of resulting in concrete action in the immediate future.

Quality assurance agencies in the three countries of CAMPUS Asia continue to engage in regular exchanges for mutual understanding. However, at this point, there is no viable initiative for developing a regional framework for quality assurance. Most Asian countries and economies, including Japan's, have highly diversified and hierarchical higher education systems. Consequently, the discussion on quality assurance becomes highly complex, in that matters such as the validity of degrees, diplomas, and qualifications, with a common understanding of learning outcomes, easily tend to spark controversy and to frustrate rhetorical appeals to "harmonization." The influence of private higher education service providers and private employers (some of them being multinational) is also strong. Increasingly, complex dynamics between and among these and other factors render it difficult to achieve a common understanding as to the composition and future of a "regional higher education arena" in East Asia.

As for the promotion of student exchanges, ten pilot projects were selected for support under the framework of CAMPUS Asia. Committee members from the three member countries implemented the selection process jointly, and selected programs are expected to enhance the quality of student exchanges among mostly top-level universities. However, the Japanese government made its selections, while considering other projects with the United States and other countries, as a means to strengthen the capacity of Japanese universities for the internationalization of university education. No single member country's policies for the internationalization of higher education are limited to its relationship with the other two participating states.

Conclusion

Forces that drive international partnerships in regard to internationalization efforts include those that are diplomatic, economic, academic, and even emotional in nature, which can rapidly alternate between overlapping and contradicting one another. At the same time, no country in the region believes it possible to sustain its higher education system without region-wide collaboration. The rise of an Asian economy with multiple centers, such as China, Singapore, South Korea, India, and others, inevitably requires a shift in Japanese diplomacy including in the arena of higher education from one reflecting one-sided reliance to one espousing linkages with other OECD countries, to create a balance between East and West.

We are witnessing the formation of an international dimension of Asia-Pacific higher education through primarily regional multilateral initiatives. However, at this moment, there is neither a developed policy consensus to guide the process nor explicit agreement as to what the "regional higher education arena" in East Asia and the Asia-Pacific looks like. Initiated by Japan, South Korea, and China, CAMPUS Asia may be understood as a collaborative action for developing an open, internationalized higher education among three countries. At the same time, the dominance of individual "leaders" in Asia will always be challenged by strong or up-and-coming countries, or economies. Recent competition to become higher education "hubs" in Southeast Asia (i.e., Hong Kong, Singapore, and Malaysia) (Knight 2010) could be understood as an example of such phenomena. Mutual exchange and collaboration between higher education institutions and individual academics and students are already widespread and developing rapidly. By facing these common challenges, more or less, almost all higher education systems in East Asia and the world will be involved in open and multilateral, mutual reliance in higher education.

Notes

1. Central Intelligence Agency (CIA) World Factbook. Available at:www.cia.gov/library/publications/the-world-factbook/. Accessed March 27, 2012.
2. Academic Ranking of World Universities (ARWU). Available at:www.shanghairanking.com/ARWU2011.html. Accessed March 27, 2012.
3. Japan Student Services Organization (JASSO). Available at:www.jasso.go.jp/statistics/intl_student/data10_E.html. Accessed March 27, 2012.
4. Japan Student Services Organization (JASSO). Available at:www.jasso.go.jp/statistics/intl_student/data11_E.html. Accessed March 27, 2012.
5. Ministry of Education, Culture, Sports, Science and Technology (MEXT). Available at: www.mext.go.jp/english/koutou/1292773.htm. Accessed March 27, 2012.

References

Altbach, P. G., and J. Balán, eds. 2007. *World Class Worldwide: Transforming Research Universities in Asia and Latin America*. Baltimore, MD: Johns Hopkins University Press.

Dore, R. 1997. "Reflections on the Diploma Disease Twenty Years Later." *Assessment in Education: Principles, Policy & Practice* 4 (1): 189–206.

Duke, B. 1986. *The Japanese School: Lessons for Industrial America*. New York: Praeger.

Honda, Y. 2009. Kyoiku no Shokugyo teki Igi (The Meaning of Vocational Education). Tokyo: Chikuma Shobo (in Japanese).

Knight, J. 2010. "Quality Dilemma with Regional Education Hubs and Cities." In *Quality Assurance and University Rankings in Higher Education in the Asia Pacific*, ed. S. Kaur, M. Sirat, and W. G. Tierny. Penang, Malaysia: USM Press, pp. 99–119.

Kuznetsov, Y., ed. 2006. *Diaspora Networks and the International Migration and Skills*. Washington, DC: World Bank Institute

McVeigh, B. J. 2002. *Japanese Higher Education as Myth*. Armonk, NY: M. E. Sharpe.

Marginson, S., and M. Van der Wende. 2007. "Globalization and Higher Education." Working Paper No. 8, OECD Organization for Economic Cooperation and Development Conference, Paris.

Mok, K., and R. James, eds. 2005. *Globalization and Higher Education in East Asia*. New York, NY: Marshall Cavendish Academic.

Morita A. 1966. *Gakureki Muyo Ron (On the Uselessness of Academic Credentials)*. Tokyo: Bungei Shunju (in Japanese).

OECD 2010. *Education at a Glance 2010*, Paris: OECD.

Stevenson, H., and J. W. Stigler. 1992. *The Learning Gap: Why Our Schools are Failing and What We Can Learn from Japanese and Chinese Education*. Toronto: Summit Books.

Stevenson, H., H. Asuma, and K. Hakuta, eds. 1986. *Child Development and Education in Japan*. New York, NY: Freedman.

Sunami, A. 2010. "Expansion of Training Opportunities for Young Japanese Researchers." In *Japan Society for the Promotion of Science* (ed.), *Strategic Fund for Establishing International Headquarters in Universities*. Tokyo: JSPS, pp. 231–266.

US Department of Education. 1987. *Japanese Education Today*. Washington, DC: US Department of Education.

Vogel, E. F. 1979. *Japan as Number One: Lessons for America*. Cambridge, MA: Harvard University Press.

Yonezawa, A. 2003. "Making 'World-class Universities': Japan's Experiment." *Higher Education Management and Policy* 15 (2): 9–23.

Yonezawa, A. 2007. "Stability amidst a Storm of Evaluation: Policy Trends and Practice in Higher Education Evaluation in Japan." In *Quality Assessment for Higher Education in Europe*, ed. A. Cavalli. London: Portland Press, pp. 95–103.

Yoshimoto, K., and H. Yamada. 2007. "University Education and Its Relevance to Working Life: Selection, Education and Career Effects," in J. Allen et al. (eds), *Competencies, Higher Education and Career in Japan and the Netherlands*. New York: Springer, pp. 97–127.

Chapter 6

China in the Emerging Reality of Asia Regional Higher Education
Wen Wen

Introduction[1]

Although many scholars are skeptical of regional cooperation in Asia on the basis that the expansive cultural and social diversity in this region and its loose framework of associations provide no credible plan among Asian governments for building regionalism (Aggarwal and Koo 2007), regulatory regionalism is evolving in the region. This seems especially the case for Asian countries when taking into account the rise of China coupled with the current economic difficulties of the United States and Japan and the possible effect of these on their ability to influence regional engagement. Among the different forms of regionalization that may emerge, economic integration is key, as it is definitely accelerating. The initiation of the Association of South East Asian Nations (ASEAN)–China Free Trade Area in 2010 has great potential to produce huge benefits on all sides. In South Asia, the Dhaka Declaration of the South Asian Association for Regional Cooperation (SAARC) was established in 2005 to relieve poverty in this region. Kazakhstan, Kyrgy, Tajikistan, and Uzbekistan have signed an agreement to pursue a strategy for the development of the Central Asian economic community to facilitate a free-trade area, a customs union, and a unified labor market. All these regional economic cooperation establishments play an important role in promoting economic development in Asia, witness the overall value of exports in ASEAN in 2008 amounting to US$180 billion, while imports reached US$202.6 billion. The value of exports of SAARC was US$109.1 billion with the value of imports at US$100.5 billion (Song 2008).

The booming economic integration that has taken place in Asia requires intellectual and technical support that only a regional cooperative and integrated higher education system can provide. For higher education in specific, two forms of regional cooperation have emerged: one is regional networks, examples of which include the Southeast Asian Ministers of Education Organization (SEAMEO), the ASEAN University Network, the Southeast Asia Engineering Education Development Network (SEAEEDN), the Association of Pacific Rim Universities (APRU), the Asia-Pacific Network (APN), and so on. The other type of regional higher education cooperation is the university cooperation program that is conducted through interorganizational agreements, such as the Campus Asia program. These educational establishments have facilitated the wider process of harmonizing Asian higher education. However, compared with other world regions, efforts toward developing a harmonized higher education regime in Asia still lag far behind.

As one of the biggest powers in this region, China is moving fast on its way toward internationalization. China entered the World Trade Organization (WTO) in 2002, and successfully hosted the 2008 Olympics. Since 2008, China has responded in a responsible manner to the global financial crisis, and has established and supported numerous Confucius Institutes located throughout the world in response to the rapidly increasing demand for promoting Chinese language and culture. All these examples testify to the country's growing status and importance in international affairs. Its growing engagement in international affairs demands a higher education system that can nurture international talents. The country also needs to be more open to the world to allow others to understand its history, culture, and society. Though not much stressed by the central government, international student mobility is an important approach in this regard, allowing for greater openness to come into effect.

Student mobility in China is truly diverse. Although the outflow to English-speaking countries continues to grow, the country's international education market is booming, attracting much attention from other countries in this region and those of other regions. China is becoming fully engaged in what has become the acquisition battle for international students as a prerequisite to become an international hub of human resource development.

This chapter examines China's role in the emerging reality of Asian regional higher education mainly from the perspective of international student mobility. It assesses the composition of China's international education market, identifies the opportunities and challenges that the country faces, and finally examines the main issues of engagement in higher education regionalization.

Background to International Education in China

China's international education started to develop in the 1950s and 1960s, shortly after the founding of the People's Republic of China in 1949. During this period, most international students were drawn from neighboring Asian and African countries. From 1950 to 1966, China received 7,259 foreign students from 68 countries. Among these, 39.5 percent came from Vietnam, North Korea, and Albania, and 7.3 percent from African and Latin African countries. Only 1.9 percent were from Japan, Western Europe, and North America, all of whom were enrolled through nongovernmental agencies. Political considerations were the determining factor at that time. Indeed, 90.8 percent of the international students in China during the 1950s and 1960s came from 12 socialist countries.

The past three decades have seen rapid shifts in China's international education landscape, as changes intensify in alignment with China's dramatic economic development and active engagement in international issues. In particular, after 2001 and its entry into the WTO, China's gross domestic product (GDP) surpassed that of Germany to become the world's second largest economy. Overall, China's higher education has become open to an unprecedented extent, motivated in part by its need to face the challenges and opportunities brought about by globalization. Between 2000 and 2008, the average annual growth rate of international students studying in China exceeded 20 percent with the annual net growth reaching 30,000. 2008 became a landmark year as the number of international students exceeded 200,000 for the first time—equal to 180 times the number of international students in 1978 (1,200), 38 times the number in 1988 (5,835), and 5 times that in 1998 (43,084) (see Figure 6.1).[2]

Institutions enrolling international students have increased in number, size, and diversification. In 1979, only 23 academic institutions enrolled international students, compared to 363 in 2001. In 2008, the number of educational institutions serving international students had grown to 592. Besides the existence and growth of public colleges and universities, many research institutes and private educational institutions also moved to admit international students, such as the Chinese Academy of Sciences and the China Civil Aviation Management Institute (Jiang and Ma 2011).

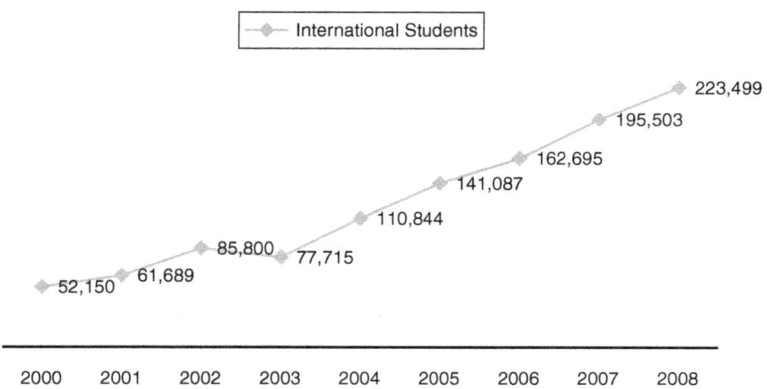

Figure 6.1 Growth of international students in China (2000–2008).

The International Education Market in China—Asian Dominance

International students studying in China come from 189 countries throughout the world with students from Asia accounting for approximately 68 percent (see Figure 6.2). According to available data, the percentage of Asian students reached 82 percent, its highest, in 2003, then declined to 68 percent in 2008 (mainly due to a decrease in the number of students sent by Japan). Among those countries that send students to China, Korea and Japan account for the largest numbers, as the sum of Korean and Japanese students together exceeds one-third of all the international students.

Among the top seven sending countries, five are Asian: Korea, Japan, Indonesia, Thailand, and Vietnam. However, for the first time in 2008, the number of American students exceeded those from Japan (see Figure 6.3). It is estimated that this trend will continue, particularly after the United States outlined a plan, announced during President Obama's visit to China in late 2009, to send 100,000 American students to study in China over the following four years.

An obvious trend when one looks at student nationalities is the increase in student numbers from ASEAN countries, from 4,155 in 2000 to 25,956 in 2008 for an annual increase rate of 65.6 percent. This total almost equaled that for European countries. In terms of the annual increasing rate, ASEAN countries enjoy the highest rate at 66.3 percent; the United

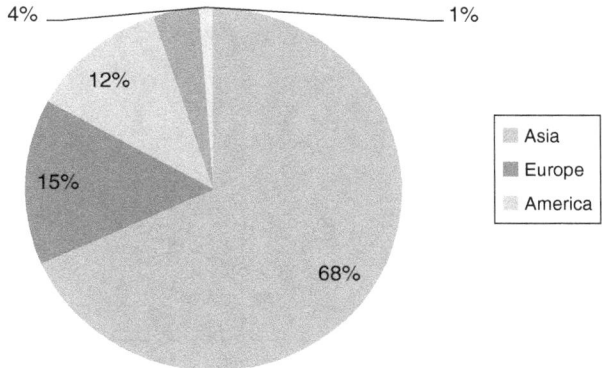

Figure 6.2 Percentage of international students according to world regions.

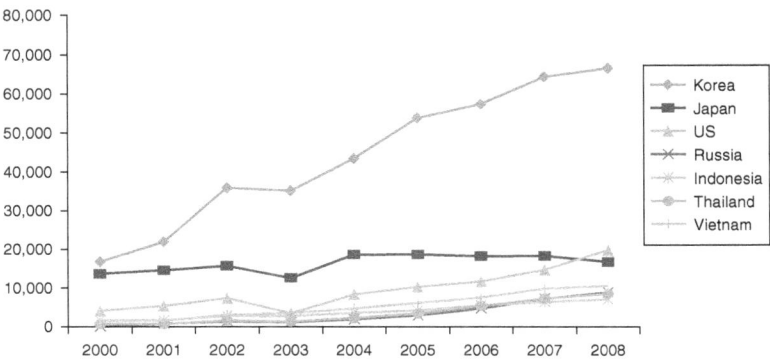

Figure 6.3 Origin countries of international students in China (2000–2008).

States, 45.7 percent; European countries, 57.2 percent; Korea and Japan, 21.6 percent (see Figure 6.4).

As for study fields and degree program level, it has long been considered that the gap between developed and developing countries has been enlarging, and Asian countries run a risk of being marginalized in the international higher education market. As is normal when internationalization takes place, one goes from promoting the transition and development of knowledge to producing economic outcomes. Developed countries, such as the United

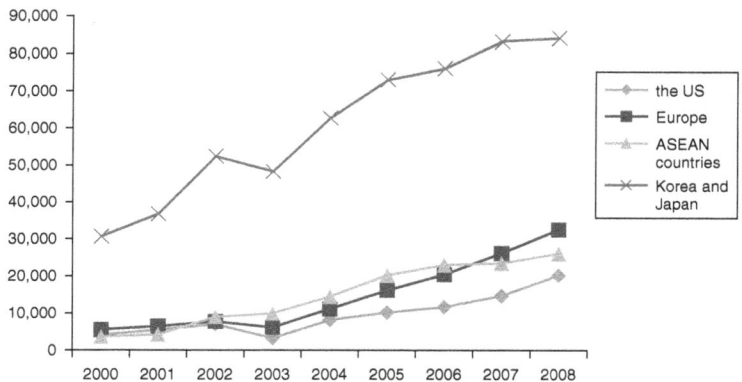

Figure 6.4 Origin regions/countries of international students in China (2000–2008).

Kingdom, Australia, New Zealand, and those of the European Union all consider higher education an important component of their service sectors, and see the internationalization of higher education as a huge market. From this perspective, they encourage their universities to compete for more international students. Universities in those countries thus develop subjects of particular instrumental value to international students, such as business, management, and biology, to render these programs more attractive. Recent data suggest that at least US$30 billion in tuition fees flow to Organization for Economic Cooperation and Development (OECD) countries from Asian countries. If living costs are included, the figure becomes US$60 billion to 80 billion (Song 2008). In the competition for international students, Asian countries stand at a relatively disadvantageous position, reflecting to a large degree the region's relative position in the international division of labor. Taiwan is an example: 10 percent of its students travel to Western countries to study high-technology-related subjects, while the majority of foreign students come to Taiwan primarily to study the Chinese language (Yu 2008). Mainland China is another example: only 6.4 percent of its international students study in postgraduate programs, while more than half of Chinese students go abroad for a master's or doctor's degree.

Overall, the level of international education in China is becoming more diversified. While most international students usually enrolled in nondegree, nonformal programs usually take Chinese-language training or a short-term study, the proportion enrolled in formal programs has increased yearly with a corresponding decline in the numbers pursuing nonformal

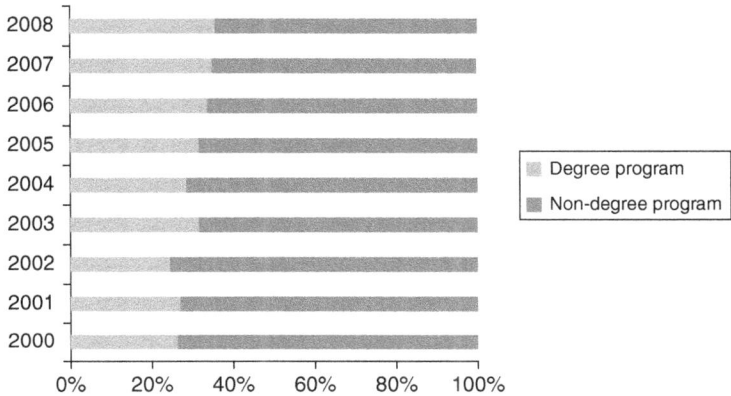

Figure 6.5 Percentage of international students in degree and nondegree programs.

programs. In 2004, of 110,844 international students in China, those in nonformal programs accounted for 71.5 percent but dropped to 64.2 percent in 2008, when the total number had increased to 223,499 with a corresponding increase in formal program enrollment from 28.5 percent in 2004 to 35.8 percent in 2008 (see Figure 6.5). Although the percentage of international students who study for a degree increased from 26.3 percent in 2000 to 35.8 percent in 2008, graduate students continue to represent a rather low proportion at only 6.4 percent.

Regarding study fields, although the percentage of students studying science and engineering rose rapidly from 3.2 percent in 2002 to 8.6 percent in 2008, it is still a rather small portion compared with language and related subjects. In 2008, a high proportion of international students continued to major in language and arts (64.1 percent), followed by other majors such as medicine and related subjects (12.8 percent), and economics and management (9.9 percent) (Figure 6.6).

To summarize, on the one hand, China's higher education has commanded a large and increasing share in the Asian market, thereby providing a good opportunity for China to play a leading role in regional higher education integration. Still, the level of international education is relatively low given the size of higher education in China, and the programs offered by higher education institutions remain limited in scope of subjects and degree. The overall effect is to restrict the number of international students flowing to China.

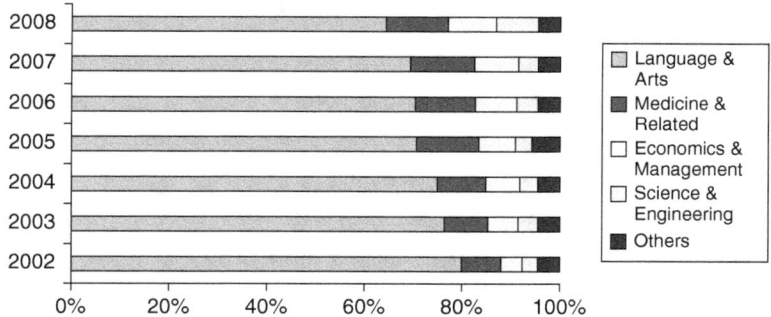

Figure 6.6 Percentage of international students by field.

Conclusion: Issues and Recommendations for China's Engagement in the Process of Higher Education Regionalization

1. *The Chinese government maintains an open position toward multilateral cooperation mechanisms.*

There is a tendency in China to say that: "China's regional interest stays with all its neighboring countries, not only in East Asia." This way of thinking clearly reflects China's stand on regionalization, namely, that China will not emphasize one mechanism as the only pillar of its regional strategy. On the contrary, in regard to different regionalization models, China has an open mind. Consequently, China has been a key participant and staunch supporter of the ASEAN + 3, the Shanghai Cooperation Organization, and the China–Japan–Korea and North East Asia cooperation mechanisms. Furthermore, central and local governments in China actively participate in various subregional cooperation mechanisms within Asia.

However, viewed from another perspective, it can be said that a wider strategic plan for regionalization is lacking at the state level. Although the Chinese government has seriously worked on promoting the internationalization of its higher education sector, efforts have mostly focused on improving research and teaching up to world-class standards. In fact, much stress has been placed on enhancing research cooperation, exchanges, and nurturing domestic students to become global citizens with an international vision, and to be competitive in the international labor market, while education for international students in China has been less emphasized.

Framed differently, much emphasis has been placed on internationalizing Chinese students, rather than improving the Chinese higher education market for international students. Realizing that it is far lagging behind its counterparts in North America, East Asia, and Europe in the international education market, China has moved to elevate international education on its agenda. In the recently released outline of China's National Plan for Medium and Long-term Education Reform and Development (2010–2020), the explicit goal is for China to become the biggest hosting country for international students in Asia and a major destination in the world. By maintaining an annual growth rate of 7 percent, it is expected that international students will reach 500,000 by 2020.

2. *"Province leading with the state approving"—a Chinese approach to regionalization*

The centralized structure of China's political system locates diplomatic power, theoretically, in the hands of the central government. However, in terms of regional cooperation and integration, provincial governments in practice enjoy considerable autonomy with provincial governments actively participating in various subregional cooperation establishments (Su 2010). In this structure, provinces in China are powerful financial hubs, equal in size to small state economies in the region. By comparing the GDP of Chinese provinces with neighboring countries, it can be seen that: (1) among the top 20 biggest economies in the Asia-Pacific Rim, 11 are countries and 9 are Chinese provinces; (2) among the 40 biggest economies in Asia-Pacific Rim, 16 are countries, while 24 are Chinese provinces; and (3) the GDP of Chinese border provinces is close or even higher than that of their neighboring countries.[3]

Yunnan and Guangxi provinces are instructive examples. These two Southwest China provinces possess GDPs of US$82.02 billion and 103.19 billion, respectively, and populations of 45.9 million and 46.0 million, respectively. The central government decentralizes political power to the two provinces to facilitate more efficient and effective regional cooperation, and to make them the most active participants engaging in ASEAN cooperation. In 2003, the then vice prime minister, Zeng Peiyan, publicly stressed Yunnan's position as the key player in the cooperative development of the ASEAN—Mekong Basin. Guangxi province is the main participant of the "China Vietnam two corridors and one circle" and "Nanning (the capital city of Guangxi province)-Singapore economic corridor" initiatives. With substantive autonomy, Yunan and Guangxi are the main decision-making centers for regionalization in China. The cooperation mechanism in these two provinces is extremely sophisticated, expanding from the state level to the institutional level. The "province leading, the state approving" model is thus a uniquely Chinese approach to regionalization.

3. *More autonomy is needed at the institutional level to facilitate substantive regional cooperation in higher education.*

Given that the diversities within Asia far exceed the commonalities, an outstanding feature of the dominant Asian cooperation mechanism is its composition of various complex formal and informal institutions. This could be explained as follows: As Asia is nowhere near the cultural affinities of West Europe (Terada 2003), a flexible informal institution/soft law construct that is usually formed in a "bottom-up" way, rather than the regulatory, compulsory formal institution/hard law approach is more acceptable to Asian countries when engaging in processes of regionalization.

Regarding higher education cooperation, the informal institutions, such as the Association of East Asian Research Universities (AEARU), APRU, BESETOHA,[4] and so on, which are initiated by universities, work much more effectively than formal institutions. Chinese universities are seriously engaged in regional cooperation by participating in the regional university associations mentioned above, receiving Asian students, supporting Chinese students and faculties to study or work in other Asian universities, conducting relevant research, and so on. However, as some aspects in higher education management are still under the control of the minister of education and provincial education administrations, individual universities enjoy limited autonomy, such as enrollment, degree conferring, subject establishment, and so on, and regional cooperation is somewhat restricted. Therefore, it is necessary for the Chinese government, at both national and provincial levels, to change the governance structures of its higher education system, and distribute more freedom to universities, such as encouraging higher education institutions to select partners based on their own features and advantage, to participate in multilateral organizations, and to initiate the process of regionalization.

4. *Lack of regional identity recognition is a crucial problem.*

The attention being given to regional identity stems from the belief that a strong regional identity is an important foundation for political and security cooperation (Johnston 2010). Higher education plays an important role in promoting regional awareness through student/scholar mobility, partnerships, and exchange of knowledge among academics. China has successfully instilled a sense of "national citizenship" to its people, and has worked hard to promote internationalization and the spirit of "global citizenship" among young people—witness, for example, the success of the 2008 Beijing Olympics. However, a lack of public awareness in China of its Asian identity persists. A survey to examine what percentage of the population has a sense of Asian identity found that only 43.5 percent of Chinese people admit that they have a sense of Asian identity, ranking

China far behind other Asian countries, namely Vietnam, Cambodia, Taiwan, Philippines, and Thailand (Johnston 2010). Therefore, balancing "global identity," "regional identity," and "national identity" is an urgent task for China. On a positive note, some efforts to address this imbalance have already begun. For example, Asian study centers have been established in many Chinese universities, and special scholarship quotas have been established for students from ASEAN countries to study in China.

Notes

1. The author would like to acknowledge sponsors of this research. Support was provided by the Humanities and Social Sciences Youth Fund of Ministry of Education of China （教育部人文社会科学研究青年基金项目）(Project No.: 11YJC880124) and the Tsinghua University Independent Research Fund （清华大学自主科研计划） （Project No.:2011Z04107）.
2. Data source for all figures: *China Education Statistic Yearbook* (2000–2008).
3. Data resource: http://ddp-ext.worldbank.org/ext/DDPQQ/member.do?method=get Members &userid=1& queryId =135.
4. A forum in which four representative East Asian Universities—Peking University, Seoul National University, the University of Tokyo, and Hanoi National University—met to discuss the present state and future directions of higher education in East Asia. The BESETOHA forum takes its name from the first two letters of the English names of the attending universities.

References

Aggarwal, V. K., and M. G. Koo. 2007. "The Evolution of Regionalism in East Asia." *Journal of East Asian Studies* 7: 360–369.

Jiang, K., and X. Ma. 2011. "Overseas Education in China: Changing Landscape and Policies." *International Higher Education* 63: 6–8.

Johnston, A. 2010. "Obstacles to Governance in East Asia: The Case of Security Communities." In *Security Cooperation and Regional Integration in Asia Conference Proceedings*, Global Institute for Asian Regional Integration, Waseda University, Tokyo, Japan, pp. 78–92.

Song, H. 2008. "A Review of Issues of Higher Education Internationalization," *Academics in China* 133: 17–24.

Su, C. 2010. "Bring Chinese Local Governments Back in Sub-regionalization." *World Politics* 5: 4–24.

Terada, T. 2003. "Constructing an 'East Asian' Concept and Growing Regional Identity: From EAEC to ASEAN=3." *The Pacific Review* 16 (2): 251–277.

Chapter 7

Locating Indonesia within the Emergent Regionalism of Southeast Asian Higher Education
Anthony R. Welch

The Indonesian higher education system presents a series of challenges to the growth of regionalism, underlining empirically that different states have differing capacities to engage with regional developments and agendas. While a key member of the Association of South East Asian Nations (ASEAN), and part of associated initiatives in regional higher education, such as the ASEAN Universities Network (AUN), the Association of Universities of Asia and the Pacific (AUAP), and the Association of Pacific Rim Universities (APRU), Indonesia's relatively peripheral status in the global knowledge system, as also domestic issues of institutional governance, limited regulatory capacity, quality, corruption, and financial constraints, all serve to inhibit a more robust engagement in regional initiatives. In this sense, the analysis here largely concurs with that of Jayasuriya (2003), in which he argues that much of the existing analysis of South East Asian regionalism, including at times by ASEAN member countries themselves, has been both triumphalist and too focused on "formal regional 'institutions',... to the detriment of the understanding of the domestic political mainsprings of regional governance" (Jayasuriya 2003, 199). Moreover, these regional initiatives themselves lack the more established character of their European Union (EU) counterparts, thereby limiting the capacity of what has been called regulatory regionalism. In this sense, ASEAN regionalism is at a less-mature stage compared to Europe, which, as Robertson points out, is now at times itself operating as a state actor (Jayasuriya 2010;

Mok 2010, 100; Robertson 2010, 25, 35). In another sense, however, both ASEAN and the EU recently had to face a similar challenge—the rise of China (Robertson 2010, 30; Jarvis and Welch 2011).

Simply put, as Jayasuriya points out, instituting regulatory regionalism in ASEAN

> will prove difficult in a region where there is scant evidence of a history of policy coordination and, moreover, where levels of economic development and the organization of...systems differ considerably. (Jayasuriya 2003, 209–210)

and where

> a substantial gap exists between formal policy pronouncements and their subsequent implementation. (Jayasuriya 2003, 210)

This is also clearly the case within Indonesia. Indeed, it can be argued that Indonesia's current state architecture is still developing and in particular has not entirely instituted the "complex systems of multi-level regulation, meta-governance, and systems of soft law" about which Jayasuriya speaks (Jayasuriya 2010, 128), as illustrated below in its regulation of higher education. Decentralization of governance in the post-Suharto era poses a further challenge to regionalism for Indonesia (Surakhmad 2002; Amirrachman et al. 2008), while its relatively peripheral status in the global knowledge network means that the panoply of regulatory regionalism that is evident in parts of East and Southeast Asia is less evident in Indonesia (Mok 2010; Yang and Welch 2012). This is arguably even more the case for the private sector, and Islamic higher education institutions (HEIs) under the control of the Ministry of Religious Affairs (MORA).

However, there are other elements of Indonesia's culture, history, identity, and international higher education engagement that further challenge traditional conceptions of regionalization. Two are treated as follows: extra-ASEAN partnerships, for example, with Australia, China, and Europe; and Islamic higher education, which has both strongly regional dimensions as well as links to Gulf States and the Middle East. Domestic constraints form the third test of regionalism, in particular, Indonesia's capacity for robust engagement.

The Indonesian Context

Higher education in Indonesia currently faces a number of interrelated challenges—of governance, demographics, and finance—each of which limits the capacity to engage robustly in regionalization. The world's largest majority-Muslim nation, a country of around 230 million inhabitants (of whom around one quarter are under the age of 15 years), with a higher education population totalling around 3.4 million, was hit hard by the regional economic crisis of the late 1990s, leading to a debt burden of major proportions, from which it is now emerging strongly.[1] The postcrisis bailout of some US$23 billion by the International Monetary Fund (IMF), World Bank, and Asian Development Bank came with the usual strings attached—strong pressure to restructure specific industries, as well as the conventional package of "adjustment programs,... de-regulation and trade reforms" (Purwadi 2001, 64). As is now acknowledged, the intervention made matters worse. Real wages fell a calamitous 44 percent in Indonesia in 1997–1998. Poverty, already very unevenly distributed, exploded: "In Indonesia,...the incidence of poverty, (measured on the basis of the national poverty line) rose from 11 percent to 18 percent between 1996 and 1999" (Agenor 2002, 30). The true scale of this catastrophe is realized when one considers that this represented not merely a rise of more than 63 percent, but embraced almost 40 million individuals, nationally. Inevitably, there were significant effects in higher education: "both on the economic capability of parents to pay...and on the government's capacity to provide subsidy" (Purwadi 2001, 61). At other levels of education, it is estimated that 3 million children dropped out of school, during 1998/1999, while a further 3.5 million were given scholarships to tide them over. School enrollment ratios fell from 78 percent to 54 percent over the period. Literacy rates, already strongly gendered (World Bank 2001), also fell significantly.

Poverty, which fell from 40 percent to about 10 percent during the Suharto regime, spiked at 23 percent after the regional crisis—and still hovers at around 18 percent. Forty-two percent of Indonesians are estimated to live on between US$1 and US$2 per day (UNDP 2005; *The Australian* 2007). At the same time, however, its economy grew by an estimated 6 percent in 2007 (before the onset of the global financial crisis [GFC]), and it has risen to similar levels since. It is further estimated that remittances by Indonesian workers abroad now contribute 1 percent of Indonesia's gross domestic product (GDP).

Often thought of as monolithic, Indonesia is extraordinarily diverse, as its official motto implies: *Bhinekka Tunggal Ika* (Unity in Diversity). Embracing 500 ethnic groups, and some 14,000 islands, population density varies from 1,302 people per square mile in Java to 6.4 in Irian Jaya (Bray and Murray Thomas 1998; Purwadi and Muljoatmodjo 2000). Hindu minorities (principally in Bali) mix with animist traditions, modest-sized Christian sects, and a small Buddhist minority, but the dominant Muslim population comprises the vast majority. The respective sizes of the religious groupings are as follows: Muslims, 88 percent; Christians, 8 percent; Hindus, 2 percent; Buddhists, 1 percent; others, 1 percent (Purwadi and Muljoatmodjo 2000).

Mainstream Islam in Indonesia remains syncretic, generally moderate, outward looking, and supportive of scholarship (*Newsweek* 2005; *Sydney Morning Herald* 2005; SBS 2011). At the same time, several fundamentalist organizations, such as *Laskar Jihad* and *Jemaah Islamiah*, have fostered educational institutions, specifically *Pesantren* (Islamic boarding schools), and each has put forward its notions of a purified Islamic society, or transforming Indonesia into an Islamic state:

> Since the fall of Soeharto in 1998, a bewildering array of Indonesian groups has sprung up which are committed to building an Islamic realm. (*Sydney Morning Herald* 2003b)

Whether one agrees with the latter sentiment or not, such events as the horrific bombings in Bali in October 2002, which resulted in around 200 deaths, and in Jakarta in mid-2003, underlined the danger of Islamic fundamentalist suicide squads, and depressed, if temporarily, both the important Balinese tourism industry and foreign investment generally. While foreign direct investment has grown again more recently, some remain nervous, at least in part due to occasional outbreaks of more extreme religious sentiments, via groups such as *Laskar Jihad* and *Jemaah Islamiah*, which can, inter alia, threaten more robust regional engagement.

Bahasa Indonesia is the official language, even though almost 600 languages or dialects are spoken across the archipelago's 6,000 inhabited islands. Long-standing moves for regional independence and deep suspicion of central domination from Jakarta persist, from Aceh (Sumatra), at one end of the archipelago in the Moluccas, to West Papua, at the other end of the archipelago, and there is some basis for these local concerns, since a substantial history exists of rulers in Jakarta using education as a weapon with which to forge national identity, at times against the wishes of local inhabitants (Leigh 1993). Hence, state building in Indonesian education may be seen, at least in part, as explicable in terms of some version of Archer's processes of domination and assertion (Leigh 1993; Aspinall 2004), a process that has clear implications for (regulatory) regionalism.

Both domestic and external analysts have criticized the process of "big bang" decentralization for decentralizing corruption (*The Australian* 2009; *Sydney Morning Herald* 2011), although Indonesia's *Transparency International* (2006) rating has improved somewhat lately (*The Australian* 2008; see also *Sydney Morning Herald* 2008). The corrupt and authoritarian Suharto regime was succeeded by a range of short-term political leaders with varying allegiances, some committed to building civil society (Aspinall 2004; *New York Times* 2008) but at times uncertain leadership qualities. Hence, while there is now a vigorous free press, and active civil society, after some 30 years of authoritarian rule, and only a decade of democratic experiment, "the challenge now is to consolidate democracy" (Madjid 2003), and not allowing decentralization to be co-opted by local authorities (sometimes called "little kings" in Indonesia), for their own ends. In the much-anticipated 2009 parliamentary and presidential elections, 180 million Indonesians were eligible to vote and, while the impact of KKN (*Korupsi, Kolusi, dan Nepotisme*) cannot be excluded, the process of democratic accountability will proceed. Since the process of decentralization has been implemented, only around 30 percent of members have been reelected, which may indicate that local politicians are being made more accountable. Again, however, the rise of independent local movements under a more decentralized Indonesian state can weaken or fragment a coordinated involvement in regionalism.

Indonesian Higher Education

Higher education in Indonesia is under the control of two separate ministries—the Ministry of National Education (MNE) and the MORA—of which one is decentralized and the other is not. In addition, ongoing financial constraints, together with spiraling demand for higher education, have underpinned the growth of private higher education, at the expense of public institutions—which in turn are adopting some of the strategies of the private sector (Welch 2011a). Private-sector enrollments now total some 1.9 million, over 60 percent of the total (Buchori and Malik 2004, 250).

Born of an internal mismatch between limited state capacity on one hand and burgeoning demand on the other, private higher education is, as several scholars have pointed out, at its most powerful in Asia, including in neighboring ASEAN member countries such as the Philippines (Altbach 1996, 1999a; Levy 2002; Welch 2011a and b). However, the balance between public and private higher education in Indonesia has shifted appreciably over the past two decades, in part aided by external pressures for more structural adjustment on the part of international agencies such as the World Bank, particularly after the late 1990s' Asian currency crisis (Welch and Mok 2003; Varghese 2004a and b). Regionalization initiatives discussed in this chapter, notably those involving ASEAN and South East Asian Ministers of Education Organization (SEAMEO), largely exclude the substantial private sector.

Decentralization, implemented somewhat hastily, and according to several sources, at least partly in response to rising demands for regional autonomy from several areas, has also had an impact on education (Aspinall 2004, 7; Amirrachman et al. 2008). A degree of confusion resulted, with many tasks being transferred to the local level without warning or preparation, and in the face of a substantial lack of professional staff at local levels (Amirrachman et al. 2008). It is clear, however, that the reins will not be entirely loosened, and that "steering from a distance" will be practiced (Brodjonegoro, n.d.).

Introduced after the enactment of Law 22, in 1999, the principle of educational decentralization was subsequently extended in a pilot scheme to five major public HEIs, all in Java, which were accorded the new status of *Badan Hukum Milik Negera* (BHMN), or "State Owned Legal Institution." By virtue of this new status, the selected HEIs were empowered to create new patterns of student recruitment, which would, inter alia, have the effect of garnering greater financial support from students and their families (see below). Certainly, there are reports of significant struggles between the Department of National Education (DNE), which is enthusiastic about decentralization, and the resistance manifested by the Departments of Finance and Home Affairs, as well as the MORA, which retains an important role in education but, unlike DNE, remains centralized. By early 2003, the legislation had still not been enacted; nonetheless, the institutions had all lifted their fees (*Kompas* 2003).

Concerns have been raised recently that the trend toward privatization and mercerization of education are at odds with constitutional guarantees to provide good-quality education for all citizens. The private higher education sector, officially sanctioned and encouraged for more than a decade by the Ministry of Education and Culture, can reasonably be expected to expand further over the coming years, but as indicated above, is less involved in the formal regionalization initiatives listed here.

Educational opportunities, especially to enter institutions of good quality, are still concentrated on Java, although progress has been made in distributing higher education more widely. Literacy rates, too, for example, are also unequal, being clearly segmented along gender lines (although progress has been made for both males and females in recent years). In higher education, however, gender disparities are not as great as might be expected, with women totaling 1.5 million in 2001 (Buchori and Malik 2004, 250), or over 44 percent of total enrollments. This overall figure, however, masks persistent stark disparities in areas such as engineering. Participation rates by social class reveal a huge social cleft, with the proportion of enrollments by the highest quintile almost 10 times that of the lowest quintile (Welch 2011a).

Regional Engagement in Higher Education

As the largest ASEAN member nation, and Chair for 2011, Indonesia has a strong regional presence, including in explicitly regional organizations such as ASEAN and Asia Pacific Economic Cooperation (APEC), and associated educational programs. In addition, it is a member of the SEAMEO, and an active participant in the SEAMEO Regional Institute of Higher Education (RIHED). This includes, for example, a recent regional initiative to boost student mobility, the Malaysia–Indonesia–Thailand (MIT) student mobility project, coordinated by the respective national higher education organs and SEAMEO RIHED that commenced in 2010. A pilot project, it was part of the wider aim to promote a higher education common space in Southeast Asia through developing a harmonization process (Aphijanyatham 2010). The process began in 2008 with the *Exploration of a Common Space* conference, and was followed by recommendations from the Third Director General/Secretary General/Commissioner for Higher Education in Southeast Asia Region meeting, held in Bangkok in January 2009. One hundred and fifty students, 50 from selected subject areas, in each of the three countries, were to be involved. Eleven Indonesian HEIs were selected to be part of the program. As of August 2010, of the 50 students to have participated, 6 inbound students had completed their studies in Indonesia, while 7 outbound students were studying in one of the other systems. Of the Indonesian component, 9 inbound and outbound students were scheduled to take part in the program, with up to another 18 from both categories awaiting confirmation (SEAMEO RIHED 2010). Student mobility is seen by regional leaders, including in Indonesia, as promoting both regional development and "a multicultural space where people respect differences in culture, language and religion while aware of the common values and unity of the ASEAN nations" (SEAMEO RIHED 2010, 5). In turn, Indonesia's engagement is part of a wider push toward harmonization of regional higher education, and the development of a South East Asian Credit Transfer system (SEA-CTS), which takes inspiration and experience from the EU's Bologna initiative. The fact that, as indicated above, the higher education system is administered by two separated ministries does not seem to have affected Indonesia's involvement, although it is likely that few of the Indonesian participants alluded to above would have stemmed from MORA-administered HEIs, which are generally seen to be academically weaker than their MNE-administered cousins.

Regional initiatives and partnerships also include Indonesia's membership in AUN, with member HEIs being *Universitas Indonesia, Gadjah*

Madah, Institut Teknologi Bandung, and Universitas Airlangga. Both *Gadjah Madah* and *Universitas Indonesia* offer scholarships, the former between seven and ten for either its Masters of Public Administration (MPA) or Religion and Cross Cultural Studies Program, and the latter ten for its regular undergraduate or graduate programs (AUN website 2010).

Limits of Regionalism—(1) Islamic Higher Education

There are a number of limits to Indonesian regionalism. Islamic higher education constitutes both an illustration of, and challenge to, our understanding of regionalism in Indonesian higher education. Islamic higher learning in the region now known as Malaysia and Indonesia is centuries old, and pockets of Islamic influence and higher learning exist in the south of the Philippines and Thailand, as are connections to trans-regional centers of Islamic scholarship, for example, the venerable *Al Azhar* in Egypt (Ridell 2001; Azra 2004; Welch 2008, 2012). The earliest forms of Indonesian higher learning were indeed Islamic, with some of its brightest pupils going on to postgraduate studies at universities in the Middle East, notably *Al-Azhar*, which was founded in Cairo circa 970 CE. The persistence of this long-standing pattern of trans-regional mobility was evident when visiting that institution in 2009, although as the Indonesian students I met there acknowledged, studying in Arabic constituted a significant barrier.

Paralleling colonial institutions, private Islamic institutions were developed, such as the Indonesian Islamic University in Jogjakarta, founded in the immediate postwar year of 1946 (Buchori and Malik 2004). Private higher education was first given legal mandate in Indonesia in the immediate postindependence era—through the Basic Education Law of 1950 (later ratified as Law 12 of 1954). Islamic higher education was enshrined with the creation of *Akademi Dinas Ilmu Agama* (ADIA) or the Academy of Religious Sciences in 1950, subsequently subsumed into the Institute of Islamic Higher Learning (IAIN) in 1960:

> Following the principle that every citizen enjoys the right to pursue whatever religious or philosophical convictions he chooses, citizens likewise have the freedom to establish and conduct private schools. (Murray Thomas 1973, 146)

Law UU 15 of 1961 gave to each citizen the power to found a new private institution. Demand for Islamic higher education was high, especially in the provinces, while the structure, content, and duration of degrees broadly paralleled those of public HEIs. IAIN graduates have equivalent status to public HEI graduates.

Of major Islamic organizations with an interest in education, *Muhammadijah* (The Way of Muhammad) is one of the better known. With a membership now some 30 million strong, it has offered modern education to indigent Muslims since 1912, including institutionalized training for Islamic teachers. Originally based on a modernist Islam imported from the Middle East (a source of radical anticolonialism in Indonesia), many *Muhammadijah* universities have now been established throughout the archipelago, through the efforts of its supporters. Education and "modernist social action" were high priorities from its inception, albeit tempered at times with "a conservative-fundamentalist theology" (Murray Thomas 1973, 166; Jones 2003), but *Muhammadijah* was critical of the traditional private boarding school, or *pondok pesantren's* confinement of education to religious subjects, and was responsible for the introduction of the *madrasah*, an alternative that married Western learning with Islamic knowledge (Murray Thomas 1973, 166; see also Nakamura and Nishino 1995). *Muhammadijah* University was founded in Jakarta in 1955, and subsequently expanded to include branch campuses in other parts of Java, as well as Padang (Sumatra), Makassar, and Bandjermasin (Kalimantan).

Taman Siswa (Pupils' Garden), established by a radical nationalist and follower of Montessori in 1922,[2] was another such organization. Closely related to the struggle for national independence, it also included teacher training among its offerings. "In 1930, there were 40 branches of this institution, including those in Sumatra and Kalimantan, which enrolled about 5,140 students" (Purwadi and Muljoatmodjo 2000, 81). A third organization, *Nahdatul 'Ulaama* [NU] (Awakening of Islamic Scholars), founded in 1926, was more closely associated with the traditional syncretic Islam of Java, than *Muhammadijah*. Now some 40 million strong, it is associated more with Abdurrahman Wahid, former Indonesian president, and considered one of the most prominent modern Islamic thinkers and activists in Indonesia.[3]

Currently, six universities are under the control of the MORA: *UIN Sunan Kalijaga Yogyakarta*; *UIN Syarif Hidayatullah Jakarta*; *UIN Alauddin Makasar (South Sulawesi)*; *UIN Maulana Malik Ibrahim Malang (East Java)*; *UIN Bandung*; and *UIN Sultan Syarif Kasim* in Sumatra. It is notable that none was among those listed above as among Indonesian HEIs in the AUN network.

Key regional elements underpin Islamic higher education. Several thousand Indonesian students now study in Malaysian universities, a pattern encouraged by Malaysian universities' expositions in Indonesia (and Brunei), coordinated by the Malaysian Ministry of Education. Indeed, by 2007, notwithstanding Malaysia's efforts to recruit substantial number of students from China, Indonesia had replaced China as the largest source of international students from the region (Welch 2011a, 71). 2010 figures indicated a total of 9,888 Indonesian enrollments in Malaysian universities, 6,119 in private HEIs and 3,769 in public HEIs (Department of Higher Education 2010; Welch 2012), and this is likely to include diploma and certificate enrollments, which are far more numerous in the private sector than in the public sector. Only a small proportion of these students are studying in designated Islamic HEIs, such as the International Islamic University of Malaysia (IIUM). Some Malaysian private HEIs have also developed branch campuses in Indonesia. Indonesian students were also the third most numerous among international enrollments in Philippine HEIs in 2003–2004, although it is not clear how many of these were engaged in Islamic studies, or enrolled in Islamic HEIs (Welch 2011a, 125). It is also likely that some Indonesian students are enrolled at the small number of Islamic HEIs in the south of Thailand, although actual numbers are hard to discern (Welch 2011a, 100–101).

Indonesia is also part of several pan-Islamic higher education networks. Several Indonesian HEIs are members of the Federation of the Universities of the Islamic World, notably the *Universitas Islam Indonesia, University of Indonesia, University Swadaya Gunung Jati, University of Ibnu Khaldun, Riau Islamic University, Muhammadiyah University of Magelang, Sharif Hidayatullah State Islamic University, State Institute for Islamic Studies Sunan Gunung Djati, Gadjah Mada University, Institute Agarah Negeri Islam Mataram,* and *Bandung Islamic University* (Federation of Universities of the Islamic World, n.d.). Indonesia is also part of a pan-Islamic network of the Organisation of the Islamic Conference (OIC), on quality assurance and accreditation in higher education, which met in Damascus in March 2011, and aims to boost the quality of Islamic HEIs, a long-standing problem that sees only one institution (Istanbul University) listed among the Shanghai Jiaotong top 500; and in a relatively low position (University World News [UWN] 2009). As part of a wider quality problem among universities in OIC member countries, it was pointed out that:

> The entire Muslim world comprised one-fifth of humanity but had less than 1% of its scientists who generated less than 5% of its science and made barely 0.1% of the world's original research discoveries each year.
> Islamic countries had a negligble percentage of patent registrations in the US, Europe and Japan. Even more serious was the fact that the R&D

manpower of Muslim countries was only 1.18% of the total science and technology manpower. (UWN 2009a, see also OIC 2010)

In sum, then, Islamic higher education in Indonesia broaches the bounds of regionalism, with both regional and trans-regional dimensions. Its origins were clearly from the Middle East, and a long-standing tradition persists among some of the more serious scholars of Islamic higher learning, to pursue their studies at august institutions in the Middle East, notably Al Azhar. At the same time, a strongly regional dimension pervades Islamic higher education in Indonesia, with substantial numbers of Indonesian students studying in Malaysia, as well as smaller numbers in Thailand and the Philippines.

As indicated above, a more forceful instance of the trans-regional dimension in Islamic higher education is evident in neighboring Malaysia. Beyond the Indonesian examples cited above, Malaysia has been explicit about marketing its Islamic environment to prospective international students, as a contribution to the development of fellow Muslim countries (Welch 2011a, 2011b, 2012). As is seen in Table 7.1, of the total of 87,000 international students listed as enrolled in Malaysian universities and colleges for 2010 (mostly in private-sector HEIs), 10,024 stemmed from the Middle East and North Africa (MENA), with Iran (11,823), Yemen (5,311), and Libya (4,627) comprising the three largest source countries. Nigerian enrollments are also substantial (5,080), but while it is likely that Muslims form a substantial proportion, precise data are not available

Table 7.1 Top ten source countries, Malaysian higher education, public and private, 2010

Country	Public sector total	Private sector total	Total
China	2,168	8,046	10,214
Iran	4,814	7,009	11,823
Indonesia	6,119	3,769	9,888
Nigeria	737	5,080	5,817
Yemen	1,809	3,522	5,331
Libya	1,125	2,805	3,930
Sudan	596	2,241	2,837
Botswana	–	1,909	1,909
Saudi Arabia	668	1,584	2,252
Bangladesh	538	1,503	2,041
Total	18,574	37,468	56,042

Source: Ministry of Higher Education, 2010a, 2010b.

(Department of Higher Education 2010). Of the 10,214 students from China, it is highly unlikely that more than a few were Muslims.

Limits of Regionalism—(2) Relations with China

China has for centuries been part of Southeast Asia. Geographical and historical linkages are substantial and long-standing (Jarvis and Welch 2011). China, it should be recalled, is bounded on its southern border by several Southeast Asian states: Vietnam, Burma (Myanmar), and Laos, while also sharing sea borders with all of the Southeast Asian countries, with the exception of Burma.

While the history of China's trade with Southeast Asia is, according to one of the major scholars of the relationship, over 2,000 years old, beginning around the third century BC, and extending in the Three Kingdoms period (220–280) and again during the Tang dynasty (618–906), it was not until much later that it grew significantly (Wang 2000). Historical records indicate trade with current-day Vietnam, Cambodia, Java, and Sumatra during the first millennium AD, voyages of exploration from China to Southeast Asia, during the third century AD, and significant contact between Buddhists in China and counterparts in Southeast Asia during the fifth and sixth centuries.

Expansion of such contacts occurred during the Tang dynasty, including by Buddhist priests and scholars, some of whom settled permanently in Southeast Asia. Equally, Confucianism exercised a profound influence over Vietnam, for example, in terms of social structure, aesthetics and architecture, law, and higher learning (Welch 2010). This was partly because when Vietnam (called Nam Viet by the Chinese) broke away and became quasi-independent around the fall of the Tang dynasty, some Chinese stayed rather than return to China. Later, in the late thirteenth and fourteenth centuries, traders, including non-Han Muslims, settled in current Vietnam, Cambodia, around the Gulf of Thailand and in Java and Sumatra. The voyages of the great admiral of the Ming dynasty, *Zheng He*, to Southeast Asia during the period 1405–1433 provided perhaps the apex of Chinese naval history, although sadly, records of the voyages were deliberately destroyed, a result of an imperial decision to end further maritime expeditions. Although brakes were deliberately applied periodically, a weakened government in Beijing from the 1620s to the end of the Ming dynasty in 1644 provided more opportunities for traders, often Hokkien, or Fujianese. Records of the time indicated thousands living in Java, Vietnam, Thailand, Cambodia, and the Malay archipelago. The peak of

Hokkien migration to ports of Southeast Asia in the late-seventeenth and first half of the eighteenth centuries was paralleled by massacres of Chinese settlers in Manila and Batavia (the former name for Jakarta) (Reid 2008).

The legacy of Chinese exploration, trade, and settlement in Southeast Asia is readily seen. Chinese minorities in Southeast Asia exercise a disproportionate influence on many regional economies, which perhaps goes some way to explain the periodic purges conducted against ethnic Chinese that have been conducted in some of those societies. (China's previous support for parties such as *Parti Kommunist Indonesia* [KPI] also cost local Chinese dearly, of course, as well as setting back China–Indonesia relations by decades [Suryadinata 2003; Wang 2005, 196].) Diplomatic relations between the two, established in April 1950, were suspended in October 1967, after the "September 30th event." Formal diplomatic relations were not reestablished until August 1990. Even today, forms of discrimination are practiced against ethnic Chinese in Southeast Asia, despite the fact that over 25 percent of Malaysians are of Chinese ethnicity, and perhaps 60 percent of Singaporeans (Welch 2011b). Hence, while the Chinese diaspora, estimated by Chang (2008) at perhaps 16 million strong across Southeast Asia, represents a potential bridge for China–ASEAN regionalism, the prospects for its further development are affected by China's greater unification (now again more like it was at the end of the Qing dynasty in 1910), the relatively weak ASEAN structures, with modest integration, and some nervousness, and consequent hedging, regarding the extent of China's rise on the part of ASEAN nations (*International Herald Tribune* 2010; Sutter 2011; *The Australian* 2011).

Just as ethnic Chinese were disproportionately important in the economies of Southeast Asia, including Indonesia, so too were they more numerous in Indonesian higher education than their mere numbers suggested. Sometimes, this prominence brought unwanted attention, as in the anti-Chinese demonstrations and purges that occurred in Indonesia in the 1960s. An example occurred at the *Res Publica* University, founded in Jakarta in 1960, and sponsored by a group known as *Baperki*, primarily Indonesian citizens of Chinese descent, and comprised in practice largely of members of the Indonesian Communist Party (*Partai Komunis Indonesia* [PKI]). The institution was founded in response to the introduction of ethnic quotas on enrollments, implemented in the 1950s by Indonesian authorities concerned with the disproportionate numbers of Chinese students attending Indonesian HEIs. It was estimated that, although Chinese formed only about 3 percent of the national population, that at some HEIs, they comprised approximately 25 percent of enrollments (Murray Thomas 1973). When, in 1965, anti-Communist youths invaded the *Res Publica* campus, on the pretext that it was a "headquarters for training communist forces... purportedly allied with the activists that had murdered the generals on September 30" (Murray Thomas 1973, 150), students barricaded themselves in the College of Technology building: It was then burnt to the ground, by the mob. The incident naturally forced the institution into the limelight, and, responding to the climate of the time, the Minister of Higher Education decreed the establishment of a new private HEI on the same site, to be known as *Trisakti*. One-third of the students who had been enrolled were banned from renewing their enrollment, "because of their alleged affiliation with the communist movement" (Murray Thomas 1973, 151). While the number of students of ethnic Chinese descent remained high, the proportion of ethnic Indonesian students rose appreciably over the next few years.

Despite some lingering reservations regarding the influence of ethnic Chinese Indonesians, higher education relations have expanded substantially in recent years, as part of a much wider engagement between China and ASEAN in many fields including higher education (Jarvis and Welch 2011). In 2008-2009, Indonesia was the eighth largest source of international enrollments for Chinese universities, with a share of 3.3 percent, or some 7,900 of the almost 240,000 total. While this percent had remained stable at 3.3 percent, actual enrollments had risen from 2,565 in 2003, when Indonesia was ranked the fifth largest source country for China (Institute of International Education 2010).

Indonesia–China relations present another test of regionalism in higher education. Although the relationship is a long-standing one, including in the realm of higher learning and knowledge mobility, it has not been altogether a smooth one, with periods of real tension. Currently, like some of its ASEAN neighbors, Indonesia not only wants to take advantage of the opportunities presented by China's rise in the region, including the establishment of the first Confucius Institute in Jakarta, in September 2007, and via mechanisms such as the ASEAN China Rectors Conferences (Welch, in Jarvis and Welch 2011), but is also hedging against China's rise, by forging links with other countries. While as illustrated above, relations between China and Indonesia have origins that date back to centuries, they highlight the limits of regionalism, which in some ways is more focused on the ASEAN region. (The same point could be made regarding relations with Japan, which is scheduled to join the MIT mobility program in 2012.)

Limits to Regionalism—(3) Domestic Constraints

Each of the two instances of external engagement raises issues regarding the strength of regionalism in Indonesian higher education. At the same time, as the introduction made clear in relation to Southeast Asia, regionalism is still at an emergent and somewhat emergent phase, with rhetorical commitments not always matched by actual outcomes.

Notwithstanding earnest efforts, domestic constraints in Indonesian higher education can be seen similarly, and hence arguably constitute a further limit on robust regional engagement. Several such domestic issues are treated below, and are argued to form a third effective limit to Indonesia's capacity to robustly engage in regional initiatives.

Limited Governance, Especially of Private Higher Education

Indonesia's higher education system has expanded massively over the past decade or two, with the private HEIs constituting the larger sector. The rise of the private sector is an acknowledgment of the fact that state budgets remain inadequate to cater to burgeoning demand in higher education (Hadijardaja 1996; Welch 2011b). Private enrollments form more than 60 percent of the total. The differences are seen much more starkly in institutional terms, and illustrate some of the difficulties of governance. More than 2,700 private HEIs are spread across the archipelago, compared with around 100 public HEIs. The expansion of higher education has not always been well regulated, and poses questions of domestic governance, which also form limits to effective regional engagement. Even now, there are effectively two categories of private HEIs, one of which is not accredited (*tidak terakreditasi*). This may mean that students are studying subjects that have not been accredited for that institution. The government was so concerned about the weakness of some of these institutions, and their failure to conform to regulatory guidelines, that in 2009, it threatened some 700 with closure unless they ended links with their *yayasans* (foundations), and re-registered, under the 2009 Law on Educational Decentralization. It is widely thought that many will fail to make the grade and will effectively be deemed illegal and cease to operate (Welch 2012, 38–39).

Compounding limits to effective governance and regulation is competition between the Directorate of Private Higher Education, which is formally responsible for the coordination of private HEIs, and the National Accreditation Committee (*Badan Akreditasi Nasional* or BAN). Private HEIs, managed by either a foundation (*yayasan*) or a corporation, did not traditionally receive public monies from government (and even now receive little), but may be eligible for certain forms of subsidy, or incentives, in the form of buildings, or staff seconded from public-sector HEIs. Perhaps, 10 percent of academic staff at private HEIs are paid by government (Buchori and Malik 2004, 251). Fees make up a considerable proportion of income, and donations are also sought (but often remain modest). Private HEIs are usually founded and in large part sustained by *yayasans* or foundations, which mostly merely manage the resources garnered from fees and donations, without adding (much) to resource levels. While a few private-sector HEIs are among the strongest in the country, the overall level of private higher education is weak, and could contribute little if anything to effective regional engagement. Staff at most private HEIs are poorly qualified, while the institutions themselves are much more poorly resourced relative to public-sector HEIs, with limited internal efficiency.

Effective governance is also limited by the fact that, as indicated above, of two ministries responsible for higher education, one (MNE) has decentralized, while the other (MORA) has not. Regulatory capacity is also not aided by Indonesia's geography, which poses "administrative problems for the officials who direct the operation of the country's...education system...Communication and transportation are particularly difficult. Large sections of Kalimantan and Irian Jaya have few roads...As for data collection, the geographic barriers to obtaining timely and accurate information about enrolments, staffing and buildings" are significant, and do not assist the ease and efficiency with which the regulatory regime can be implemented (Bray and Murray Thomas 1998, 2–3). The spread of private HEIs, including 75 in Moluccas and Papua alone (Dikti 2007), further exacerbates regulatory difficulties.

Quality of Higher Education

In general, in terms of what has been termed the global knowledge system (Altbach 1998, 2003), Indonesian higher education, while a large system, remains relatively peripheral. Not only has growth largely outstripped the qualification levels of academic staff, but working conditions are also often poor, as is remuneration. Periodic economic crises, from the mid-1960s to the late 1990s have had marked effects on the Indonesian professoriate, paralleled by at times precipitous declines in the *rupiah*. Inevitably, this has had effects on quality. An earlier characterization of the financial dilemma faced by faculty remains largely pertinent today, when public-sector salaries remain insufficient to sustain the family.

> A college instructor would put the minimum number of hours required at his institution,...then...use all the remaining available time teaching a course or two...at a private college. In addition, he might sell second-hand

autos, edit manuscripts for a publisher, sell real estate, tutor students, write for a newspaper or carry out any number of other activities (to) supplement his income. (Murray Thomas 1973, 202)

Persistent academic "moonlighting" was confirmed by World Bank estimates that "well over half" of public-sector academic staff maintained a second job, at a private HEI and/or elsewhere (World Bank 1996, 5). Poor remuneration means that many staff spend more energy and time on off-campus work, or business, at times including management or teaching at private HEIs, than their work at public-sector HEIs. The situation in the private sector, with lower proportions of qualified and full-time staff, is "even worse" (Buchori and Malik 2004, 261). The overall effect is reduced quality in the public-sector HEIs (which loses much of the time and energy of key staff), as in private HEIs, where the same individuals also work. In practice, many private HEIs "would not be able to survive without" public HEI staff (World Bank 1996, 5). In practice, it is difficult to even know actual staff numbers, since a number of faculty falsely claim to be working full time, at two separate institutions. Research, teaching, and students suffer accordingly, in both public and private sectors, and the low investment and per-pupil spending rates, poorer facilities and equipment, together with the lower quality of teaching staff, and lower-quality intakes of the latter mean that students usually take longer to complete their studies (World Bank 1996; Welch 2012). Islamic HEIs under MORA control are also less well funded than their MNE peers, and tend to have less well-qualified faculty.

Transparency

In addition, corruption is a widespread phenomenon, much criticized by Indonesians, especially now when a more open civil society and vigorous free press often highlight such practices. The effects are evident in higher education, where the need for a more effective regulatory regime is now widely acknowledged, against a background where the widespread culture of *korupsi, kolusi, dan nepotisme* (KKN) often undermines the effective quality assurance procedures (*Kompas* 2002c; *Jakarta Post* 2005; Transparency International 2006; University World News 2008). Students who do not attend special "after hours" classes find their marks slipping, "no matter how smart they are or how hard they work" (*Sydney Morning Herald* 2008). Private HEIs formally need to submit an annual report to the authorities, but some falsify their data "to maintain their current status or standing,... the Office of Private Higher Education cannot check and match every detail with the PHEI's physical entities due to the limited number of staff, and because there are a great number of universities' (Hadijardaja 1996, 44). Welch (2012, 16–17) cites a typical example, designed to circumvent effective regulation of quality (see also Buchori and Malik 2004, 262). The effects are to reduce quality and to limit the extension of regulatory regionalism in the higher education sector.

Financing Higher Education

It is not merely the case that the large and diverse private sector is funded at a much lower rate, perhaps 20 per cent of that accorded to public-sector HEIs. The widening gap between spiraling enrollments and declining state support, at least in per-student terms has meant that public-sector HEIs, too, are increasingly reliant upon fees (*Jakarta Post* 2006; Welch 2011a, 42–46).

Responding to finite resources but increasing demand, institutions have, for example, expanded fee-paying programs—for which success at the very competitive public university entrance examinations is not required—at the expense of regular courses (*Kompas* 2002b). Such "extension courses" attract new students—but further undermine quality, offering much the same qualification with much lower entry requirements.

That such courses are taught by public-sector staff, moonlighting from their mother institution, further weakens the quality of teaching and research, as seen above. But in addition, the phenomenon dubbed *Jalur Khusus* ("Special Passage") has been much criticized (*Tempo* 2003, 54–55). Under such schemes, public-sector HEIs reserve some places for wealthy students, who can pay high fees. At one prestigious public-sector HEI, for example, highly sought-after places in Engineeering were advertised at 225 million Rupiah (or US$26,470) each, including an annual student fee of 3.5 million. Another set fees for *Jalur Khusus* entry into its Faculty of Medicine at 150 million Rupiah (around US$17,650). Other examples highlighted in the press in 2008 included 28 percent of 34,000 students sitting for the entry examination at a major national university in 2008, being found to have paid substantial "brokerage" fees (of up to US$22,000), for guaranteed places (University World News 2008). By no means uncommon, such practices can at times involve individuals from the institutions concerned (*Jakarta Post* 2005). While major national public-sector HEIs, notably those designated BHMN, may offer higher salaries than their less-prestigious peers, salaries alone are unlikely to dissipate the need to mooonlight, or earn additional income. Despite a

2010 decision by the Constitutional Court that declared an earlier (2008) law, which in effect licensed the charging of differential fees by public HEIs, unconstitutional, there is little evidence that the practice has ended. Although the government indicated they would "obey the court ruling," the minister for national education, Mohammad Nuh, indicated that he needed to study the verdict before commenting, but unless finances were substantially boosted, public HEIs would be hard hit by the ban on differential fees (*Kompas* 2002a; Jakarta Globe 2010).

Institutional leaders of such major public-sector HEIs would claim that they have no choice but to recruit such students at high-fee levels, in order to compensate, at least in part, for declining government support:

> Since the only source of funding other than government appropriation is student tuition, it is unavoidable to demand (a) higher rate. The need for higher parents' contribution is also apparent. (Brodjonegoro, n.d., 11)

Such measures, however, effectively exclude poor but able students (notwithstanding the practice of making some of the income generated available in the form of scholarships). Such students, already excluded from the good-quality private-sector HEIs due to high fees, now increasingly find themselves frozen out of public HEIs, too, on the same grounds. It is already the case that, of the 5.41 million pupils who entered elementary education in 1989, a mere 724,940 made it into higher education, after 12 years of schooling, and these retention rates were massively skewed toward wealthier groups, whereas only 3.3 percent of higher education students stem from the lowest 20 percent of income groups, 30.9 percent are from the highest quintile (Nazim 2006, 42–43). Compounding the problem, it is not always certain that all funds generated by "Extension" courses, or *Jalur Khusus*, are used for university developmental purposes.

Conclusion

It has been argued above that both regional and domestic constraints limit the effectiveness with which Indonesian higher education can robustly engage in regionalism. This includes a somewhat less-developed domestic regulatory architecture, as indicated above. While Islamic higher education revealed regional dimensions, significant elements were trans-regional in character, as has long been the case. As the arguably weaker cousin of MNE-administered HEIs, those under the control of MORA are probably less influential in regionalization initiatives instituted by ASEAN and SEAMEO, as is the private sector. Indonesia's engagement with China also tested the limits of regionalism, while issues of domestic capacity, corruption, and quality, mainly, but by no means only in the private sector, also limit effective and robust regional engagement. Indonesia's continued importance; economic growth; and size and weight within the region, including within ASEAN and associated higher education networks, ensure a significant place at the regional table; yet, each of the three elements discussed above forms different limits to that regionalism. Overall, the instruments of regulatory regionalism are, as yet, less well developed than in either the Anglo-American systems or in other parts of Asia, such as Singapore, China, Taiwan, or Korea. While signs of both state control and neoliberal influences exist (most particularly in terms of the extension of income diversification among HEIs), accountability measures are less comprehensive and transparent than in some other systems, while the relatively peripheral status of Indonesia's knowledge system also acts as a brake on the extension of regulatory regionalism.

Not only is the development of an ASEAN higher education space at a less-developed stage, relative to the EU for example, but the considerable diversity, as well as lack of transparency and generally less internationally competitive HEIs within Indonesia, also means a lesser degree of internal regulatory capacity, while also inhibiting fuller engagement in wider regionalization.

Notes

1. Public-sector debt to GDP ratio was estimated at a low 26.4% in 2010, see www.cia.gov/library/publications/the-world-factbook/geos/id.html. Accessed March 3, 2012.
2. I am grateful to Keith Foulcher, formerly of the Indonesian Department of the University of Sydney, for this point.
3. Abdurahmin Wahid's National Awakening Party (PKB) was created by core members of NU, while the leaders of Muhammahiyah fostered the National Mandate Party (PAN).

References

Agenor, P. 2002. "Why Crises are Bad for the Poor." *Development Outreach* 4 (1): 30–32.
Altbach, Philip. 1998. "Gigantic Peripheries: India and China in the World Knowledge System." In *Comparative Higher Education. Knowledge, the University and Development*, ed. P. Altbach. Greenwich, CT: Ablex, pp. 133–146.

Altbach, P. 1999a. "Private Higher Education: Themes and Variations in Comparative Perspective." In *Private Prometheus: Private Higher Education and Development in the 21st Century*, ed. P. G. Altbach. London: Greenwood Press.

Altbach, P. 2003. "Centres and Peripheries in the Academic Profession:The Special Challenges of Developing Countries." In *The Decline of the Guru. The Academic Profession in Developing and Middle Income Countries*, ed. P. G. Altbach. New York: Palgrave, pp. 1–21.

Amirrachman, A., S. Syafi ' i, and A. Welch. 2008. "Decentralising Indonesian Education. The Promise and the Price." *World Studies in Education* 9 (1): 31–54.

Aphijanyatham, R. 2010. *East Asian Internationalisation of Higher Education. A Key to Regional Integration.* SEAMEO RIHED Programme Report No 25. December.

ASEAN Universities Network (AUN). 2010. *Updated Information on AUN Student Exchange Program 2010.* Available at: www.aunsec.org/site/scholarship2011/2011AUNStudentExchangeProgramme.pdf. Accessed March 9, 2012.

Aspinall, E. 2004. "Indonesia: Transformation of Civil Society and Democratic Breakthrough." In *Civil Society and Political Change in Asia: Expanding and Contracting Democratic Space*, ed. M. Alagappa. Stanford, CA: Stanford University Press, pp. 62–78.

Bray, M., and Thomas, R. Murray, eds. 1998. *Financing of Education in Indonesia.* Manila: Asian Development Bank.

Brodjonegoro, S. n.d. *Higher Education Reform in Indonesia.* Available at: www.tfhe.net/resources/satryo_soemantrI_brodjonegoro2.htm. Accessed March 24, 2012.

Buchori, M., and A. Malik. 2004. "Higher Education in Indonesia." In *Asian Universities: Historical Perspectives and Contemporary Challenges*, ed. P. G. Altbach and T. Umakoshi. Baltimore: Johns Hopkins University Press, pp. 377 p.

Chang, S-D. 2008. "The Distribution and Occupations of Overseas Chinese." In *The Chinese Diaspora in the Pacific*, ed. A. Reid. Aldershot: Ashgate, pp. 33–51.

Department of Higher Education (Malaysia). 2010. *Public Higher Education Institutions.* Available at: www.mohe.gov.my/educationmsia/index.php?article=dept. Accessed March 9, 2012.

Dikti (D. o. H. E., Indonesia). 2007. *Profil Perguruan Tinggi.* Available at: www.dikti.org. Accessed March 9, 2012.

Federation of Universities of the Islamic World (FUIW). n.d. Available at: www.fuiw.org/en/universites_membres.php. Accessed March 9, 2012.

Hadijardaja, J. 1996. "Private Higher Education in Indonesia. Current Developments and Existing Problems." In *Private Higher Education in Asia and the Pacific. Final Report. Summary and Recommendations*, ed. T.-I. Wongsotorn and Y-B. Wang. Bangkok: UNESCO PROAP and SEAMEO RIHED.

Institute of International Education. 2010. *Atlas of Student Mobility: China.* Available at: www.atlas.iienetwork.org/page/72248/. Accessed March 9, 2012.

International Herald Tribune (IHT). 2010, September 29. "Asia's Clouded Horizon."

Jakarta Globe. 2010. "Historic Ruling Throws Out Law on Indonesian Universities." Available at: www.thejakartaglobe.com/home/historic-rulin g-throws-out-law-on-indonesian-universities/366993. Accessed March 9, 2012.
Jakarta Post. April 23, 2005. "Haluoleo Uncovers Admissions Scandal." *Jakarta Post.* Retrieved from www.thejakartapost.com/news/2005/04/23/haluoleo-un-covers-admissions-scandal.html
Jakarta Post. November 7, 2006. "Commercialization of the Country's Higher Education."
Jarvis, D., and A. Welch, eds. 2011. *ASEAN Industries and the Challenge from China.* London: Palgrave Macmillan.
Jayasuriya, K. 2003. "Introduction: Governing the Asia Pacific—beyond the 'New Regionalism'," *Third World Quarterly* 24 (2): 199–215.
Jayasuriya, K. 2010. "Learning by the Market: Regulatory Regionalism, Bologna, and Accountability Communities." *Globalisation, Societies and Education* 8 (1): 7–22.
Jones, Sydney. 2003. "Jemaah Islamiah in South East Asia. Damaged but still Dangerous." International Crisis Group Report No 63, August 26, 2003.
Kompas. 2002a. Anggaran Pendidikan Minimal 20 Persen dari APBN dan APBD (Education Budget Should be at least 20 Percent).
Kompas. October 3, 2002b. Kian marak, Program Ekstensi di Universitas Indonesia, Honorarium Dosen Lebih Menjanjikan (More and More Extension Programs at University of Indonesia, Lecturers Secure Greater Financial Benefits).
Kompas. August 15, 2002c. Tampa Kontrol, Peningkatan Anggaran Pendidikan Bisa Berbahaya (Without Controls, Increasing the Education Budget Could be Dangerous).
Kompas. February 5, 2003. Soal RUU Sisdiknas: Setnig Harus Pahami Aspirasi Masyarakat (About the Education Law: State Secretariat Must be Sensitive to People's Aspirations).
Leigh, B. 1993. *The Growth of the Education System in the Making of the State: A Case Study in ACEH, Indonesia.* Sydney: The University of Sydney.
Levy, D. 2002. "Unanticipated Development: Perspectives on Private Higher Education's Emerging Roles." Working Paper 1, University at Albany, State University of New York.
Madjid, N. 2003. *Speech, University of New South Wales.* Sydney: Ministry of Higher Education.
Ministry of Higher Education (MOHE). 2010a. *Institusi Pengajian Tinggi Swasta (IPTS).* Private Higher Education Institution (Private HEI), Malaysia: Ministry of Higher Education.
Ministry of Higher Education [MOHE] 2010b. *Institusi Pengajian Tinggi Awam (IPTA).* Public Higher Education Institution (Public HEI) Malaysia: Ministry of Higher Education.
Mok, K.-H. 2010. "Emerging Regulatory Regionalism in University Governance: A Case Study of China and Taiwan." *Globalisation, Societies and Education* 8 (1): 87–103.

Murray Thomas, R. 1973. *A Chronicle of Indonesian Higher Education*. Singapore: Chopmen Enterprises.
Nakamura, M., and Nishino, S. 1995. "Development of Islamic Higher Education in Indonesia." In *East Asian Higher Education: Traditions and Transformations*, ed. A. H. Yee. 1st ed. Oxford, UK; New York: Published for the IAU Press by Pergamon.
Nazim. 2006. *Indonesia. Higher Education in South-East Asia*. Bangkok: SEAMEO RIHED, pp. 35–68.
New York Times. 2008. "Suharto Dies at 86; Indonesian Dictator Brought Order and Bloodshed." Available at: www.nytimes.com/2008/01/28/world/asia/28suharto.html?pagewanted=all. Accessed August 20, 2012.
Newsweek. October 17, 2005. "Looks Can be Deceiving." *Newsweek*, 24–25.
Organisation of the Islamic Conference (OIC). 2010. *Report of the Secretary General, COMSTECH*. Available at: comstech.org/LinkClick.aspx?fileticket=NBe_TJ0EuJc%3D...english. Accessed August 20, 2012.
Purwadi, A. 2001. "Impact of the Economic Crisis on Higher Education in Indonesia." In *Impact of the Economic Crisis on Higher Education in East Asia*, ed. IIEP. Paris: IIEP/UNESCO, pp. 61–75.
Purwadi A., and S. Muljoatmodjo. 2000. "Education in Indonesia: Coping with Challenges in the third Millenium." *Journal of South East Asian Education* 1 (1): 79–102.
Reid, A. 2008. "Introduction." In *The Chinese Diaspora in the Pacific*, ed. A. Reid. Aldershot: Ashgate, pp. xv-xxviii.
Robertson, S. 2010. "The EU, 'Regulatory State Regionalism' and New Modes of Higher Education Governance'." *Globalisation, Societies and Education* 8(1): 23–37.
SBS. 2011. "Islam's Deadly Divide." Available at: www.sbs.com.au/dateline/story/watch/id/601076/n/Islam-s-Deadly-Divide. Accessed March 9, 2012.
South East Asian Ministers of Education (SEAMEO) Regional Institute for Higher Education (RIHED). 2010. *SEAMEO RIHED and the M-I-T*. Bangkok: SEAMEO RIHED. Available at: www.schwartzman.org.br/simon/jakarta.htm. Accessed August 20, 2012.
"(Malaysia–Indonesia–Thailand) Student Mobility Pilot Program—Towards the Harmonisation of Higher Education." Available at: www.rihed.seameo.org/files/harmonizMIT2.pdf. Accessed March 24, 2012.
Surakhmad, W. 2002. *Desentralising Education: A Strategy for Building Sustainable Development*. Paper presented at Conference on Autonomy in Education in the Indonesian Context, Australian National University, September 29.
Suryadinata, L. 2003. "Patterns of Political Participation in Four ASEAN States: A Comparative Study." In *The Chinese Diaspora. Selected Essays* (vol. 1), ed. L-C. Wang and G. Wang. Singapore: Eastern Universities Press, pp. 64–83.
Sutter, R. "Rising China, US Influence, and Southeast Asia—Background, Status, and Outlook." In *ASEAN Industries and the Challenge from China*, ed. D. Jarvis and A. Welch. London: Palgrave Macmillan.
Sydney Morning Herald. January 10, 2003. "We are Paying a Heavy Price for Putting our Heads in the Sand."

Sydney Morning Herald. February 8, 2005. "Terrorism Blacklist: Indonesia Confident."
Sydney Morning Herald. April 19, 2008. "We Fill Our Tanks, While They Can't Fill Their Stomachs ."
Sydney Morning Herald. April 22, 2011. "Counting the Cost of Too Much Democracy."
Tempo. June 1, 2003. "Jalur Khusus. Menembus Kampus Ternama." pp. 54–55.
The Australian. January 15, 2005. "Campus Life on Hold as Tsunami Takes its Toll."
The Australian. February 8, 2007. "A Strengthening Bond."
The Australian. October 11, 2008. "Crusader Finds Fear is the Key."
The Australian. February 14, 2009. "Democracy Proves a Winner."
The Australian. March 5, 2011. "Region Nervous as China Boosts Defence Spending."
Transparency International. 2006. *2006 Corruption Perceptions Index*. Berlin, Germany: Transparency International.
UNDP. 2005. *Human Development Report for South East Asia*. New York: United Nations Development Program.
University World News. April 27, 2008. "Indonesia: University Admissions Scandal." Available at: www.universityworldnews.com/article.php?story=20080424153208204. Accessed March 9, 2012.
University World News. June 28, 2009. "Islamic States: Network to Improve Quality Assurance." Available at: www.universityworldnews.com/article.php?story=2009062612263584. Accessed March 9, 2012.
Varghese, N. V. 2004a. *Private Higher Education*. Paris: International Institute for Educational Planning (IIEP).
Varghese, N. V. 2004b. "Private Higher Education in Africa." Paper presented at the Policy Forum on Private Higher Education in Africa, Accra, Ghana, November 2–3, 2004.
Wang, G. 2000. *The Chinese Overseas. From Earthbound China to the Quest for Autonomy*. Cambridge: Harvard University Press.
Wang, G. 2005. "China and Southeast Asia: the Context of a New Beginning." In *Power Shift. China and Asia's New Dynamics*, ed. D. Shambaugh. Berkeley, CA: University of California Press, pp. 187–204.
Welch, A. 2008. "Imagining Islam: Funding and Governance of Islamic Higher Education in Indonesia and Malaysia." *Positioning Universities in the Globalized World: Changing Governance and Coping Strategies in Asia*, University of Hong Kong, December.
Welch, A. 2011a. *Higher Education in Southeast Asia. Blurring Borders, Changing Balance*. London and New York: Routledge.
Welch, A. 2011b. *Financing Inclusive Higher Education in Asia*. Manila: Asian Development Bank.
Welch, A. 2012. "Seek Knowledge Throughout the World? Mobility in Islamic Higher Education." *Research in Comparative and International Education* [Special Issue on Academic Mobility] 7 (1): 70–80.

Welch, A., and K.-H. Mok. 2003. "Conclusion: Deep Development or Deep Division?" In *Globalisation and Educational Restructuring in the Asia Pacific Region*, ed. K.-H. Mok and A. R. Welch. London: Palgrave Macmillan, pp. 333–356.

World Bank. 1996. *Staff Appraisal Report. Indonesia. Higher Education Support Project: Development of Undergraduate Education.* Jakarta: World Bank.

World Bank. 2001. *World Bank Tables 2000. Social Indicators of Development.* Washington, DC: World Bank.

Yang, R., and A. Welch. 2012. "A World Class University in China? The Case of Tsinghua." *Higher Education* 63 (5): 645–666.

Chapter 8

The Philippines and the Global Labor Market: An Emergent Form of Trans-regional Influence on Philippine Higher Education

Regina M. Ordonez

Introduction

There is a song that goes "Money makes the world go round, the world go round, the world go round." And that is as true of the world of Philippine higher education as it is of the rest of the world. The student is driven by his/her dream to work overseas for higher pay, the higher education institution (HEI) is driven by the opportunity to capture a student market willing to pay for a degree in demand by overseas employers, and employers of global firms are still driven by the desire and ability to source cheap labor from developing countries.

Commission on Higher Education's Role and Challenge

This lure of overseas employment is the challenge today faced by the Philippine Commission on Higher Education (CHED) that governs the operation and monitors the performance of Philippine HEIs. These HEIs offer degrees and courses in high demand by college students hankering to work abroad in hopes of a better economic future. However, the chair of the Commission recently stated that she had to prune a large number of universities that had failed to provide quality education to those students who wanted to enter the global labor market (Licuanan 2011).

Unfortunately, many of the HEIs that sprouted seeing the attraction of business and financial returns were not necessarily equipped to handle such courses as nursing, teacher education, business administration, information technology, hotel and restaurant management, maritime, and other "hot" or in-demand degrees. They merely wanted to jump onto the bandwagon of market opportunity, only to graduate people with these degrees who were then tested by the appropriate government body and failed the required licensure examinations.

Given the above situation, it is essential that HEIs upgrade themselves to prepare their students for the institutional global labor market. This chapter focuses on the quality education implications for HEIs. But first, it is useful to understand the history of the Filipino worker who constitutes one of the highest suppliers in the global labor market.

The Philippine Response to the Global Labor Market

For the Philippine government and its institutions, and for overseas Filipino workers, known as OFWs, the global labor market is divided basically into two types: the domestic worker or household laborer and the company employee or institution-based laborer.

For the latter, in more recent years, part of this huge global labor market has been added to the outsourcing strategy by transnational firms of establishing offshore operations in the Philippines, hiring out at lower management cost to Filipinos such functions as accounting, marketing, legal services, supply-chain management, and other company requirements without the latter ever having to migrate. However, this chapter will only consider OFWs, those who are employed abroad, which fall under mode 4 of the General Agreement on Trade in Services (GATS), which is the movement of natural persons (to other countries).

Notwithstanding the waves of agricultural workers who sailed to the United States for a better future before the Second World War, significant labor migration began around the 1960s when financially well-off, adventurous youth began to explore the benefits of undergraduate education and then employment opportunities in developed economies, predominantly the United States (Tullao 2006).

By the 1980s, the appeal of higher salaries drew Filipino domestic helpers, or DHs, into the global workforce, first to nearby English-speaking Hong Kong and Singapore, and as the years went by, to most distant Asian and European countries. As Filipinos began to experience the political and economic pains of martial law from 1972 to 1986, they looked beyond their native land for work opportunities abroad.

Word spread among relatives and friends that foreign households were able to pay three or four times more than people would ever earn in their homeland, inducing them to hire themselves out as cooks, cleaners, and nannies. Among them were degree holders in education and teachers based in the provinces unable to earn a decent wage at home because of the economic conditions in the Philippines. However, their English communication skills were satisfactory enough for foreign employers, who preferred to delegate babysitting, family, and menial household chores to the former while they took off to their comfortable corporate offices.

At about the same period, the Middle East began its huge infrastructure buildup, requiring thousands of construction workers from the Philippines brought in by Filipino contractors who had won bids to build highways, hospitals, and ports.

From these early beginnings, Filipino migrant labor has diversified into a variety of skills ranging from professionals in medical, information technology (IT), and health, to middle-skilled labor such as caregivers, entertainers, and seafarers, to low skilled and unskilled labor, including DHs. At least 50 percent of OFWs work as DHs.

Currently, the relatively recent mushrooming of Philippine HEIs is producing thousands of teachers and college graduates who often end up in jobs that lower the perceived status of the Filipino worker since they find employment as DHs in Hong Kong and Singapore, and as entertainers (*japayuki*) in Japan. IT professionals and licensed engineers do construction work in the Middle East, and medical doctors take nursing courses so that they can get jobs as nurses in US hospitals, while accountants work as clerks or caregivers (Tullao and Cortez 2004).

A critical policy question is how can HEIs produce more Filipinos who will qualify one day to be part of the corporate, institution-based labor market, rather than the domestic worker market?

Today about 10 million Filipinos, or 10 percent of the population, work overseas in over 150 countries in six continents. About 70 percent are land based with 30 percent being sea based.

Official statistics from the Philippine Overseas Employment Administration (POEA) office that processes the departure papers of OFWs shows that about one million workers a year on average were deployed from 2003 to 2009. In 2009, 64 percent found jobs in the Middle East, 25 percent in Asia, 5 percent in Europe, 3 percent in the Americas, and 2 percent each in Africa and Oceania/Trust Territories. For the first nine months of 2010, the numbers differ but slightly; see Figure 8.1. The figures here are officially documented, and do not include those who find work overseas informally, without their going through the POEA.

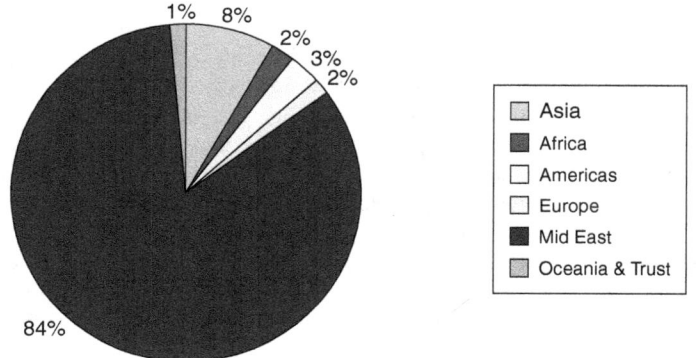

Figure 8.1 Nine-month deployment.
Source: CHED/Management and Information Systems (MIS), January 2010.

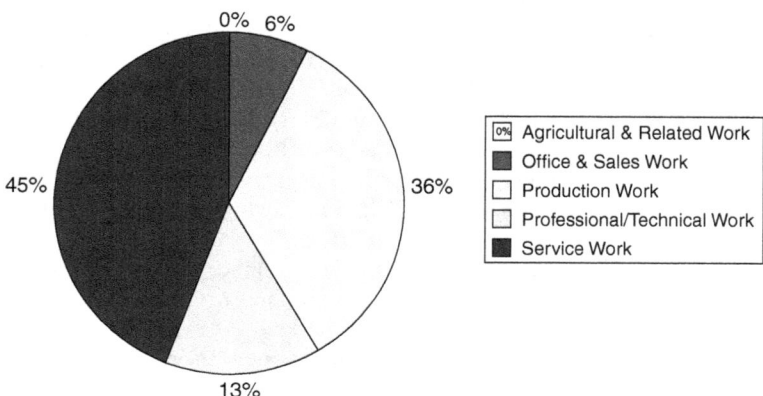

Figure 8.2 Nine-month deployment by type of work.
Source: CHED/MIS, January 2010.

Figure 8.2 indicates that professional workers comprise 13 percent of the pie. These are comprised of engineers with 5 percent of the jobs, nurses at 4 percent, while teachers make up less than 1 percent. Out of the group of service workers, which constituted most of the deployed jobs at 45 percent in 2010, household workers remain the bulk at 35 percent. Note that these numbers represent workers deployed just in the last nine months of 2010, and do not include those who already live and work overseas.

Dreams of the Filipino Youth: Work Abroad

A 2003 World Bank study found that not only was there a mismatch between the educational system and the job market, but that "the youth do not pursue the kinds of careers/occupations that are in demand in the country but instead seek to enter occupations in which there is an over-supply...they take courses in hopes of landing overseas jobs" (p. 91). Many take nursing courses not because they are interested in that career, but because their minds and hearts are set on finding employment in the United States, even as their own country has an acute lack of trained nurses employed in that profession (study cited in Sta. Maria 2003).

Young women and men enrolled in droves in nursing courses of universities and schools, legitimate and otherwise, to the point that today the Philippines has an oversupply of around 300,000 nurses, comprising about 10 percent of the 2.9 million unemployed or 3 percent of the 7.6 million underemployed, which are 7.5 percent and 19.5 percent, respectively, of the total labor force of 39 million (*Philippine Labor Force Survey* January 2011).

Degree holders or not, employable Filipinos cannot find work locally that pays sufficiently, if at all, to get them out of the poverty cycle and to support their immediate and extended families. They are thus attracted to the relatively higher wages offered by overseas jobs.

In other words, the main driving force or motivation for working abroad is: salary, salary, salary! Ironically, for workers to obtain the higher amount of pay compared to a home-based wage, they must often pay excessive fees to employment agencies that will place them in jobs after processing their papers. The agency deducts its fees and expenses owed by the OFW from his/her salary earned in the first few months – or years, in a few instances. The OFW who obtains a long-term contract of at least two to three years is lucky.

Gaining the educational qualifications to work abroad is half the battle. Other hurdles include obtaining approval for the appropriate visas and other employment and health clearances required by both home and host countries. A much smaller number of these OFWs are those who have been fortunate enough to have studied abroad and were thereafter able to arrange for work permits and/or immigrant visas.

The bright side is that this diaspora of 10 million Filipinos remitted a total of US$87.6 billion for the period 2003–2009, or an average of US$12.5 billion a year. In 2010 alone, they contributed US$18 billion to the economy, or around 12 percent of gross domestic product (GDP) (Remo 2011). Thus, OFWs are called the "unsung heroes of the Philippines" by government officials since they prop up the Philippine economy, helping the country through good and bad times, even when the rest of the world teeters on unstable political and economic uncertainties. Both elective and appointive officials continue to encourage the export of Filipino workers overseas, whether products of HEIs or not.

Governance of HEIs by the State

HEIs are governed on a national level by the CHED. CHED controls HEIs by issuing permits that allow new ones to operate, gives a certificate of recognition for the university or college to operate under temporary status, and finally accredits the programs of the HEI, either directly for the state universities and colleges (SUCs), or indirectly for the private universities and colleges (Tullao 2001b).

As of school year (SY) 2010–2011, official CHED data show that there are 1,823 private and public HEIs. However, this figure is an institutional count; the number is better appreciated if "satellite campuses" of the public institutions are included since this chapter is concerned with geographic access by higher education students from their respective places of residence. The total universe of HEIs then becomes 2,247.

Figure 8.3 indicates that private HEIs total 1,604, of which 334 are sectarian and 1,270 are nonsectarian, while public HEIs constitute 643 SUCs inclusive of their campuses.

It is interesting to note that the HEI population more than doubled by 2.6 times from 1992 to 2010 (Table 8.1). The number of public universities as a percentage of the total stayed at around 25 on average.

However, the total number of HEIs grew 2.6 times over the 18-year period from 862 to 2,247. Note that there was a big jump in the number of HEIs from just over 860 in 1992 to double that in 2001. One difference in the HEI population size between the years 1992 and 1997 was that programs in business administration and education were still the most attractive and easily available to the bulk of students taking up college

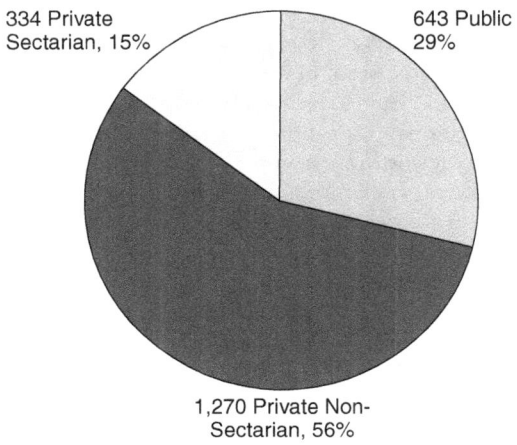

Figure 8.3 Type of HEIs.
Source: CHED/MIS, January 2010.

Table 8.1 Growth of HEIs over 18 years, from 1992 to 2010

Year	Public	Growth every period: public	Private	Growth every period: private	Total
1992	226		636		862
1997	372	146	1,114	478	1,486
2001	407	35	1,258	144	1,665
2005	451	44	1,492	234	1,943
2010	643	192	1,604	112	2,247

Source: CHED/MIS, January 2010.

degrees since offerings in those areas were generally the more common among HEIs. But rapid expansion continued until there were 2,247 in 2010 providing proof of the ever-growing demand by the global labor market. Students clamored for and got nursing, caregiving, engineering, dentistry, maritime, entertainment, and IT education. These courses offered hope and promise to the aspiring Filipinos who wanted to get employed abroad.

A 2005 study by the Philippine Survey and Research Center commissioned by the British Council Philippines cited the "unusually high number" of tertiary schools in and for the Philippines. Nevertheless, the number of HEIs ballooned to more than 2,000, with the help, persuasion, and pressure of political leaders of cities and provinces, who saw the advantages of meeting the economic needs of their constituents while reaping benefits for all. They therefore approached CHED for permits and accreditation for putting up their own institutions and program offerings.

It would be noteworthy to compare these statistics with the size or number of HEIs in other countries in the region and the rate at which they have grown, but that is beyond the scope of this chapter.

Quality Education

Quality in Philippine HEIs is assessed by a process of evaluation first by panels of experts from the different accreditation agencies, that is, the Educational Associations Federation of Accrediting Agencies of the Philippines (FAAP) for private schools or the Accrediting Agency of Chartered Colleges and Universities in the Philippines (AACUP) for public HEIs, which then recommend or endorse to CHED the quality level of the HEI.

The various factors are typical of any tertiary institute's quality assessment – quality of the faculty, number of enrollees, curriculum content, library capability, international linkages, pass rate on licensure examinations, and others. In 1998, for example, only 7 percent of the faculty members held doctorate degrees and 25 percent held master's degrees, revealing the relative academic inadequacy of the teaching faculty. Many of them were overworked, carrying heavy teaching loads per semester. This has also not changed much (Tullao 2001a).

Table 8.2 indicates the criteria employed to determine the level at which a given HEI will be rated.

Note that even while CHED relies on the federations to accredit their respective members, CHED is still mandated to "monitor and evaluate the performance of programs and institutes of higher learning for appropriate incentives and imposition of sanctions, such as, but not limited to, diminution or withdrawal of accreditation, programme termination or school closure" (Tullao 2002, 2).

The accreditation process is done at the program level and not at the institutional level. However, if at least one program is accredited, this is counted as the HEI being accredited. Table 8.3 indicates how both public and private HEIs were accredited for the year 2010–2011. Out of the 2,247 HEIs in 2011, only 20 percent had accredited programs; see Table 8.3.

The first step of the accreditation process is to enter Candidate status, where the HEI applies or requests for accreditation. Table 8.4 indicates

Table 8.2 Criteria for determining the level of HEI

Level 1	Level 2	Level 3	Level 4
Initial accreditation after a formal survey by the accrediting agency and duly certified by the accreditation federation or network, effective for a period of three years	Reaccreditation using the same processes as Level 1, effective for another period of three or five years	1. High standard of instruction 2. Strong faculty development tradition 3. Highly creditable performance of its graduates in licensure examinations 4. Highly visible community extension program – provision for a reasonable budget; quality of completed outputs; measurable result, such as publication, etc.; involvement of a significant number of faculty members; visible, tangible, and measurable impact on the community 5. Existence of working consortia or linkages with other schools and/or agencies 6. Extensive and functional library and other learning resource facilities	Same as Level 3, but in addition: 1. Carries prestige and authority comparable to similar programs in excellent foreign universities 2. Excellent research as seen in the number scope and impact of scholarly publications in referred national and international journals 3. Community service and the impact of contributions to the economic and social uplifting on both regional and national levels 4. Evidence of international linkages and consortia 5. Well-developed planning processes that support quality assurance mechanisms

Source: CHED/MIS, January 2012.

Table 8.3 HEIs with accredited programs

	Number	%
Total no. of HEIs in 2010–2011	2,247	100
No. of HEIs with accredited programs	447	20
Type of HEI:		
Public	204	9
Private	243	11

Source: CHED/MIS, January 2012.

Table 8.4 Public and private HEIs by program accreditation level

Accredited programs	Candidate status	Level 1	Level 2	Level 3	Level 4	Total
Public	375	387	419	327	0	1,508
Private	280	317	619	375	10	1,601
Total	655	704	1038	702	10	3,109

Source: CHED/MIS, January 2012.

that levels of accreditation for public HEI programs are evenly distributed among Candidate statuses: Levels 1, 2, and 3. For private HEI programs, more programs are bunched around Level 2, with Candidate status, Levels 1 and 3 taking a similar share from 17 percent to 23 percent. Less than 1 percent are at Level 4.

It seems then that the majority of HEIs are far from meeting the quality standards needed to obtain a Level 2, much less a Level 3, accreditation. A recent news article stated that

> the CHED has been slow in clamping down on substandard schools, especially private nursing schools owned by politically influential businessmen. It hasn't cracked the whip on schools whose products have consistently underperformed in licensure exams, and it hasn't really monitored the quality of historically low-performing state and local universities and colleges. (*Philippine Daily Inquirer* March 29, 2011)

Quality of the Enrollee

On the other side of the spectrum, the entering enrollee to a HEI may not have the qualifications to get through the four years of university learning, much less the professional licensure examinations. The government of the Philippines has recently seen the wisdom of conforming to the prevailing global standard on basic education, which pegs the number of years at twelve. The Philippines is currently only one of the three countries left, the two others being Djibouti and Angola in Africa, with a ten-year basic education cycle – six years of elementary education and four years of high school. This puts the country's high-school graduates behind their counterparts in most other countries in terms of quantity of learning. Although many private schools offer a Grade 7 to compensate, that is still one year short of the global standard. Thus, the Department of Education (DepEd), which handles basic education, has seen fit to increase the number of years to 12, and has named their program "K to 12." This means one year of kindergarten, six years of grade school, four years of junior high school, and two years of senior high school. The government mandate is being implemented slowly, year upon year, until the entire system will have reached full implementation by the SY 2017–2018.

Although this program has met with initial resistance from parents who say they cannot afford the extra two years of schooling for their children, and the actual participation rates for basic education have been declining over an eight-year period from 2002 to 2010, the policy is in place. The DepEd's assessment has found that due to the congested curriculum,

> secondary graduates of the current system are not adequately prepared for college. This is why most of the courses, the so-called General Education subjects, taken by first year college students are actually remedial as they should have already been mastered in high school. (Senate Economic Planning Office 2011)

Furthermore, Education Undersecretary Francis Varela justifies this change by claiming that it makes sense economically in the long run: "While a graduate of a four year high school course would earn P19,876 annually, the graduate of a six year (high school) course could earn P35,280, a difference of P15,404" (Choudhury 2012). The additional two years of secondary school would increase the chances of the entering college student to complete tertiary education, and be better equipped to meet the job requirements of employers both in the Philippines and abroad.

The DepEd is tapping HEIs to implement an adjusted curriculum for Grades 11 and 12 as well as share their facilities for a seamless transition. This would trigger an evaluation of their existing learning systems and equip and upgrade them to prepare their students for the demanding external labor market.

Internationalization of HEIs

In keeping with government policy to "seize opportunities [in the global market], minimize the costs and the risks, empower and guide the workers in their decision making, enable stakeholders, engage recruiters, foreign governments, and employers to share responsibility and mainstream the issues in development planning," CHED issued a Memo Order in early 2000, encouraging international linkages and twinning programs in coordination with the Department of Foreign Affairs and the Bureau of Immigration and Deportation ("Encouraging international linkages and twinning programs in coordination with the Department of Foreign Affairs and the Bureau of Immigration and Deportation," available at: https://www.google.com/#hl=en&output=search&sclient=psy-ab&q=Philippines+CHED+Memo+Order+encouraging+international+linkages+and+twinning+programs+in+coordination+with+the+Department+of+Foreign+Affairs+and+the+Bureau+of+Immigration+and+Deportation&oq=Phi&gs_l=hp.1.0.35i39l2j0l2.2590.3300.0.6005.3.3.0.0.0.0.156.459.0j3.3.0.crnk_fspiked..0.0...1c.Jqa06AHHxgw&pbx=1&bav=on.2,or.r_gc.r_pw.r_cp.r_qf.,cf.osb&fp=3006fb04a1a2772d&biw=1222&bih=691).
This order aims to achieve the following objectives:

- to upgrade the present quality of academic programs through collaborative activities, effective exchange of faculty, and cooperation in research;
- to strengthen educational, cultural, social, economic, and political bonds between the Philippines and foreign institutions;
- to develop pedagogical reform through international linkages in higher education and research;
- to promote and facilitate international mobility of teaching staff and students as an essential part of quality and relevance of higher education; and
- to enhance existing higher educational goals in the country.

The Memo Order laid the institutional foundation for exchange agreements between Philippine HEIs and universities abroad. Twinning programs have resulted in faculty and student exchange programs, collaborative research, scholarship grants, short- and long-term training, curriculum development and enhancement, library and laboratory enrichment and cultural exchange, offshore education, and teleconferencing – all paving the way for intercultural understanding and intellectual growth.

HEIs' participation in international networks and consortia has received the blessing and financial support of CHED. Unfortunately, only 10 high-end private HEIs are at Level 4 and are able to apply this well-intentioned policy, although more are attempting to do so. Out of the 1,604 private HEIs, only 243 have gone through the accreditation process, of which only 4 percent, which are the 10 high-end schools, can be said to have international recognition.

The names of these institutions are quite familiar to those in the field of international education and to students in the region looking for excellent schools with global standards, the likes of the University of the Philippines, De La Salle University, Ateneo University, University of Sto. Tomas, and a handful of others. The painful dilemma is that 96 percent of private HEIs are not up to par in producing high-quality graduates who can compete in the global labor market of corporate jobs; a similar scenario occurs among public HEIs.

A lack of financial resources is a major problem for most HEIs and the students who are unable to enroll in them; neither side can afford to take advantage of CHED's internationalization thrust. In fact, the majority of HEIs cannot even deliver the more basic requirement of quality education, as shown when their graduates take licensure examinations.

Performance of HEIs

Governance policy set by the HEI boards should translate into quality education. But if policy underpinnings are motivated heavily by market and monetary considerations, then the output of having produced a qualified student is not achieved. Unfortunately, many HEIs are neither equipped nor qualified to offer high-demand programs. The Professional Regulation Commission (PRC), the government agency that administers licensure examinations which strongly determine the performance of the graduates from these institutions, has published results that are disappointing.

CHED had gathered information revealing that, in 2010, only half of the nursing graduates passed their nursing board examinations. Records show that in 2009, about one-third, or 36 percent, out of 415,190 college graduates passed the examinations in 44 various professional disciplines, such as education, medicine, engineering, and other science and technology courses. Courses with the lowest passing rates were in the field of engineering – aeronautics, electronics, communications engineering, and marine engineering. Nursing, which was in high demand (at least 40 percent of all graduates, 172,000, were from nursing schools), also demonstrated a low pass rate at around 40 percent (*Philippine Daily Inquirer* March 29, 2011). The same article stated that the 2009 result was a decline from 2008, when 39 percent of 390,378 examinees passed. In other words, for the last three years, between 50 and 60 percent of college graduates failed to prove that they were qualified to obtain licenses to practice the profession in which they had received degrees.

Although only 230,000 examinees presented in 2004, by 2009, the number had grown to 415,000, almost double from five years previously, which indicates that HEIs have been crunching out graduates in huge numbers without necessarily giving them the quality education they need to pass the licensure examinations. Yet, the license is needed as an intermediate step (the next being obtaining local employment so that work experience becomes part of their resume) before they enter the ranks of those who are qualified to seek employment abroad.

The dismal record of passing rates is now being blamed on the poor quality of education given to students by the HEIs.

> The CHED has been notorious for its tendency to over-regulate course offerings and disciplines of private education at large, which does not receive anything from government, without however doing anything to stop poor-performing private nursing and engineering schools. It has also failed to check the proliferation of state and local colleges and universities, much less monitor the quality of education they offer. (*Philippine Daily Inquirer* March 29, 2011)

The numbers of HEIs had dramatically expanded because management saw the opportunity of profiting from the student demand for such courses. Even institutions known for their expertise in IT now offer nursing courses from which they gain profitably, notwithstanding the poor passing rate of their graduates in both their IT and nursing courses.

Can HEIs govern themselves? The individual HEI is under pressure to deliver. The government demands that it link with other countries/movements/associations where there is an exchange of students, faculty, curricula, materials, and equipment. However, prestigious universities abroad seek to link up only with those in the Philippines that have highly qualified faculty and staff. The Association of South East Asian Nations (ASEAN) University Network contains only a few member institutions from the Philippines.

CHED's Solution

Under the current Aquino administration, CHED has recognized the erratic quality of higher education and has begun to tighten requirements for HEIs offering such courses. The review of the over 2,000 universities and colleges indicated that many were created as an accommodation to politicians who saw both economic opportunity and a chance at recognition in having a college established during their tenure in office. Some college administrators also felt that unless the name "university" was attached to their institutions, they would be looked upon as less competent and of lower quality than those who carry that label. For SUCs, the lower number of enrollees would mean they would receive less in governmental budget support.

CHED is drawing up measures to strictly enforce standards in both private and public colleges and universities. Patrica Licuanan, the CHED chair, has indicated that the department plans to implement strategies to streamline the education system that is currently crowded with more than 2,000 institutions. These would include:

1. A moratorium on processing applications for new HEIs is in place. This had been done in the past, and for as long as there was political support from the top, it succeeded. However, if the leadership at a certain point in time has needed to win and maintain favor with certain politicians, then the moratorium was ignored, as evidenced in the latter years of the Arroyo Administration (2002–2010).
2. Closure of institutions that do not meet the minimum standards set by CHED serves as a warning to all HEIs. In 2006, the then chair of CHED was able to put a stop to the offering of nursing courses by 23 HEIs. However, many wonder if CHED has enough political will and backing to pursue, recommend, and act upon the closure of HEIs and programs that do not meet the standards of excellence without interference from the executive and legislative branches.
3. Rationalization and reclassification of HEIs into the most appropriate organizational typology, such as the university for research and/or teaching, the four-year community college, the professional college for licensing professions, the liberal arts school for the generalist outlook, and the two-year junior college, so that the nomenclature fits the various needs of different segments of the student population. A better fit between the needs of the global labor market and the HEI that can deliver the educational product should always be monitored, so that expertise is preserved without being diffused by other seemingly more popular courses.
4. Encouraging the strengthening of non-CHED accreditation and certification agencies for knowledge and skill-based competencies so that HEIs will be put under pressure to respond competitively to their mandate to offer quality programs in their schools. Other quality assurance measures such as minimizing the presence

of power brokers within CHED whom influential politicians have approached for lenient treatment in meeting standards. Perhaps, more checks and balances should be installed within the CHED system to minimize the chances of approval of requests by political personalities to open or expand the higher education offerings in their local areas of influence.

Summary

In analyzing the response of HEIs to the trans-regional, nay trans-global, phenomenon of movements of people, goods, and services across the world, the driving force of economics seems to take precedence as the prime motivator. The global labor market is characterized on the one hand by the demand of corporations for skilled foreign workers willing to accept lower wages than their local or host counterparts, and the supply of educated manpower on the other hand looking for greener financial pastures outside their respective home countries. The matching occurs when HEIs most closely attune their policies and programs to the human resource needs of that job marketplace.

This trend has been ongoing for a number of years. Many HEIs were established or upgraded because of what they saw as an opportunity for profit and fame. The CHED permitted the continuing operation of universities that did not meet academic standards, despite their mandate to regulate, monitor, and penalize. Under new leadership and direction that may change. The current government administration has ordered the cleaning up of the tertiary education system.

It must be stated, however, that the Philippines remains a model in the region in which the private sector dominates over government institutions in establishing tertiary educational institutes, outdoing the SUCs by an almost 3.5:1 ratio. Historically, a major incentive for the private sector to establish these HEIs was to service the needs of the commerce sector as it grew from the early 1950s, as business skills were demanded by that economy, as they continue to be today. This trend of need-driven quality business schools remains today.

A second factor in favor of hiring Filipino graduates is that they possess a facility with the English language that other nationals may lack. Proof of the Filipino worker's desirability is his mobility and presence in so many parts of the world, combined with his adaptability to different cultures. From this pool of graduates, global business firms look to hire the most qualified and educated applicants.

These are strengths that the HEI can leverage as long as it stays attuned to the changing labor environment as well as the demands of college students for the appropriate coursework that leads them to desirable overseas jobs. HEIs should be guided by the words of César de Prado Yepes of the United Nations University.

> The "new regionalism" paradigm is a multidimensional form of integration, which includes economic, political, social and cultural aspects and thus goes far beyond the goal of creating region-based free trade regimes or security alliances of earlier regional blocs... (and which) seeks to promote certain "world values" (for) security, economic and social development and ecological sustainability. (Yepes 2006, 1)

If the spirit of the GATS is truly to be fulfilled, the flow of education and jobs across countries should result in a more humane and more equitable global labor market.

References

Choudhury, Perla Aragon. "Who's Afraid of 'K to 12'?" *Philippine Daily Inquirer*, January 23, 2012.

Licuanan, Patricia, 2011. Interview with Chair Commission on Higher Education, April 6, 2011.

Philippine Commission on Higher Education (CHED). 2012. "Management and Information Systems Unit." Extracted from MIS data as basis for Tables 1–3, January 2012.

Philippine Labor Force Survey, January 2011. Philippine National Statistics Office, "Results from the January 2011 Labor Force Survey," No 2011–21; Income and Employment Statistics Division, data released March 15, 2011.

Philippine Overseas Employment Administration (POEA) data as basis for Figures 1–6, April 2011.

Remo, M. 2011. "OFW Remittances Hit $18.76B, an All-time High- BSP." *Philippine Daily Inquirer*, February 15, 2011.

Remo, M. 2011. "Is Labor Export Good Development Policy?" *Philippine Daily Inquirer*, March 8, 2011.

Remo, M. 2011. "Failing Grade." *Philippine Daily Inquirer*. March 29, 2011.

Sta. Maria, J., and A. G. Watts. 2003. "Public Policies and Career Development: A Framework for the Design of Career Information, Guidance and Counseling Services in Developing and Transition Countries." *Country Report on Philippines*, World Bank, June 2003.

Tullao, T. S., Jr. 2001a. "Are Filipino Professionals Ready to Meet International Competition?" *Policy Notes No. 2001–09*, Philippine Institute for Development Studies (PIDS), August 2001,

Tullao, T. S., Jr. 2001b. "Domestic Regulation and the Trade in Services: The Role of the Commission on Higher Education (CHED) and the Professional Regulation Commission (PRC)." Center for Business and Economic Research and Development Working Paper Series 2001–02, De La Salle University (DLSU)-Manila, 2002, pp. 27–28.

Tullao, T. S., Jr. 2002. "Does Domestic Regulation Promote Globally Competitive Filipino Professionals and Educational Services?" *Policy Notes No. 2002–12*, Philippine Institute for Development Studies (PIDS), December 2002, p. 3.

Tullao, T. S., Jr., and M. A. Cortez. 2004."Movement of Natural Persons between the Philippines and Japan Issues and Prospects."Discussion Paper Series No. 2004–11, Center for Business and Economic Research and Development, De La Salle University (DLSU) – Manila, March 2004, p. 18.

Tullao, T. S., Jr., and M. A. Cortez. 2006. "Issues and Prospects on the Movement of Natural Persons and Human Capital Development in the Philippine American Economic Relations." Discussion Paper Series No. 2006–07, Philippine Institute for Development Studies (PIDS), February 2006, p. 19.

Yepes, Cesar de Prado. 2006. "World Regionalization of Higher Education: Policy Proposals for International Organizations," *Higher Education Policy 19, 2006*, United Nations University, Comparative Regional Integration Studies.

Part III

Regulatory and Governance Dimensions

Chapter 9

Cooperation and Competition in Tango: Transnationalization of Higher Education and the Emergence of Regulatory Regionalism in Asia[1]

Ka Ho Mok

Introduction

Confronted with a growing pressure for internationalization, together with the strong urge for enhancing the global status in the highly competitive knowledge-based economy, many Asian governments have adopted different strategies to make their higher education (HE) more competitive through the quest for becoming a regional education hub and the transnationalization of HE in order to assert their regional/global influences. Unquestionably, the rise of transnational higher education (TNHE) and the quest for regional education hub status among Asian countries has suggested more competition. However, we have also observed more regional cooperation emerging through various kinds of bilateral and multilateral collaborations among Asian states with attempts to strengthen the regional influences in coping with the growing challenges from their counterparts in Europe and North America. One of the major trends of changing university governance is the emergence of regulatory regionalism, which is reflected by the striking features of recent developments in regional governance that transcend territorial spaces of nation states. This chapter sets out against this policy context to examine major policies introduced and strategies employed by governments in selected Asian societies – Singapore and Malaysia – in expanding TNHE programs and actively involving regional collaborations. More specifically, this chapter also reviews major developments of deepening regional cooperation among Asian countries/societies to assert their regional influences in the globalizing world.

Regional Response to Global Pressure: The Rise of Transnational Education

With a strong conviction to turn their countries/societies into regional hubs of education, the Singapore government has proactively engaged in the "global school project" to transform the city-state into "Boston of the East," while the government of Malaysia has tried to develop two mega-education cities at its capital city and a city in the South just across the border between Singapore and Malaysia (Mok 2011; Mok and Yu 2011). In view of the declining student population in high schools, together with the need to internationalize the HE system, the government in Taiwan announced a new policy in January 2011 to transform the island state into a regional education hub by recruiting more overseas students from Southeast Asia and mainland China (Chen 2011a). Similarly, we also witness other Asian governments' attempts to invest more in education to raise their international profile. South Korea has invested heavily in its "Brain 21 Project" in promoting research and scholarship, while China has continued its strategic investments in major universities through the "211," "985," and other forms of strategic development investment in grooming a few universities to rank higher in the global university ranking exercises (Chen 2011a; Mok 2012). All these measures adopted by Asian states are to enhance their global competitiveness, of which one is to pursue regional education hub projects in Asia.

The Quest for Regional Education Hub: Malaysian Experience

Malaysia's ambition to become a regional education hub was first sketchily noted in the grand development blueprint of *Wawasan 2020* (Vision 2020) initiated by the Mahathir administration in 1991.[2] According to Vision 2020, the government is keen to meet the policy target of having 40 percent of youth aged 19–24 years admitted into tertiary education. By

2020, it hopes that 60 percent of high-school students will be admitted into public universities, with the rest going to private colleges and universities. The publication of the *National Higher Education Strategic Plan 2020* and the *National Higher Education Action Plan, 2007* (both launched in August 2007) is the most recent response to the changing socioeconomic and sociopolitical circumstances in Malaysia. Given that the global higher educational environment has significantly changed, the *National Higher Education Strategic Plan 2020* outlines seven major reform objectives, which are: widening access and enhancing quality; improving the quality of teaching and learning; enhancing research and innovation; strengthening institutions of HE; intensifying internationalization; enculturation of lifelong learning; and finally, reinforcing the *MOHE's delivery system*.

In terms of the development of TNHE in Malaysia, the *Report by the Committee to Study, Review and Make Recommendations Concerning the Development and Direction of Higher Education in Malaysia (Halatuju Report)* was published in July 2005, which contained 138 recommendations. Though it was controversial (Wan Abdul Manan 2008), central to this report is the need for local higher education institutions (HEIs) to engage in self-promoting activities in the outside world. In addition, the report also recommends that the government invest more in international student and staff exchange programs, which would promote more collaborations between local and transnational education institutions. Based on inputs from the Cabinet, another report named the *Transformation of Higher Education Document* was issued in July 2007 to combine the relevant elements in the Ninth Malaysia Plan and recommendations from the *Halatuju Report*. Subsequently, the latest publication for this long-term plan, the *National Higher Education Strategic Plan*, was put together in August 2007. According to the plan, the Malaysian government was trying to attract 100,000 students from overseas by 2010.

In Malaysia, distance-learning arrangements, notably twinning programs, have long been prosperous ever since the mid-1980s. Yet, the establishment of international branch campuses could only become possible after the construction of a new legal framework in 1996.[3] Since then, various forms of TNHE have swiftly emerged in Malaysia, especially in the Klang Valley where Kuala Lumpur is located. The development of international branch campuses here is particularly impressive. In Malaysia, branch campuses of foreign universities can only be established by an invitation from the Ministry of Education or the Ministry of Higher Education (after 2004). The invited foreign universities, however, need to establish themselves as Malaysian companies, with majority Malaysian ownership, to operate their campuses. For instance, the University of Nottingham has run its programs in its Malaysia campus since 2000, with a newer campus recently set up at Semenyih, Negeri Sembilan, for the 2005–2006 academic year. The other three international branch campuses in Malaysia, to date, are all Australian universities, namely the Monash University (Petaling Jaya campus, 1998), Curtin University (Miri campus, 1999), and Swinburne University of Technology (Kuching campus, 2000). According to the Observatory on Borderless Higher Education (2002), Monash University cooperates with the Sunway Group – a pioneer of twinning arrangements in the field of education as early as the late 1980s – and the latter provides funding for its Malaysia campus. Similarly, the local partner of Swinburne University of Technology in Malaysia is the Sarawak state government, which cooperates indirectly with the university through its *Yayasan Sarawak* (Sarawak Foundation) and Sarawak Higher Education Foundation.

Malaysia's increasing cooperation with foreign universities has coincided with the increased regulation of transnational provision (Lee 1999; McBurnie and Ziguras 2001). After establishing the partnership with local corporations, foreign university campuses in Malaysia have done well. For instance, Monash University was the first to build its overseas branch campus in Malaysia. With its five faculties including Medicine and Health Sciences, Engineering, Information Technology, Business, and Arts and Sciences, the Monash University – Malaysia now offers various undergraduate and graduate programs to almost 4,000 students. Its purpose-built campus was opened in 2007, which provides a high-tech home for the University. The Nottingham Malaysia campus has also successfully recruited more than 2,700 international students from more than 50 countries. According to the Malaysian Qualifications Agency (MQA), as of April 21, 2009, there are altogether four branch campuses (having one set up by the UK university and three by Australia), running 84 programs throughout the country (interview conducted in Malaysia, April 2009). Official statistics also indicate that the private sector has played an increasingly important role in enhancing access to HE in Malaysia. In 2004, 32 percent of students were enrolled in private HEIs in Malaysia. Furthermore, 27,731 international students were studying in Malaysian private HEIs in 2004. I was also informed during a recent visit to MQA that 19 UK universities are now running 110 twinning programs accredited in the list of the Malaysian Qualifications Register (MQR), while 18 Australian universities are offering 71 programs of this kind in the country. Institutions from other countries like New Zealand, the United States, Egypt, and Jordan are also offering twinning programs in Malaysia (interview conducted in Malaysia, April 2009).

Finally, the government has also initiated a general regulatory framework for quality assurance of HE. In fact, the private education sector was initially the only focus of this regulatory framework. *Lembaga Akreditasi Negara* (National Accreditation Board) was established under the *Lembaga Akreditasi Negara* Act of 1996 as a statutory body to accredit certificate, diploma, and degree programs provided by private institutions of higher learning. Yet, later in April 2002, the Ministry of Education also set up its own Quality Assurance Division to coordinate and manage the quality assurance system in public institutions of higher learning. With the rise of transnational education programs and the rapid expansion of private HE, the government eventually sought to streamline these existing regulatory frameworks in 2003, and thereafter adopted the unified Malaysian Qualifications Framework (MQF) in 2004, governed by the newly established MQA in 2007 to accredit qualifications awarded by all institutions of HE. In short, the most recent achievements of TNHE in Malaysia are as follows:

- The two major projects by the Malaysian government to establish itself as a regional hub of education, namely, the development of Educity in Iskandar Malaysia, just next to Singapore, and the Kuala Lumpur Education City (KLEC), incorporating a new commercial and residential project in the Klang Valley south of Kuala Lumpur.
- Newcastle University in the United Kingdom was the first foreign institution signed on to be part of Educity, and the Dutch Maritime Institute also plans to offer programs with foreign degrees, while international schools such as Britain's Marlborough College will be set up in the Educity (Pekwan 2009).
- In 2007, there were 47,928 international students from around 150 countries studying in Malaysia. Among them, 14,324 enrolled in public HEIs and 33,604 enrolled in private HEIs.
- In 2007, Indonesians represented 17.6 percent (8,454) of the population of international students in Malaysia. It was followed by students from China, 13.5 percent (6,468); Nigeria, 6 percent (2,884); and Bangladesh, 5.2 percent (2,506).
- However, while the student population from Indonesia continues to expand from 2003 to 2007 (*+50.1 percent*), student population from China has shrunk significantly (*–37.5 percent*).
- The growth of the student population from the Middle East has also been hindered by the latest HE developments in the Middle East.
- The number of private universities/university colleges in Malaysia (branch campuses of foreign HEIs inclusive) has increased dramatically *from 0 in 1998 to 37 in 2007*, with a vast majority of them offering TNHE programs particularly in business and Science and Technology.

- Obviously, the two regional development projects mentioned above reveal Malaysia's ambition to develop a multiuse commercial, academic, residential complex (Ministry of Higher Education, Malaysia, 2009).

Global School House Project: Singapore Experience

As a city-state with meager natural resources, the Singapore government has always taken the quality of its human resources very seriously. Being aware of the importance of a more inclusive, energetic, and creative HE sector, it has initiated various comprehensive reviews of its HE system since the late 1980s. Two major policy directions have been set in this regard: first, the expansion of postgraduate education and research at the universities; and second, the enhancement of undergraduate curricula with a stronger emphasis given to students' creativity and thinking skills.

Yet, as far as the quest for a regional hub of education is concerned, policies of quality enhancement and the corporatization of public universities alone may be far from sufficient. The provision of more opportunities for HE, both in terms of number and variety, has to be delivered to domestic Singaporeans and foreign learners from the region. The mid-1980s' school-leaver boom saw the beginning of TNHE in Singapore, and as Richard Garrett pointed out at the time, this school-leaving cohort (20- to 24-year age group) would rise again and reach its peak around 2010 (as it did. 2005: 9). However, by 2003, Singapore's public universities and polytechnics could only enroll around 40,000 and 56,000 students respectively; while on the other hand, 119,000 students were enrolled by around 170 private tertiary providers, of which 140 offered programs in collaboration with foreign institutions and enrolled 75 percent of the total student population in this section (ibid., 9–10). The importance of transnational education provision in Singapore has therefore become obvious.

Meanwhile, in order to tap in the lucrative education market more aggressively, the Singapore government had launched its Global Schoolhouse initiative in 2002. In fact, ever since 1998, the government, through efforts taken by its Economic Development Board (EDB) instead of its Ministry of Education,[4] has strategically invited "world-class" and "reputable" universities from abroad to set up their Asian campuses in the city-state. As a result, Singapore is today home to 16 leading foreign tertiary institutions and 44 pre-tertiary schools offering international curricula.[5] The prestigious INSEAD (Institut Européen d'Administration des Affaires, established its Singapore branch campus in 2000), the University of Chicago

Booth School of Business (2000), S. P. Jain Center of Management (2006),[6] the New York University's Tisch School of the Arts (2007), and DigiPen Institute of Technology (2008) are in the list of these foreign tertiary institutions, ranging impressively from business, management arts, media, hospitality to information technology, biomedical sciences and engineering.

In 2003, a further and more integrated step was taken by the government to promote Singapore as a premier education hub. "Singapore Education," a multi-government agency initiative, is led by the EDB and supported by the Tourism Board, SPRING Singapore, International Enterprise Singapore, and the Ministry of Education. According to the official website of Singapore Education,[7] EDB is responsible for attracting "internationally renowned educational institutions to set up campuses in Singapore," whereas the Tourism Board is tasked with overseas promotion and marketing of Singapore education,[8] and the International Enterprise Singapore in charge of helping quality local education institutions (e.g., Anglo-Chinese School [International] and Raffles Education) to develop their businesses and set up campuses overseas. Last but not the least, the SPRING Singapore is given the role of administering quality accreditation for private education institutions in the city-state.

Another significant strategy adopted by the government in promoting TNHE is the joint-degree program arranged between local universities and their overseas partners. Local Singapore universities are actively collaborating with peer universities across the world in a diversified spectrum of academic programs, bringing together affluent resources in such fields. Students are granted the freedom to study at both campuses and receive supervision and teaching from faculties of both universities. A representative example is the Singapore–MIT (Massachusetts Institute of Technology) Alliance (SMA), an innovative engineering education and research enterprise jointly founded by the National University of Singapore, the Nanyang Technological University, and MIT in 1998. This alliance has so far developed five graduate degree programs, and has created a learning environment at the forefront of current technology.

Finally, as part of its policy to support TNHE, the Singapore government also offers a comprehensive package of financial aid to international students through several public channels (Cheng et al. 2009). The tuition fees for them are only 10 percent above the local rate, and they can apply for any financial assistance schemes open to local students, including scholarships provided by the "Singapore Scholarship" and tuition grants conditional on the agreement of working for a Singapore-registered company for at least three years upon graduation. Moreover, numerous bursaries are provided by individual tertiary institutions, and student loans are also available at favorable interest rates. Interviewing senior administrators of selected transnational education institutions like James Cook University Australia and ESSEC IRENE Business School (Institute for Research and Education on Education) from Paris, the author learned that both institutions have received financial subsidies and other forms of assistance such as providing them good amenities or identifying very good sites for campus buildings. Seeing great potential developing their campuses in Singapore as a solid platform reaching out to Asian students, these overseas institutions, therefore, are attracted by the preferential treatment given by the Singapore government to venture into Asian soil (filed interviews conducted in Singapore, August 2010). Recent immigration policies that aim to attract talented and skilled individuals to live and work in Singapore, in addition, have also facilitated the development of its transnational education industry. In short, the most recent achievements of TNHE in Singapore are as follows:

- In 2007, it was estimated that 86,000 international students from 120 countries were studying in Singapore, with approximately 1,120 cross-border education program arrangements in the city-state.
- Over 1,200 private HEIs and 44 pre-tertiary schools are offering international curricula in Singapore.
- *Raffles Education Corp*, the largest private education group in Asia, has established its international headquarters in Singapore. About 61,000 students are studying in its 28 colleges around the Asia-Pacific region.
- Public universities have also played a role in the quest for creating a regional hub of education. The three autonomous universities enroll 20 percent international students who mainly come from the Association of South East Asian Nations (ASEAN), China, and India. Most of them are enrolled in Engineering and Science courses.
- As of 2008, the education sector (all levels) contributed about 2 percent of Singapore's GDP and is forecasted to reach 5 percent by 2015. (*Source*: MTI 2003; Lasanowski 2009; Ministry of Education 2010)

Obviously, the Global Schoolhouse is a multifaceted and ambitious project, with multiple objectives to recruit "foreign talent," generate income, foster economic growth, and attract research and development firms as well as multinational companies specializing in knowledge economy and service industries (Gribble and McBurnie 2007). The rise of TNHE in Malaysia and Singapore in general and the quest for regional hub status in particular have clearly suggested that these Asian governments are particularly keen to expand the education market not only for income generation but also for "soft power" assertion to enhance their national competitiveness in the global marketplace. Whether such a quest for a regional education hub in Asia would promote more regional cooperation or create additional tension among Asian countries in competing for students and human capital very much depends upon whether nation states see others as competitors or partners (Lo 2011). Our above discussions clearly suggest that potential tensions among these Asian economies are growing when they are pursuing a similar agenda to assert their regional/global influences. Nonetheless, we also observe more regional cooperation being fostered among Asian countries through different forms of regional collaborative frameworks.

The Emergence of Regulatory Regionalism

Having examined recent HE transformations and the rise of TNHE in Asia, we could analyze such changes as part of the wider contemporary trend to "reinvent the state" or to enhance the "competition state" projects in the globalizing world (Mok 2008). Yet another contemporary inclination, as we can see in the accelerated integration of the European Union (EU), is regionalism within the wider context of globalization. Thus, accordingly, is there any sign of the emergence of regulatory regionalism in terms of East Asian HE? The following will examine whether and how regulatory regionalism has emerged in Asia.

Admittedly, not only in East Asia, the whole of European HE has also been dwarfed by its American counterpart since the end of World War II. This successful American model, particularly in regard to research universities, has increasingly posed a challenge to the relatively stagnant and conservative European institutions based largely on their heritage from the eighteenth and nineteenth centuries. In face of these pressures, one of the recent responses from the EU is its attempts at regulatory regionalism that try to synergize the competitive edge of European universities. The quest for world-class universities is particularly relevant in this regard, and the first effort set to improve the research quality of European universities could be found in the "Lisbon Strategy" first initiated by the European Council in Lisbon in March 2000 (Deem et al. 2008).[9] The 1999 Bologna Declaration[10] and its subsequent "Bologna Process"[11] could be regarded as the second effort concerning university learning and teaching, as well as the creation of a common HE market and research area. The academic degree structures of EU universities have henceforth been harmonized to enable learner and worker mobility, facilitate credit transfers, and ensure quality assurance (Robertson 2008, 2009). More importantly, the Bologna Declaration, with its goal of achieving a "European Higher

Education Area" by 2010, has for the first time created a common ground for the EU to promote its HE in a global market, particularly to Asia. Since Russia and southeast Europe are now also part of the European Higher Education Area, it thus extends far beyond the EU as a constitutional entity (Robertson 2009, 8).

In comparison, to date, mechanisms to promote East Asian integration in HE have not yet been developed. However, signs of regulatory regionalism could be traced in related collaborations via certain regional organizations, or in the institutional interactions undertaken within a wider framework of ASEAN + 1 or ASEAN + 3. For example, the formation of the ASEAN as a regional collaborative framework is a case in point.

ASEAN and cooperation in HE

ASEAN was established in August 1967 as a formal regional intergovernmental collaboration between five noncommunist countries in South Asia primarily over issues of security in the region but later expanded to have ten members. Originally, it was not intended as a legal entity with sovereign power but only an organization with regional member countries to discuss common issues and come up with regional approaches to solve these issues. However, ASEAN evolved into a legal entity with the signing of the ASEAN Charter with its members in November 20, 2007. This Charter elaborates principles and rules for ASEAN, giving it a stronger collective voice in the international community and promoting compliance with ASEAN agreements. Adhering to the principles of the United Nations Charter, ASEAN's purpose is to collaborate in accelerating economic growth, social progress, and cultural development in the region, especially by promoting regional peace and stability among the countries in the region. ASEAN works through the process toward a regional agenda to attain goals revolving around dialogues, understanding common problems/interests, identifying mutual gains to be derived from regional cooperation, and achieving compatible national approaches by member countries (ASEAN 2004).

In 1997, the ASEAN Vision for 2020 was to create a concert of Southeast Asian nations, bonded together in a partnership of dynamic development, outward looking, peaceful, stable, and prosperous in a community of caring societies. The three pillars of the ASEAN community – ASEAN security community (ASC), ASEAN economic community (AEC), and the ASEAN socio-cultural community (ASCC) – were also established. The ASCC was tasked to ensure that its workforce shall be prepared for and benefit from economic integration by investing more resources for basic and HE, training, science and technology development, job creation, and social protection. The ASCC believes that the development and enhancement of human resources is a key strategy for employment generation, alleviating poverty and socioeconomic disparities, and ensuring economic growth with equity (www.aseansec.org).

In order to strengthen the cultural cooperation among its member states, ASEAN identified a few areas including manpower development, teacher education, and the education system for deep collaboration in 1977. However, it took a while to further develop the ideas into a concrete deep cooperation. Until the January 1992 summit, coinciding with the creation of Asian Free Trade Area (AFTA), that cooperation in the field of HE began among ASEAN member states. Deeper cooperation also led to the establishment of the ASEAN University Network (AUN) in November 1995 with the objectives to promote cooperation, develop academic and professional human resources in the region through information dissemination among the ASEAN academic community, as well as enhancing the ASEAN identity among member countries.

In December 1998, ASEAN passed the Hanoi Plan of Action, which further suggested the priorities for education under the heading *Promote Human Resource Development*. According to the Plan, ASEAN members are committed to strengthen the AUN and move forward to transform it into the ASEAN University. To realize the goal of deep collaboration among member states, major foci were identified on equal access to education, establishing and strengthening networks in education and training by 2004. More importantly, the Bali Concord II, adopted in October 2003 under the AEC heading, clearly stated "the realization of a fully integrated economic community…There is a need to enhance cooperation & integration on activities in other areas, human resource development & capacity building; recognition of educational qualifications…and enhancing private sector involvement."

More importantly, the Vientiane Action Program 2004–2010 (VAP) adopted by ASEAN members further enhances deep cooperation among member states in education. According to the document, it clearly states:

> There is a need to enhance human resource development through the networking of skills training institutions and the development of regional assessment and training programs and the development of mutual recognition arrangements shall facilitate labor mobility in the region and will support the realization of the AEC. (p. 2)

Stressing regional assessment, training programmes, and mutual recognition arrangements, ASEAN's HE agenda is closely connected to achieving its economic goals to promote the regional economic community to compete in the global environment. With particular reference to HE structural reforms in the area of governance, access to HE, focus on science and technology, and private-sector participation, and geared toward manpower development, ASEAN is keen to promote human resource development and capacity building among member states. Accreditation, quality assurance, and internationalization of HE are part of the ASEAN's agenda of getting the programmes recognized internationally.[12]

ASEAN not only works with other countries in East Asia, but has also branched out to work with regional nongovernmental organizations (NGOs). For example, the Association of Southeast Asian Institutions of Higher Learning (ASAIHL) has covered major public universities from all the selected East Asian territories except mainland China and South Korea as its members, and serves to foster academic cooperation among its member institutions particularly through regional fellowships and academic exchange programs. A newer yet more relevant organization, the Association of East Asian Research Universities (AEARU), was founded in January 1996 as a forum for presidents of the leading research universities in East Asia, which also carries out mutual exchanges among these institutions. AEARU has put an emphasis on the common academic and cultural backgrounds of its member universities; thus, it is composed of the leading universities from only five territories in East Asia, namely mainland China, Japan, Korea, Hong Kong, and Taiwan, which could also be seen as an university union specifically for the Confucian Cultural Sphere. Nevertheless, AEARU is hitherto a rather loose union with only a total of 17 participating leading research universities from the region.[13]

Compared with the nongovernmental ASAIHL and AEARU, the Southeast Asian Ministers of Education Organization (SEAMEO) has offered another framework of collaboration with semiofficial functions in the region. Given the fact that all its members, except Timor-Leste, are also members of ASEAN, SEAMEO by and large acts as the educational wing of ASEAN. Moreover, among its 19 specialized regional centers, the Regional Institute for Higher Education and Development (SEAMEO-RIHED) is particularly relevant in initiating regional reforms in HE governance. For instance, SEAMEO-RIHED has recently tried to establish an ASEAN Quality Assurance Network (AQAN) for the future development of a common set of quality assurance guidelines. After the first ASEAN Quality Assurance Roundtable Meeting at Kuala Lumpur in July 2008,[14] the "Kuala Lumpur Declaration" was adopted to recognize the crucial role of quality assurance in advancing the process of harmonization in regional HE. Moreover, overseas study visits, regional workshops, and seminars regarding university governance or institutional restructuring have also been held frequently by SEAMEO-RIHED over the past few years (SEAMEO-RIHED 2009).[15]

SEAMEO-RIHED moved a step further in exploring the ideas of creating a common space of HE in Southeast Asia when it published *Harmonisation of Higher Education: Lessons Learned from the Bologna Process* (Supachai and Nopraenue 2008) after a preliminary study. A further research project on that theme was then followed, and SEAMEO-RIHED subsequently initiated a conference series to raise "awareness" among the key stakeholders in the process of HE harmonization in Southeast Asia (SEAMEO-RIHED 2009, 6). However, as the phrase "raising awareness" implies, though discourse on constructing an overall HE framework within this region is now underway, if compared with the EU's Bologna Process, concrete achievements remain to be seen in ASEAN.[16] In fact, before 2007, many of the initiatives regarding HE in ASEAN were centered around creating a level-up playing field for its Indo-China members (Vietnam, Cambodia, Laos, and Myanmar) with others in terms of infrastructure and human resource development, rather than a systematic mechanism for policy harmonization (IPPTN 2008: 1).

Deep Interuniversity Collaborations in Asia

To strengthen their global competitiveness, major Asian universities have proactively reached out not only to the major university systems of Europe, Australia, and North America but also to the region. For instance, Yonsei University in South Korea has set up an international college offering Korean studies in English to attract overseas students. Meanwhile, Yonsei has also reached a regional collaboration with the Faculty of Social Sciences, the University of Hong Kong, and Keio University in Japan to launch a three-campus program in Comparative Asian Studies by recruiting students from these three partnering institutions targeted to enhance students' learning experiences and overseas exposure (Faculty of Social Sciences, The University of Hong Kong 2009). Similarly, more regional collaborations are emerging among various university systems in Asia such as the founding of a new regional research consortium related to Asian Education and Development Studies in Asia, with participation of major comparative education societies in Asia including Japan, mainland China, Hong Kong, Taiwan, Singapore, South Korea, Australia, and New Zealand (National Chung Cheng University 2009). Since forming the consortium in 2009, this new regional research network has expended with the launch of a new international journal titled *Asian Education and Development Studies*, published by an international publisher, Emerald, in an effort to create a platform to engage academics in the region to rediscover the unique contributions of Asian scholarship.

Meanwhile, we also witness more frequent collaborations and interactions among university systems of mainland China, Hong Kong, and Taiwan, with more student and staff mobility through academic exchange and research collaborations. The author of this chapter is also involved in setting up a new research consortium with major emphasis on comparative Greater China Studies, with positive responses from institutions based in mainland China, Hong Kong, and Taiwan, through which they hope to become leading institutions offering research programs in Greater China Studies. During a recent visit to Taiwan, the author met the Dean of College of Social Sciences of National Taiwan University to discuss further collaborations in terms of joint programs. One possible area for joint venture is related to an executive master degree for civil servants from mainland China, Taiwan, and Hong Kong. In view of the improved relationship between mainland China and Taiwan, the academic institutions consider Hong Kong as an ideal platform to facilitate academic exchange and professional training for students and civil servants from Taiwan and mainland China. Hong Kong, being seen as a place practicing political neutrality, is well positioned to facilitate more regional collaborations for Greater China. Meanwhile, Taiwan has started developing its own Taiwan Social Science Citation Index (TSSCI) as an indicator for assessing publications in Chinese, while the academics in mainland China have also engaged in developing a China Social Science Citation Index (CSSCI) to benchmark refereed publications written in Chinese. As Lo (2011) has rightly pointed out, with the growing number of publications entering these indexes promoted by Taiwan and mainland China, together with the growing influence of the Greater China area (including mainland China, Taiwan, Hong Kong, Macau, and other overseas Chinese communities like Singapore), such newly developed research performance indicators would become increasingly important to form a regional platform ("Chinese axis" in Lo's term) to offer alternative benchmarking for Asian scholars.

In addition, we have also witnessed similar trends evolving in Asia through the efforts to establish regional hubs of education. Our above discussions have already highlighted that Singapore, Malaysia, and Hong Kong are particularly keen to turn their societies into regional hubs of education, making education services part of their economic pillars and state capacity building in terms of strengthening "soft power" (Mok 2011). In order to diversify their university systems, TNHE is becoming increasingly popular not only among the above candidates for regional hubs of education but also among developing economies like mainland China, India, and other Southeast Asian countries. Realizing that depending on the state alone would not be sufficient in terms of capacity to meet the pressing educational demands/needs, different Asian societies have allowed overseas academic institutions to mount offshore programs in order to create additional education opportunities.

One major regional cooperation initiative is the United Board for Christian Higher Education in Asia. With a strong conviction to support a Christian presence in colleges and universities in Asia, the United Board was founded in 1922 as a Christian organization that works in partnership with HEIs across Asia to express values such as justice, reconciliation, and harmony between ethnic and religious communities; gender equity; care for the environment and civil society. With more than 100 partners in Cambodia, China, East Timor, Hong Kong, India, Indonesia, Japan, Korea, Myanmar, the Philippines, Taiwan, Thailand, and Vietnam, the United Board works closely with its partners to promote Christian values in HE across Asia, it has been successfully organizing leadership training, faculty development, and various programs addressing issues related to globalization and HE (United Board 2011). The author was invited as a member of the task force of the United Board since 2010. Through the involvement in the United Board meetings and activities, the author has witnessed the growing importance of such a regional network of Asian universities. Having a common vision and mission, these partnering institutions have worked together to promote core values in which they believe. The synergy released from this regional cooperation framework has clearly suggested another form of regulatory regionalism in the forming (field observation in New York, April 2011). Overall, the developments outlined above have clearly shown that recent changes in university governance have given rise to the emergence of regionalism in HE, by which we mean closer collaborations have been fostered among major university systems in the region and similar regional trends are evolving in HE developments in Asia.

Given the rapid expansion and improvement of HE in East Asia as a whole, in particular, the prosperity of the region's network of TNHE, together with a gradual convergence of the modes of HE governance, it is expected that this trend for East Asian regulatory regionalism will persist. Moreover, in prospect, China may gradually become the center in this regional drive in repositioning HE because of its remarkable size in the first place, and its aggressive strategies to achieve world-class status and applying HE as a means to exert its cultural "soft power" in the second. The most probable platform for further integration, in this respect, may well be the mechanism of ASEAN + 3.

More importantly, regional cooperation has not been confined only to education among ASEAN members but it has moved beyond to other aspects as cooperation has also moved beyond ASEAN members. Growing out of the annual ASEAN summit meeting are the ASEAN Plus Three (APT) process, with the involvement of China, Japan, and South Korea. In addition, other forms of regional cooperation have emerged such as the ASEAN-sponsored East Asian Summits (EAS) with the added participation of India, Australia, and New Zealand to the APT (Arase 2011). ASEAN further extends beyond the East Asia region by organizing multilateral consultations through the participation in the 21-member Asia-Pacific Economic Cooperation (APEC) meeting. ASEAN also sponsors the 27-member ASEAN Regional Forum (ARF) to promote dialogue and consultation on political and security issues of common interest and concern in the Asia and Pacific region.

The Emergence of Regulatory Regionalism and New Governance

Our above observations/discussions have suggested that new modes of HE governance are emerging in Asia, characterized by evolving features of "regulatory regionalism." Based on Ravenhill's (2005) definition of regionalism as a formal intergovernmental collaboration between two or more states, Robertson (2008, 720) further enhances this definition by arguing that regionalism should be viewed as an outcome of integration processes involving a coalition of social forces such as markets, private trade, investment flows, policies and decisions of organizations, and state-led initiatives. ASEAN, being an organization with a formal collaboration among ten member countries that involves coalitions with the East Asia Big Three and other forms of regional cooperation has clearly indicated not only the growing stature of this regional international organization but also emerging regional forces fostering for a more consolidated regional cooperation platform.

One point that deserves particular attention is that when analyzing regional cooperation or competition among Asian universities in general and governmental cooperation in particular, we must not treat such processes as mutually exclusive. We need to see them as the regional platforms that Asian governments have involved like ASEAN and other regional cooperative frameworks that closely interact with the regional cooperation venues spontaneously emerging from academic and research organizations such as different forms of academic and research associations, societies, or consortia. I would conceptualize government-driven regional cooperation efforts like ASEAN and APEC as a "hard approach," while the regional collaborations initiating from individuals and universities or other kinds of research/academic organizations as the "soft approach" toward regional cooperation. The central characteristic of the hard approach is that it is top down, normally driven by the nation state and the governance style is much more "centralized." Unlike the hard approach, the soft approach is far more bottom up, normally driven by local forces and organic in nature, with emphasis on network governance. We may argue that the hard approach would shape national policy directly; however, the soft approach would also influence national strategy and policy since neither governmentally nor nongovernmentally driven cooperation is entirely exclusive but rather complementary to each other.

Deepening regional cooperation in the context of an increasingly competitive environment would certainly require both a structural and soft approach in interaction to maximize the "political capital" generated from the governmentally driven cooperation frameworks and the "network capital" generated from the organically formed regional cooperation platforms. Empirical evidence can be found in support of the interactive relationship between hard and soft approaches when analyzing regional cooperation in Asia. Taiwan, for instance, which has encountered difficulty in asserting its national status because of the "One China" issue, has discovered different ways to assert its influence through engagement along a variety of regional/international cooperation venues such as academic/research consortia, associations, and societies; while mainland China has also taken a more active approach in asserting its regional and global leadership through participation in different forms of regional organizations spontaneously evolving from local/regional communities (Chen 2011b).

Another major observation that needs to be highlighted here is that when analyzing regional cooperation, we must note that regionalism is not a single phenomenon but complex and complicated processes, demonstrating that subregionalism emerges from regionalism, which requires us to closely examine the different forms and nature of regional cooperative frameworks.

Concluding Remarks: Cooperation or Competition as Two Sides of the Same Coin

As Arase (2011) points out, "ASEAN is the linchpin of the most important regional cooperation processes" (p. 36), while Ellen Frost (2008, 251) remarks that "Asian governments cannot afford not to pursue the integration because the consequences of not doing so are too risky." Without engaging in regional cooperation, the region would be destabilizing, which would leave smaller countries in the region at the mercy of unrestrained rivalry among the regional powers, particularly in the context of the rise of China and the potential rift between the rim democracies and nondemocratic forces.

Although many political scientists or political economists are still skeptical of regional cooperation in Asia, questioning such a loose framework has no credible plan among Asian governments in building regionalism (Solingen 2005; Aggarwal and Koo 2007). Similarly, Paul Evans (2005, 211) argues "East Asian regionalism is at a modest and early stage of development, faces formidable obstacles, and is unlikely to be a key factor in the balance of economic and political power in the region," while Edward Lincoln (2004, 251, 232) writes that because East Asia is so diverse and dependent on trade with the United States, East Asian regionalism as presently constituted amounts to little more than "Talking and becoming familiar with one another." Nonetheless, our above discussion has suggested that regulatory regionalism is evolving in Asia, especially when the Asian countries have realized that the rise of China and the economic difficulties confronted by the United States and Japan would certainly influence their engagement in regional cooperation (particularly in the context that China has made serious efforts in extending its influence in the region). After the Asian financial crisis, Hu notes that ASEAN-led efforts have begun to gain substance since

> these projects were driven by the shared sense of purpose among East Asian countries to construct a more Asian-oriented community, with the emerging ASEAN+3 process as its anchoring framework. As the countries in East Asia have become increasingly interdependent, leaders in the region have become more determined to build a framework for greater regional cooperation and integration. (Hu 2009, 3)

Similarly, Oros (2011) also argues along the same line that Asian countries have put aside personal prejudices or political dogmas in favor of practical and forward-looking cooperation. For instance, the now annual "Asian Davos" meeting of the World Trade Economic Forum in China provides a good platform for leaders from the region to engage in dialogue and conversation to devise solutions to pressing regional and global problems outside of rigid government-led dialogues. More frequent meetings among leaders in the region such as attending the opening of the United Nations General Assembly, Asia–Europe Meeting leaders meeting in Brussels, the Group of 20 meeting in Seoul, and the Asia Pacific Economic Cooperation (APEC) annual meeting would certainly promote better understanding among leaders in Asia and Pacific. Other organizations such as Proliferation

Security Initiatives (PSI) and the Shanghai Cooperation Organization (SCO) further enhance regional understanding and cooperation in Asia.

Our above discussion has shown how Malaysia and Singapore have sought to become regional leaders in education and, along cultural dimensions, the development of which may induce more intense competition among these Asian economies. However, we have also witnessed regional cooperation not only in the economic aspect but also along political, security, social, and cultural dimensions flourishing through the ASEAN-sponsored projects or other regional collaborative frameworks outlined above. Although the question related to "whether the emerging regulatory regionalism is strong enough to promote regional integration" is a legitimate one, the above empirical evidence clearly shows more frequent dialogues and interactions happening among Asian leaders and people. We would appreciate that deep collaboration among Asian countries could result in both competition and cooperation. In contrast, Asian states are well aware of the importance of asserting themselves in the growing influences of global regionalization, particularly when they realize the significant implications of having established a stronger voice and leadership through engaging in deep collaborations with other partners in the same region in order to form a more cohesive and united regional framework in coping with the growing interregional competition and rivalry.

In conclusion, our above discussions have clearly indicated that more regional collaborations have begun and different forms of regional cooperation frameworks are in the making in Asia to assert "soft power" through the rediscovery of Asian scholarship projects operating in Asia. Despite the fact that global regionalization is only at a relatively inception phase in Asia, we should not underestimate the importance of the growing prominence of these regional collaboration initiatives especially when these forms of organizational/institutional arrangements may well facilitate a new governance model through "network governance." The growing hybridization of organizations being involved in shaping global regionalization processes would considerably render the conventional governance model inappropriate and new forms of governance would lead to the emergence of super- or mega-regional governance structures to govern the growing complexity of regionalized activities and increasingly transnationalized education offerings in Asia (Ball 2009).

NOTES

1. This chapter is based upon a research project funded by the Government of the Hong Kong Special Administrative Region. The author wants to thank

the Research Grant Council for offering financial support to enable him to undertake the present report (HKIEd 7005-PPR-6). Thanks must be extended to Dr Ong Kok Chung for offering research assistance to the present project.
2. *Wawasan 2020* as an ambitious national goal of development was introduced by the then prime minister of Malaysia, Mahathir Mohamad, during the tabling of the Sixth Malaysia Plan in 1991. The vision envisages the achievement of a self-sufficient, industrialized, and well-developed Malaysia by the year 2020. In terms of economy, it set the target of eightfold stronger by 2020 than the economy in the early 1990s.
3. Before 1996, private HEIs in Malaysia had no degree-awarding power. Even right after the enactment of the Private Higher Education Act 1996, the undergraduate degree program could only be offered by private institutions with their degree-awarding foreign partners, with students being required to transfer between Malaysia and another country to complete their studies (Quality Assurance Agency for Higher Education 1999). It was only since 1998 that the Ministry of Education allowed private institutions to deliver degree programs through the so-called 3+0 arrangement with their foreign partners.
4. The Economic Development Board of Singapore is a statutory body overseen by the Ministry of Trade and Industry. Its involvement in the Global Schoolhouse initiative is a clear indication that the Singapore government has redefined higher education as industry and business.
5. Data from the official website of the Global Schoolhouse initiative (last accessed on August 30, 2009).
6. The transnational programs offered by the S. P. Jain Center of Management in Singapore are particularly worth mentioning. The center offers a truly Global MBA program conducted jointly from both its campuses in Dubai (2004) and Singapore. Students choosing Finance or Information Technology (IT) streams would first complete their core curriculum in Dubai, and then transfer to Singapore campus for their specialized curriculum; while those from the streams of Marketing, Global Logistics, and Human Resources Management will do the reverse. In addition to study in Dubai and Singapore, students enrolling in either category would also be given the option to study core curriculum in Toronto. This one-year-three-cities program thus exposes students to varied business cultures, multinational companies, cross-national networking, and international market challenges.
7. http://www.singaporeedu.gov.sg/htm/abo/abo01.htm (accessed on August 24, 2009).
8. This task is entrusted to its Education Services Division.
9. The Lisbon Strategy aims at making the EU the world's "most dynamic and competitive economy," and in respect of higher education, it has particularly focused on the challenges of knowledge economy and the necessity of innovation.
10. In 1999, the education ministers of 29 European countries and European university heads met to discuss the future development of European higher education, and subsequently issued the Bologna Declaration.

11. "Convinced that the establishment of the European area of higher education required constant support, supervision and adaptation to the continuously evolving needs" (Bologna Declaration 1999), the European education ministers decided to meet regularly to assess progress, thus transforming this commitment into an ongoing policy process.
12. Discussion related to the ASEAN in the text is based on historical documents and policy documents from the official website of ASEAN.
13. AEARU's membership includes five top research universities from mainland China (Peking, Tsinghua, Fudan, Nanjing, and University of Science & Technology of China); six from Japan (Tokyo, Kyoto, Osaka, Tohoku, Tsukuba, and Tokyo Institute of Technology); three from South Korea (Seoul National University, Korea Advanced Institute of Science & Technology, and Pohang University of Science & Technology); two from Taiwan (Taiwan and Tsing Hua); and one from Hong Kong (Hong Kong University of Science & Technology).
14. This round-table meeting in 2008 was co-organized by SEAMEO-RIHED and the Malaysian Qualifications Agency (MQA). Since then, it has become an annual round-table meeting with a specific theme related to quality assurance of the region's higher education.
15. For instance, the Regional Seminar on University Governance in Southeast Asian Countries was held at Luang Prabang, Laos, on October 14, 2008 (SEAMEO-RIHED 2009).
16. For example, while academic mobility within the region has been improved and efforts have also been taken toward establishing a regional quality assurance system, there is by far no regional agreement on the comparability of degree programs.

REFERENCES

Aggarwal, V. K., and M. G. Koo. 2007. "The Evolution of Regionalism in East Asia." *Journal of East Asian Studies* 7: 360–369.

Arase, D. 2011. "Korea, ASEAN, and East Asian Regionalism." *Joint U.S.-Korea Academic Studies* 21: 33–52.

Ball, S. 2009. "Global Education, Heterarchies and Hybrid Organizations." Paper presented at the 2009 Asian-Pacific Forum on *Sociology of Education: Social Change and Education Reform*, May 6–8, 2009, National University of Tainan.

Bologna Declaration. 1999. "The European Higher Education Area." Joint Declaration of the European Ministers of Education Convened in Bologna, June 19, 1999.

Chen, S. J. 2011a. "The Quest for World Class Status: The Reposition of Universities in East Asian Region." Paper presented at the symposium of *Managing the Global Pressure for University Ranking: Responses from East Asian Region* at the Annual Conference of the Comparative Education Society

of Hong Kong 2011, The Hong Kong Institute of Education, Hong Kong, February 19, 2011.
Chen, S. J. 2011b. "Convergence or Divergence? The Asian Way in Internationalizing Higher Education." Paper presented at the 2011 regional symposium on *Asian Education and Development Studies*, National Chung Cheng University, Taiwan, November 5, 2011.
Cheng, Y. C., S. W. Ng, and C. K. Cheung. 2009. *A Technical Research Report on the Development of Hong Kong as a Regional Education Hub*. Hong Kong: Hong Kong Institute of Education.
Deem, R., K. H. Mok, and L. Lucas. 2008. "Transforming Higher Education in Whose Image? Exploring the Concept of the 'World-Class' University in Europe and Asia." *Higher Education Policy* 21 (1): 83–97.
Economic Development Board, Singapore Government. 2009. *Global Schoolhouse*. Available at: www.edb.gov.sg/edb/sg/en_uk/index/industry_sectors/education/global_schoolhouse.html. Accessed August 30, 2010.
Evans, P. 2005. "Between Regionalism and Regionalization: Policy Networks and the Nascent East Asian Institutional Identity." In *Remapping East Asia: The Construction of a Region*, ed. Pempel, T. J. Ithaca: Cornell University Press.
Faculty of Social Sciences, The University of Hong Kong. 2009. "3 Campus Programme in Comparative Asian Studies, Website of Faculty of Social Sciences, HKU." Available at: www.hku.hk/socsc. Accessed August 5, 2011.
Frost, E. 2008. *Asia's New Regionalism*. Boulder: Lynne Rienner.
Garrett, R. 2005. "The Rise and Fall of Transnational Higher Education in Singapore." *International Higher Education* 39: 9–10.
Gribble, C., and G. McBurnie. 2007. "Problems with Singapore's Global Schoolhouse." *International Higher Education* 48 (summer): 89–112.
Hu, W. X. 2009. "Building Asia-Pacific Architecture: The Challenge of Hybrid Regionalism." Washington, DC: Brookings Institution, Center for Northeast Asian Policy Studies.
IPPTN (Institut Penyelidikan Pendidikan Tinggi Negara). 2008. "Harmonisation of Higher Education (Part 2): Initiatives and the Future for Southeast Asia." *IPPTN Updates on Global Higher Education* no. 39, September 15, 2008. Penang, Malaysia: IPPTN, Universiti Sains Malaysia.
Lasanowski, V. 2009. *International Student Mobility: Status Report*. London: The Observatory on Borderless Higher Education.
Lee, M. N. N. 1999. "Corporatization, Privatization, and Internationalization of Higher Education in Malaysia." In *Private Prometheus: Private Higher Education and Development in the 21st Century*, ed. P. G. Altbach. New York: Greenwood Press.
Lincoln, E. 2004. *East Asian Economic Regionalism*. Washington, DC: Brookings Institution.
Lo, Y. W. 2011. "The Emerging Chinese Axis in Higher Education." Paper presented at the AAS Conference 2011, March 31 to April 3, 2011, Honolulu, Hawaii.
McBurnie, G., and C. Ziguras. 2001. "The Regulation of Transnational Higher Education in Southeast Asia: Case Studies of Hong Kong, Malaysia and Australia." *Higher Education* 42: 85–105.

Ministry of Education, Singapore. 2010. "List of External Degree Programme." Available at: www.moe.gov.sg/education/private-education/edp-list. Accessed July 15, 2010.

Ministry of Higher Education Malaysia. 2009. *Statistics of Higher Education 2009*. KL: Ministry of Higher Education.

Ministry of Trade and Industry (MTI). 2003. "Executive Summary – Developing Singapore's Education Industry." Available at: http://app.mti.gov.sg/default.asp?id507. Accessed April 18, 2011.

Mok, K. H. 2008. "Varieties of Regulatory Regimes in Asia: The Liberalization of the Higher Education Market and Changing Governance in Hong Kong, Singapore and Malaysia." *The Pacific Review* 21 (2): 147–170.

Mok, K.H. 2011. "The Quest for Regional Hub of Education: Growing Heterarchies, Organizational Hybridization and New Governance in Singapore and Malaysia." *Journal of Education Policy* 26 (1): 61–81.

Mok, K. H. 2012. "Bringing the State Back In: Privatization or Restatization of Higher Education in China." *Journal of European Education* 47 (2): 228–241.

Mok, K. H., and K. C. Ong. 2012. "Asserting Brain Power and Expanding Education Services: Searching for New Governance and Regulatory Regimes in Singapore, Hong Kong and Malaysia." In *The Emergent Knowledge Economy and the Future of Higher Education: Asian Perspectives*, ed. D. Neubauer. London: Routledge.

Mok, K. H., and K. M. Yu. 2011. "The Quest of Regional Education Hubs and Transnational Higher Education: Challenges for Managing Human Capital in Asia." *Asia Pacific Journal of Education* 31 (3): 229–248.

National Chung Cheng University, Graduate Institute of Education. 2009. "Comparative Education and Development Studies Research Consortium." Paper presented at the Comparative Education and Development Regional Symposium, September 2009, National Chung Cheng University, Chaiyi, Taiwan.

Observatory on Borderless Higher Education. 2002. *International Branch Campuses: Scale and Significance*. London: Observatory on Borderless Higher Education.

Oros, A. L. 2011. "Tomorrow's East Asia Today: Regional Security Cooperation for the 21st Century." *Joint US-Korea Academic Studies* 21: 1–14.

Pekwan. 2009. Global Education Hub in Johor: Marlborough College Campus Opens in 2010, *The Malay Mail*. Available at: www.mmail.com.my/content/1 7504-global-education-hub-johor. Accessed July 15, 2010.

Quality Assurance Agency for Higher Education. 1999. *Overview Report: Malaysia*, Gloucester, UK: Author. Available at: www.qaa.ac.uk/reviews/reports/overseas/Overview_malaysia99.asp. Accessed August 29, 2009.

Ravenhill, F. 2005. "Regionalism." In *Global Political Economy*, ed. John Ravenhill. New York: Oxford University Press, pp. 116–147.

Robertson, S. L. 2008. " 'Europe/Asia' Regionalism, Higher Education and the Production of World Order." *Policy Futures in Education* 6 (6): 718–729.

Robertson, S. L. 2009. "The EU, 'Regulatory State Regionalism' and New Modes of Higher Education Governance." Paper presented to the panel on *Constituting the Knowledge Economy: Governing the New Regional Spaces of Higher Education*, International Studies Association Conference, New York.

SEAMEO-RIHED. 2009. *Annual Report*. Bangkok: Regional Centre for Higher Education and Development, Southeast Asian Ministers of Education Organization (SEAMEO-RIHED). Available at: www.seameo.org/images/stories /SEAMEO_General/About_SEAMEO/SEAMEO%20Units/Centres_Annual _Rpt/RIHED_Executive_Summary_2008_2009.pdf. Accessed September 6, 2011.

Singapore Education. 2006. "Singapore Education." Available at: www.singaporeedu.gov.sg/htm/abo/abo01.htm. Accessed August 24, 2009.

Solingen, E. 2005. "East Asian Regional Institutions: Characteristics, Sources, Distinctiveness." In *Remapping East Asia. The Construction of a Region*, ed. T. J. Pempel. Ithaca, London: Cornell University Press.

Supachai, Y., and S. D. Nopraenue. 2008. *Harmonisation of Higher Education: Lessons Learned from the Bologna Process*. Bangkok: SEAMEO-RIHED.

United Board. 2011. *2010 Annual Report*. New York: United Board.

Wan, Abdul Manan Wan Muda. 2008. "The Malaysian National Higher Education Action Plan: Redefining Autonomy and Academic Freedom Under the APEX Experiment." Paper presented at the ASAIHL Conference, University Autonomy: Interpretation and Variation, Universiti Sains Malaysia, December 12–14, 2008.

Chapter 10

Institutional Autonomy in the Restructuring of University Governance

Molly Nyet Ngo Lee

Introduction

The context of higher education in the Asia-Pacific region is changing rapidly. With some exceptions, many higher education systems are expanding in response to increasing social demand for higher education. As higher education systems expand, they become more bureaucratic and regulated so as to ensure consistency of treatment in various areas pertaining to the management of these systems. These higher education systems also become more complex, comprising a wide variety of institutions with different missions, scattered in different geographical locations, and thus making it increasingly difficult to be managed centrally. Therefore, a more decentralized management may be needed to cope with the challenges of an expanding higher education system. Furthermore, governments are forced to seek diverse sources such as the private sector, community, philanthropic organizations, foreign students, and others to fund the expansion of their higher education systems.

This chapter is an analysis of the reforms in university governance and management that have been taking place in several selected countries in the region, focusing on the trade-off between institutional autonomy and public accountability; the policy mechanisms used by different governments in granting autonomy to higher education institutions; and highlighting some of the common features of these reforms.

Changing Relationship between Universities and the State

The relationship between higher education institutions and the state revolves around the issues of autonomy and accountability. The state and higher education institutions are constantly engaged in redefining their mutual relationship, with the state demanding more accountability on the one hand and the higher education institutions insisting on more autonomy on the other hand (Neave and van Vught 1991). An emerging trend is an increase in institutional autonomy in return for more public accountability.

The ideal contract between society and universities is that universities should be responsive and responsible (Tierney 1998). Universities usually have multiple functions and multiple stakeholders, which include the state, parents, unions, businesses, and students. It is crucial that universities should listen to their multiple stakeholders. Universities are often called upon to contribute to the needs of a knowledge-based society by training students and researchers, doing relevant research, safeguarding equality of access, and maintaining the "purchase" price of education as low as possible. Universities are expected to operate efficiently with transparency, relevancy, and quality in teaching and research. They should also assume crucial responsibilities toward society. Traditionally, universities remain by far the best-placed institutions: (1) to secure and transmit the knowledge acquired by the cultural heritage of a society; (2) to create new knowledge; (3) to have the professional competence and the right status to analyze societal problems independently, scientifically, and critically; (4) to produce public intellectuals who are at the forefront of bringing about societal change. This is true even if universities face increasing competition from other types of higher learning institutions like corporate universities, industrial laboratories, and other non-university research sites. It is, therefore, not surprising that universities are among the oldest surviving institutions in Western societies, though universities are relatively new institutions in Asian societies.

The driving forces behind the continued interest in autonomy and accountability stem from several factors. In adopting neoliberal ideology, many governments are cutting back on their public and social expenditure, which has resulted in drastic budget cuts in government funding to universities. To overcome these budgetary constraints, universities need to seek alternative sources of funding and they are being given the freedom to generate their own revenues through engaging in different kinds of market-related activities. As universities find themselves operating increasingly in a competitive and market-oriented environment, they need to be flexible and to respond quickly to market pressures. Therefore, many academic leaders recognize these pressures and have started searching for ways to make their institutions more entrepreneurial and autonomous. As many universities continue to grow and expand with limited resources, their stakeholders, including the state, are concerned with the quality of education they provide. Thus, universities are increasingly subjected to external pressures to achieve greater accountability for their performances.

Conceptual Clarification

A brief review of the literature reveals an important distinction between academic freedom and institutional autonomy. The term "autonomy" means "the power to govern without outside controls" and the term "accountability" means "the requirement to demonstrate responsible actions to some external constituenc(y)ies" (Berdahl 1990, 171). The balance between "autonomy" and "accountability" is very important because too much autonomy might lead to universities being unresponsive to society, and too much accountability might destroy the necessary academic ethos in the universities. It is also important to note that academic freedom and institutional autonomy are not synonymous, for an increase in institutional autonomy may not necessarily mean more academic freedom (sometimes the reverse can happen). "Academic freedom" is "that freedom of the individual scholar in his/her teaching and research to pursue the truth...without fear of punishment or termination of employment" (Berdahl 1990, 171–172).

To further clarify the autonomy issue, Berdahl has identified two aspects of institutional autonomy, namely, (1) *substantive autonomy* and (2) *procedural autonomy*. "Substantive autonomy" is the power of the university to determine its own goals and programs, that is, the "what of academe"; whereas the "procedural autonomy" is the power of the university to determine the means by which its goals and programs will be pursued, that is, the "how of academe" (Berdahl 1990, 172). It is important to ask that if the state intervenes in university affairs, are the government actions affecting the substantive goals of the academe or are they just intervening in procedural matter? Similarly, if a university is given institutional autonomy, is it substantive autonomy or procedural autonomy or both?

A report on higher education governance reforms in Europe conceptualizes institutional autonomy as comprised of four dimensions, namely, organizational, policy, interventional, and financial autonomy (CHEPS, INCHER-Kassel, and NIFU-STEPS 2012). Universities with *organizational autonomy* have the right to decide on their own internal governance structures and on their internal authority, responsibility, and accountability structures, as well as to select their institutional leadership. *Policy autonomy* is the ability of universities to constitute themselves as academic communities in terms of student intake and staff recruitment and to design their educational and research programs. *Financial autonomy* is the ability to decide on the internal allocation of public and private funds, to diversify sources of income, to build reserves, and to borrow funds on the capital market. *Interventional autonomy* refers to the extent to which universities are free from accountability requirements.

It is interesting to observe that different policy initiatives may allow different kinds of autonomy to higher education institutions.

Broadly speaking, there are three approaches to guarantee more autonomy to higher education institutions:

1. *Deregulation*, which means that the regulation and requirements concerning higher education have either been cut back or abolished altogether, for example, in areas such as requirements concerning university admission, university facilities, university budget, and other areas;
2. *Corporatization*, which means that universities are operated like business organizations wherein they are allowed to engage in market-related activities and to generate their own revenues, and to be governed by a board of directors or trustees who are seemingly independent from the government;
3. *Privatization* is an approach where public enterprises are being privatized and run like private companies such that both the control and ownership lie outside the purview of the government.

As expected, the level of autonomy is highest in private higher education institutions. An autonomous university should be free to select its student intakes, design its study programs, develop its research programs, hire its staff, appoint its leaders, and be administratively autonomous.

There are a number of aspects of higher education where autonomy can be granted. One is through changes in the university governance structure. Whether a university is governed by the Ministry of Education or by an independent Board of Trustees or Directors can determine how autonomous it is. The amount of institutional autonomy is also reflected by how the university's vice-chancellor, president, or rector is appointed and how much power he/she has. Another area is how decisions are made on academic matters. How much autonomy does a university have to chart its mission, to offer academic programs compatible with its mission, to control the instructional and research activities in the campus, and to set its own standards for admission and degree requirements (Volkwein 1987)? A third area is financial flexibility, indicating how much control a university has in the preparation and allocation of its budget, how free it is to be able to generate revenues and manage its expenditure with few external restrictions. A fourth area is appointive powers, which govern such activities as the hiring and promotion of personnel and the conditions of employment. A fifth area is university management, which can produce a collegial academic culture or a bureaucratic culture or even a corporate culture. The amount of autonomy an academic has varies according to the position he/she holds in the organizational structure and the type of culture the campus has.

With this conceptual framework, I analyze recent higher education reforms that have taken place in a number of Asian countries with the goal of ascertaining those aspects of higher education in which autonomy has been increased.

Higher Education Reforms in Selected Countries

Corporatization of Public Universities in Malaysia

In Malaysia, the corporatization of public universities started with five public universities in 1998 and later spread to all the public universities in the country. In 1995, the Universities and University Colleges Act of 1971 was amended to lay the framework for all public universities to be corporatized. Through corporatization, public universities are freed from the shackles of government bureaucratic regulations and are run like business corporations (Lee 2004). Corporatized universities are empowered to engage in market-related activities and to generate revenue for part of their operating costs. Under the new set of amendments, the university governance structure is changed with the university council being replaced by a board of directors; the size of the senate is reduced; and the vice-chancellor is given strong executive power equivalent to that of a chief executive officer (CEO).

Malaysian corporatized universities have subsequently institutionalized a whole range of corporate managerial practices such as strategic planning, total quality management, ISO certification, and benchmarking in their attempts to improve accountability, efficiency, and productivity. Besides internal accountability, external accountability has resulted from the Ministry of Education's establishment of the Malaysian Qualifications Agency (MQA) in 2006 to manage and supervise the quality assurance systems of public universities.

Corporatized Universities in Singapore

The Singapore government carried out a review of public university governance and funding in 2000. Based on this review, universities in Singapore, which are mostly public, have been encouraged to become entrepreneurial universities so as to diversify their financial resources. The government also established a University Endowment Fund to encourage National University Singapore (NUS) and Nanyang Technological University (NTU) to attract philanthropic donations as an alternative source of income apart from government grants and tuition fees. With an emphasis on the principle of public and financial accountability, the Singapore government announced in 2000 that NUS and NTU would be given greater operational autonomy especially in financial management within a more accountability framework. The allocation of public funds would be made according to the universities' internal and external quality reviews. Similarly, faculties are delinked from civil service salary structures and they no longer enjoy automatic annual increments and are instead subjected to performance-based increments. In 2005, NUS and NTU were to follow the footsteps of Singapore Management University (SMU) and were corporatized into not-for-profit companies, whereby the governing councils and management are to take on greater responsibilities for key decisions.

Autonomous Universities in Indonesia

In 1999, the Indonesian government passed two laws in the field of higher education (PP60 and PP61) that aimed at moving Indonesian universities toward greater autonomy. The new paradigm in Indonesian higher education management consists of five pillars, namely, quality, autonomy, accountability, accreditation, and evaluation. As of January 2000, four public universities – Universitas Indonesia (UI), Institute of Agriculture Bogor (*Institut Pertanian Bogor* [IPB]), Institute of Technology Bandung (ITB), and Universitas Gadjah Mada in Yogyakarta (UGM) – were selected to function as "guides" in Indonesia's move toward greater academic and financial autonomy (Beerkens 2002). These four universities became separate legal entities, with each being accountable to a Board of Trustees instead of reporting directly to the Ministry of Education as they had in the past. The university rector is no longer appointed by the Ministry, but by the Board of Trustees. Changes were also made to university funding as in place of itemized line budgeting, block grants and formula-based funding were introduced. In addition, the universities were allowed to collect tuition fees directly from the students, and were themselves to set tuition fees. The autonomous universities, which have since increased from four to seven, have a more corporate-like management. They can appoint their own rectors, develop new study programs, and mobilize resources.

Autonomous Universities in Thailand

Thailand initiated various higher education reforms since 1990 based on The Higher Education Long Range Plan (1990–2004). The Long Range Plan addressed four major issues of Thai higher education, namely, equity, efficiency, excellence, and internationalization. One of the six policy recommendations was to change existing public universities into autonomous universities and all new public universities to be created would be autonomous from the beginning (Kritikara 2004). The Ninth Higher Education Development Plan (2002–2006) provided clear guidelines to promote university autonomy. The plan stated that every higher education institution should improve its internal management systems in the academic, personnel, and financial areas. All public universities were supposed to evolve into autonomous institutions. In 2008, the Thai government conducted a comprehensive retrospective of higher education performance and laid out a new vision in the Second 15-year Long Term Plan for Higher Education (2008–2022). Part of this plan deals specifically with issues related to the higher education system, including changing university governance and administration, financing higher education, staff and personnel development, strengthening university networks, and higher education infrastructure development.

One of the main features of Thai autonomous universities is delinking the faculty from the civil service and subjecting them to competitive compensation. Autonomous universities are freed from government's bureaucratic restrictions on their financial and administrative autonomy. However, under the reform, public universities are required to be assessed by an external agency, the Office of the National Education Standards and Quality Assessment (ONESQA), which was established in 2000 to ensure that high academic standards are maintained. Despite recent efforts to change the regulations between government agencies and universities, the majority of Thai universities are not autonomous. Currently, there are only 11 autonomous public universities.

Charter Universities in the Philippines

In the Philippines, the responsibilities of higher education come under the Commission of Higher Education (CHED), which was created through the Higher Education Act of 1994. The governance arrangements of public and private institutions by CHED have some peculiar distinctions. Basically, public higher education institutions, while financially supported by the government, can retain all generated income from tuition and service fees, while private higher education institutions can be granted autonomous and deregulated status by CHED. The autonomous status grants several privileges, particularly exemption from regular CHED monitoring and evaluation, gaining priority in grants and incentives from CHED, autonomy over curriculua, and the ability to establish satellite campuses. As of 2011, 44 higher education institutions in the Philippines had been granted autonomous status.

A major initiative to address the problems facing higher education was the April 2000 report of the Philippines Commission on Education Reform. The report addressed major concerns such as the optimization and better allocation of scarce financial resources, improving the quality of higher education by providing better preuniversity preparation, a strong faculty development program, and developing an effective system of accreditation. State universities and colleges in the Philippines have their own charters, and much that goes on in universities is strongly influenced by the board examinations administered by the associations of different professions. Besides this form of quality control, universities in the Philippines are highly regulated by the government. There are also several accreditation bodies and the CHED gives both financial grants and administrative deregulation privileges to institutions that merit certain levels of accreditation (Gonzales 2004).

Consolidation of Higher Education in Vietnam

In the case of Vietnam, the transition from a state-planned to a free-market economy has resulted in higher education reforms, which include the introduction of tuition fees, consolidating state research institutes with universities, development of large national multidisciplinary universities through the amalgamation of institutions, decentralized management, and the discontinuation of the central system of job placement of university graduates (Huong and Fry 2004).

Universities now make their own decisions on basic issues such as student enrollments and graduation requirements, academic curricula, budget allocation, and faculty recruitment. However, the delegation of power from the center to the universities has not been accompanied by an increased accountability on the part of the universities. The absence of adequate checks and balances has led to declining quality of instruction in the universities (Tran 1999). Vietnam is still in the process of setting up a functional quality assurance agency. Not all higher education institutions in Vietnam were given the same level of autonomy, with the two national universities in Hanoi and Ho Chi Min City having the highest.

Consolidation of Higher Education in Cambodia

Cambodia has a fragmented higher education system with 31 public higher education institutions under 12 different ministries. From 1988 onward, Cambodia started to change its economic system from a command to a demand economy. By 1997, private higher education institutions started to mushroom and now there are about more private universities than public universities, that is, 46 private higher education institutions. In 1997, a Royal Decree on the Legal Status of Public Administrative Institutions was introduced. It established the procedure and criteria for public agencies/institutions called "Public Administrative Institutions" (PAI). As a result, changes in university governance and management have occurred in a number of Cambodian public higher education institutions. In 2010, eight public higher education institutions were operating under PAI status, in which a higher education institution has more authority and power to administer itself under the direction of a governing board, rather than under the direct management of a parent ministry.

In 2007, a new law on education was passed that exists as a legal instrument for effective and efficient reform of governance and development of the Cambodian education sector, including the higher education subsector. The higher education reforms that have been initiated include official recognition of private postsecondary institutions, institutionalization of tuition fees, implementation of a credit transfer system, and the establishment of the Accreditation Committee of Cambodia (Ford 2003). Despite all these ongoing reforms, central government control is still very much in place.

Higher Education Reforms in China

Like other socialist countries in the region, higher education in China is also undergoing consolidation and restructuring. The move is away from the Soviet model of higher education in which there are many single-discipline higher education institutions under the supervision of different ministries to comprehensive universities. The process of institutionalizing the new framework of higher education involved changes in governance and administration, the nature of the government and university relationship, the legal status of higher education institutions, university autonomy, and the focus on socioeconomic development and labor market demands (Ming 2004). Systematic reforms in financing higher education were implemented and these include developing a cost-sharing and cost-recovery system in which Chinese universities started to charge tuition fees. Since the mid-1980s, universities are allowed to make use of their human resources and capacities in science and technology to generate revenue for their institutions.

Restructuring higher education in China required eliminating excessive government control over higher education institutions and granting universities more autonomy in the management of programs and resources, propelled by the belief that extending greater autonomy and decision-making power to universities and colleges will make them more innovative, creative, and responsive to development processes. The Chinese government adopted a two-pronged approach to university governance reforms, namely, decentralization and reorganization. Decentralization is the redistribution of power from central government authorities to provincial governments in supervising and supporting higher education institutions, as well as increasing the institutional autonomy of universities. Four models of structural reorganization were adopted (Yang 2002):

- *Joint construction*: Provincial authorities are invited to participate in the sponsorship and management of centrally controlled institutions. By 1999, 200 higher education institutions had been involved.
- *Jurisdiction transference*: Transferring affiliation signified a complete change from central ownership to provincial ownership. By 2002, 250 universities have been transferred from central ministries to local administration.
- *Institutional amalgamation*: Mergers among higher education institutions are intended to consolidate small institutions into comprehensive universities. By 2002, 597 higher education institutions had been involved in mergers, resulting 267 new institutions.

- *Institutional cooperation*: This model can denote various kinds of cooperation between institutions of different jurisdictions and types, on a voluntary basis, with their financial resources remaining unchanged.

National University Corporations in Japan

In April 2004, Japanese universities were corporatized and became independent administrative corporations in the country's move to revitalize the university system and in its attempt to create dynamic universities that are internationally competitive (Yamamoto 2012). Corporatization is meant to encourage national universities to develop independently and autonomously in the hope of opening pathways to a diverse range of national universities instead of just one prototype. National university corporations are to clarify their management responsibility so as to strengthen management frameworks within the universities to establish top-down decision-making mechanisms centering on presidents and deans. Instead of being elected by peers, university presidents are to be appointed by the Ministry of Education, Culture, Sport, Science and Technology (MEXT).

With the expansion of independence and autonomy of university administration, there will be internal audits to establish self-discipline and self-responsibility, including financial administration of each university. In 2004, the National Accreditation System was established to carry out external assessment and evaluation. At the same time, national university corporations can invest in other corporations by outsourcing their operations, development of business plans, and financing from multiple sources through revenue-associated business. The employees of the national university corporations will adopt a non–public servant status and be subjected to impartial performance evaluation and rewarded with an incentive system built into the salary schemes.

University Restructuring in South Korea

Like Japan, South Korea is also working very hard to raise the competitiveness of its universities through university restructuring. South Korea is one of those few countries in Asia experiencing higher education contraction from falling enrollments due to the leveling off of population growth. Therefore, universities are being encouraged to specialize in selected areas by means of university mergers, acquisitions, or strategic alliance. Steps were taken to reorganize university governance by introducing the method of indirect president elections so as to minimize the negative effects of the current direct election system. The Ministry of Education, Science and Technology is examining the possibility of changing national universities into corporate bodies like the case of Japan. The Ministry will also provide strong financial support to universities that are at the forefront of restructuring endeavors.

Higher Education in Crisis in India

India has the second-largest national system of higher education in Asia after China with 214 universities, 38 institutions "deemed-to-be" universities, 11 institutes of national importance, 9,703 colleges, and 887 polytechnics with 321,000 teachers and 6.7 million students (Jayaram 2004). The nature of its educational crisis can be summarized as "overproduction of educated persons, increasing educated unemployment, weakening of student motivation, increasing unrest and indiscipline on the campuses, frequent collapse of administration, deterioration of standards, and above all, the demoralizing effect of the irrelevance and purposelessness of most of what is being done" (Naik 1982, 163).

The way open and distance education programs are run in most universities is far from satisfactory. The unrealistic aspirations and unfulfilled promises undermine many of the programs. The poor quality of the study materials, ineffectiveness of the contact programs, and lack of study-center facilities have virtually ritualized such programs. There is ineffective quality control by the University Grants Commission, even though an autonomous body called the National Assessment and Accreditation Council (NAAC) was set up in 1994 because the idea of external assessment and accreditation was not well received by many universities and colleges.

As in many other countries, public investment in education in India has always been inadequate to meet social demand, and efforts to privatize higher education by encouraging private agencies to set up higher education institutions have met with limited success in general education and nonprofessional courses. Thus, the state universities and their affiliated colleges are the ones in financial crisis. In short, there is a lack of coherent long-term policy pertaining to higher education reforms in India today. While there are many ad hoc policies and a multiplicity of actors – the central and state governments, the emergent private sector – they are all dealing with higher education in different ways and thus creating an uncertain future to the higher education system in India.

Common Features of Higher Education Reforms

It is possible to draw some generalizations from these case studies that suggest the overall commonalities operating within the Asia-Pacific region. First, corporatized and autonomous universities have increased institutional autonomy in which university heads act like CEOs, making quick decisions without being restricted by bureaucratic regulations or much consultation with the academics if they choose not to seek such. Second, in many of these restructured universities, the traditional collegial methods of decision making have been replaced by top-down executive decisions taken within the central administration of universities. Third, restructured universities are under pressure to seek diversified sources of funding and they are allowed to engage in market-related activities so as to generate revenues for their operating costs. Most governments still continue to fund their public universities, but the funding mechanisms have changed from rigid line budgeting to block grants or formula-based funding or competitive funding. Public universities in many of these countries are subjected to more internal and external quality control and in all the cases, some forms of quality assurance agencies or accreditation bodies have been established to perform these tasks. Thailand, Singapore, and Japan are examples of countries that have delinked the faculty from the civil service.

The higher education reforms that have taken place in the Asia-Pacific region have resulted in expanding the role of the state vis-à-vis higher education. The state can play different roles, as a provider, protector, regulator, or advisor, in different contexts and at different points in time (Lee 2000). As a provider, the state allocates resources to higher education institutions. As a protector, it takes on the function of consumer advocacy by improving access to higher education, formulating policies to promote social equality, and by monitoring the quality of academic programs. As regulator, the state ensures oversight of new and emerging institutions through institutional accreditation and program licensing. It also steers the development of higher education by structuring the market for higher education services to produce outcomes consistent with government priorities. Most governments are interested in influencing the behavior of higher education institutions to achieve certain objectives such as quality, efficiency, accountability, and productivity. In some of the Asian countries, the state has moved from being the sole provider of higher education to take on new roles such as regulator and protector, and in other countries, it is performing the supervisory role instead of the regulatory role by letting public universities become autonomous and encouraging the private sector to play a more active role in providing higher education.

Despite the increase in institutional autonomy given to universities, overall, the role of academics in their governance has been reduced. The prevalence of bureaucratic and corporate culture in universities will continue to erode the academic tradition of the professoriate, and in the new working environment, the scholar is constantly being transformed into a bureaucrat or entrepreneur.

REFERENCES

Beerkens, Eric. 2002. "Moving Towards Autonomy in Indonesian Higher Education." *International Higher Education* Fall (29): 24–25.

Berdahl, Robert. 1990. "Academic Freedom, Autonomy and Accountability in British Universities." *Studies in Higher Education* 15 (2): 169–180.

CHEPS, INCHER-Kassel, NIFU-STEPS. 2012. *Progress in Higher Education Reform across Europe, Volume I: Governance Reforms*. Available at: http://ec.europa.eu/education/higher-education/doc/governance/sum_En.pdf. Accessed March 15, 2012.

Ford, David 2003. "Cambodian Accreditation: An Uncertain Beginning." *International Higher Education* Fall (33): 12–14.

Gonzales, Andrew. 2004. "The Philippines: Past, Present, and Future Dimensions of Higher Education." In *Asian Universities: Historical Perspectives and Contemporary Challenges*, ed. Philip G. Altbach and Toru Umakoshi. Baltimore: The John Hopkins University Press, pp. 279–298.

Huong, Pham Lan, and Gerald W. Fry. 2004. "Universities in Vietnam: Legacies, Challenges, and Prospects." In *Asian Universities: Historical Perspectives and Contemporary Challenges*, ed. Philip G. Altbach and Toru Umakoshi. Baltimore: The John Hopkins University Press, pp. 301–331.

Jayaram, N. 2004. "Higher Education in India: Massification and Change." In *Asian Universities: Historical Perspectives and Contemporary Challenges*, ed. Philip G. Altbach and Toru Umakoshi. Baltimore: The John Hopkins University Press, pp. 85–112.

Kritikara, Krissanapong. 2004. *Transition from a University under the Bureaucratic System to an Autonomous University: Reflections on Concepts and Experience of King Mongkut's University of Technology Thonburi*. Bangkok: Office of Education Council, Ministry of Education.

Lee, Molly N. N. 2000. "Expanding the State Role in Malaysian Higher Education." *International Higher Education* Summer (20): 20–21.

Lee, Molly N. N. 2004. *Restructuring Higher Education in Malaysia*. Monograph Series 4/2004. Penang: School of Educational Studies, Universiti Sains Malaysia.

Ming, Weifang. 2004. "Chinese Higher Education: The Legacy of the Past and the Context of the Future." In *Asian Universities: Historical Perspectives and Contemporary Challenges*, ed. Philip G. Altbach and Toru Umakoshi. Baltimore: The John Hopkins University Press, pp. 53–83.

Naik, J. P. 1982. *The Education Commission and after*. New Delhi: Allied.

Neave, G., and Frans A. van Vught, eds. 1991. *Prometheus Bound: The Changing Relationship between Government and Higher Education in Western Europe*. Oxford: Pergamon Press.

Tierney, William G. 1998. *The Responsive University: Restructuring for High Performance*. Baltimore: The John Hopkins University Press.

Tran, Hoa. 1999. "Vietnam: Higher Education in Search of Identity." *International Higher Education* Spring (15): 20–21.

Volkwein, J. Fredericks. 1987. "State Regulation and Campus Autonomy." In *Higher Education: Handbook of Theory and Research*, ed. J. C. Smart. Volume III. NY: Agathon Press.

Yamamoto, Kiyoshi. 2012. "Corporatization of National Universities in Japan: An Analysis of the Impact on Governance and Finance." Available at: http://ump.p.u-tokyo.ac.jp/crump/resource/crump_wp_no3.pdf. Accessed March 17, 2012.

Yang, Rui. 2002. *Third Delight: The Internationalization of Higher Education in China*. New York, London: Routledge.

Chapter 11

The Challenges of Regionalism and Harmonization for Higher Education in Asia

John N. Hawkins

The higher educational systems that exist throughout Asia/Pacific are numerous and diverse. In recent years, there have been efforts on the part of policy makers and others in the region to think of ways to harmonize these systems to allow for a more fluid flow of students and scholars. These efforts, however, have often run up against powerful nation-specific priorities. Nevertheless, some progress has been made by regional organizations (ROs) and through bilateral agreements to harmonize aspects of higher education (HE). Wesley (2003) estimates that there are well over 100 ROs engaged in such efforts but it remains to be seen how substantive these efforts are and will become.

Regionalization and HE: Some Conceptual Considerations

Is economic regionalization a trend for the future? As this happens, does it herald educational regionalization, thus uniting economic internationalization and education? There is sufficient disagreement over these propositions to warrant a certain amount of skepticism regarding the viability of economic, social, and cultural regionalization. Some have argued that this trend is already visible in the Caribbean, the European Union (EU), and one could argue, in the Association of South East Asian Nations (ASEAN) (Forest 1995). Others have argued that nationalism remains a powerful counter force, placing boundaries that regionalization dare not cross (De Witt 1995) – what here will be called *centrifugal* forces for those that pull away from regionalization and harmonization of HE, and *centripetal* for those that pull toward this vision. These, of course, are not necessarily new arguments. Clark Kerr, former president of the University of California system stated over 20 years ago that there are two laws of motion that are moving in opposite directions – internationalization of learning and knowledge, and the nationalization of the purposes of HE (Kerr 1990). It has been noted elsewhere that quality assurance (QA) within the HE movement is increasingly driven by economic agendas with its prevalent emphasis on metrics and learning outcomes that align with the world of business (Neubauer and Hawkins 2009). The influence of neoliberalism has driven higher education institutions (HEIs) toward justifying their existence and funding on how well they serve national if not local interests, a far cry from cross-national regional concerns. The expansive and convergent discourses of globalization so prevalent in framing HE policy discussion in Asia Pacific are often belied by the national sense of what it takes to gain "global recognition," which is to be recognized as having "globally competitive" (and ranked) universities. Within more narrow economic frames of reference, the seemingly robust and boundless energies that produced the World Trade Organization (WTO) extended to regional counterparts have within the past ten years been supplemented by large numbers of bilateral agreements (Naya and Plummer 2005; Aggarwal and Urata 2006). So where do ROs and HE fit in? Are these two forms of organization meant to serve truly international and regional interests, or more exclusive local concerns?

An interesting hypothesis might be that forms of regional HE organization and governance are more likely to occur in a narrow rather than broad sense. Furthermore, the nation state continues to be a centrifugal force when it comes to regionalization, largely because of neoliberalism, economic competition, accountability, QA, and alignment issues. In other words, as economics becomes more globalized, HE tries to follow (as Forest suggests) but gets caught up in the centrifugal local forces mentioned above. It is useful to recognize that both things are happening simultaneously and will continue to happen: The point is to try not to mistake the observation of instances for what may/will turn out to be enduring patterns. Alternatively, we need to forge a sensible conceptual language that permits us to understand that both forces are in continual and constant dynamic tension. As Steger has argued citing many others, this attribute seemingly typifies globalization as a phenomenon, or as a set of aggregate phenomena (Steger 2009).

Ezra Vogel (2010) makes another kind of argument for centrifugal forces that work against the further expansion of ROs especially in Asia, and therefore, the notion of regional HEIs. Here, he reminds us that we need to consider the historical context in which regionalization must take root and be nurtured. The argument is that two difficult issues exist in East Asia that remain unresolved and pose a major barrier to the establishment of a successful RO that would involve the participation of the three largest social and economic powerhouses in the region (Japan, Korea, and China): historical disputes and military balance of power. Unless and until these three nations reach some agreements on these long-standing disputes (which does not seem imminent in Vogel's view), harmonizing their HEIs in any substantive sense is less than likely and may not even be desirable. Thus, he concludes that the small-scale structures that already exist and the one large-scale structure (ASEAN) are probably sufficient for now and policy energy and funding should not be wasted on efforts to create any new ROs designed to somehow "harmonize" HE in the region.

Forms of Regionalism in Asia: Phases and Types

Regionalism may focus on political structures, security and international relations, economics, geography, literature, art and architecture, popular culture and sport, and education to name just a few. (For other ways of conceptualizing such distinctions, see Jane Knight's contribution to this volume, Chapter 2.) Following Neubauer's framework in Chapter 1 of this volume, generally speaking, two main phases of regionalism can be identified in the Asian region: old and new. The early phases (old) spanned three decades from 1950 to 1980 and consisted of country groupings of peer economies, intra-regional interactions, trade and security, and education. ASEAN is the prime example of this exclusive form. From 1980 on (new), we see the reflection of neoliberalism, economic liberalism, and market deregulation in the rise of broader-based interregional organizations such as the Asian Pacific Economic Cooperation (APEC), the Asia/Europe Meeting (ASEM), the Asia Cooperation Dialogue (ACD), ASEAN + 3, and so on. Educational regionalism has been built on organizations such as these, in particular, the Southeast Asian Ministers of Education Organizations (SEAMEO) Regional Institute for Higher Education and Development (RIHED), the Association of Southeast Asian Institutions of Higher Learning (ASAIHL), among others. These groupings focus on a diverse set of HE issues such as QA, collaborative research and development, teaching and learning, student mobility, and do not exclude interacting with national settings outside of the Asian orbit (the United States and Australia) (Shameel 2003; Robertson 2007). So we see here, in these two phases, a wide range of ROs from exclusive to inclusive, from intra-regional to interregional, and covering an equally wide range of social issues, one of which is education and especially HE.

All of this raises a number of issues that will warrant ongoing research and observation as ROs continue to grow and develop and HE is increasingly a component of this phenomenon. Yepes (2006) points out that the relationship between regionalism and HE in Asia is developing in the context of interaction between the ROs and those regional efforts in other global settings. The exemplar and paradigm that are most often mentioned are Europe, the EU, and the Bologna Process and related activities. It is worthwhile to recap some of this to put the Asian efforts into a more comparative perspective and judge to some degree how relevant such a comparison is.

Europe passed through several phases of regionalization that many in Asia hope to mimic. In the mid-1980s and through the 1990s, two initiatives were taken largely focused on mobility. The Socrates and Erasmus programs engaged in student mobility efforts and some programs focused on curriculum development across various HEIs. They engaged in addition to HEIs, European-wide professional associations (medicine, law, business), technical colleges, and online delivery efforts, all being considered inputs into the regionalization process. By 2000, these two programs plus Comenius at the K-12 level and Grundtvig (adult education) focused on five areas of harmonization (mobility, students, faculty, credit rationalization, and European university systems). By the time the Bologna Process began, 1998 and onward, the goal had magnified to establish a new Magna Charta of European Area of Higher Education still focused largely on mobility including efforts to harmonize a variety of HE features such as comparable degrees, a European credit transfer system, cooperative QA systems, and a European dimension to the curriculum.

Clearly, the EU and its HE harmonization efforts have represented a very important reform with significant implications for the role that ROs can play in HE. However, whether or not the reforms are a relevant model for Asia to emulate is another question. A recent critical study and evaluation of the entire process in Europe reached the broad conclusion that ERASMUS and Bologna were essentially "used" by national governments to implement reforms they would otherwise have had difficulty imposing on their academic communities, or they were diverted by the academic communities so that policies remained essentially unchanged (Scot 2011). In essence, most national systems remained relatively untouched by the harmonization effort – especially France where the two-tier system remains strong (Musselin 2006). ERASMUS, SOCRATES, and other mobility programs have not provided the intercultural exchange that was expected but *have* been used by national systems for their own purposes. Other aspects of Bologna, designed to harmonize credits, faculty exchange, and provide a HE architecture for the region have, in the words of Musselin, "been hijacked" by the academic community and national HE systems to satisfy their own "national" needs. This is not to say that nothing changed. However, these studies do say that the idea that a paradigm change has occurred, or that a model has emerged to be emulated by other regions is vastly overstating this effort. The notion that new circuits of exchange have been developed is best described by Scot (2011) as "circuits frustrated."

So where does this leave the Asian effort? We turn now to a closer look at the sequence of events in Asia through which regionalization and HE have progressed during the past couple of decades.

Asia, Regionalization, and HE

Efforts have been made to include HE in existing ROs since at least the 1950s when ASEAN explored collaboration with East Asia by establishing the ASAIHL in 1956. In the 1960s, United Nations Education, Scientific, and Cultural Organization's (UNESCO) Asian and Pacific Regional Bureau for Education began to work with SEAMEO to better integrate HE in the region. Expanded to include Japan and other non-ASEAN nations, the RIHED was established to "respond to needs related to policy and planning, administration and management of higher education" (Yepes 2006, 7). For its part, ASEAN established the ASEAN University Network (AUN) in 1995, housed at Chulalongkorn University in Thailand, to manage collaborative exchanges of students, faculty, and grant scholarships and to provide information networking, joint research, and an ASEAN wide-course syllabus, and is now seeking to establish links with Japan, China, Korea, the EU, India, and Russia.

The list goes on, with University Mobility in Asia and the Pacific (UMAP) in 1990s, ASEAN–EU University Network Programme in 2000, the Asia Link Program around that same time, all designed to create regional opportunities and knowledge between Asia and other world regions. There are regional and interregional initiatives directly involved with HE cooperation such as the East Asia Vision Group (EAVG) established in 1995, and in 2001, Kim Daejung proposed to combine ASEAN + 3 with HE harmonization and the EAVG to produce a strong regional identity and "East Asian Consciousness" (Yepes 2006, 8). When the goals and objectives of these various regional HE efforts are summarized, they collectively focus on such issues as regional lifelong learning, credit transfer systems, financial assistance mobility, cooperative research and development efforts, and QA regional cooperation among others.

These goals are remarkably similar to those proposed by the Bologna Process. However, in the Asian case, there has been little in the way of coordination of these various efforts and indeed many of the initiatives mentioned above (and there are more that have not been mentioned) have either stalled or are no longer very active. To resolve this lack of progress, Yepes (2006) proposes that an organization such as UNESCO could provide the umbrella coordinating organization, WTO could provide assistance with reviewing regional conventions on diplomas and degrees, and the World Bank or the Asian Development Bank could provide funding for such an effort; but this scenario does not appear likely.

Other scholars have concluded that true regionalization in Asia will not occur as long as the previous exclusive organizations (i.e., ASEAN, SEAMEO, etc.) are unable to effectively draw in the "big two" East Asian nations (China and Japan) and find a way reasonably to include the United States (Rozman 2005). The argument is made that Japan and China's difficulty in resolving historical tensions and animosities has presented a major obstacle to moving forward with a form of regionalism that would include harmonization of HE: "The problematic state of relations between Beijing and Tokyo has increasingly emerged as the foremost hurdle for East Asian regionalism" (Rozman 2005, 402). That includes the usual areas such as student mobility: "Study abroad by Chinese [in the region] is now more often associated with impoverished living leading to crime rather than goodwill ambassadors returning home to foster closer ties" (Rozman 2005, 402–403). Given that half of the global gross domestic product (GDP) and one-third of the world's population are in Japan, China, and the United States, in many respects, these three countries represent the core of the emerging twenty-first-century global political economy, including many of the HE indicators of concern to those proponents of HE regionalization. The successes of ASEAN and all of the other regional associations put together are highly dependent on these three countries and the models they represent. Rozman concludes that regionalism is likely not the wave of the future, at least in Asia, and probably not in the EU as well. Given the economic and increasingly cultural interdependency of the region, there may well be a slow, tortuous path to a regional community, but if that is put up against the rise in nationalism on the part of all three of these core nations, it is not likely to be meaningfully successful. History and cultural memory cast a huge shadow over trust in such areas as HE harmonization, shared curriculum, and other educational policies.

This rather bleak projection of bringing together East Asia and Southeast Asia (ignoring for the moment South Asia) into some form of educational harmonized relationship was echoed by such scholars as Robert Scalapino who argues that "the diversities within Asia far exceed the commonalities...Asia has nowhere near the cultural affinities of West Europe" (Terada 2003, 273). A counterargument, looking at the issue from the inside, is that the Asian nations have much more in common with each other than they do with the West and therefore, there is a basis for forging substantive regional affiliations (a *centripetal* force).

Whichever view is proposed, it is not clear at this time that there is a substantive regional identity between East and Southeast Asia. A regional-centric approach, based on exclusion as proposed by Prime Minster Mahathir in 1990, and disparaging referred to by Australia as "cultural regionalism" was a nonstarter (Terada 2003). East Asia Economic Community (EAEC) failed because it was retaliatory to the West, based on trade, and had a cultural aspect to it. It was not until Japan was able to support ASEAN + 3 (and its various other permutations: +6, +8, etc.) that some progress was made. Still, a full-fledged Asian RO capable of harmonizing HE in East and Southeast Asia with member countries participating on an equal basis has not emerged (Terada 2003). If anything, the tension between Japan and China as the latter has rapidly developed has increased. In addition, the numerous Foreign Trade Agreements (FTAs) that have emerged especially in the Northeast subregion and which are largely uncoordinated have worked against a regional Asia concept (another *centrifugal* force).[1]

Although efforts have been made to make sense out of the many ROs and partnerships that have developed and are emerging in the broad region of East Asia and the implications thereof for a more harmonized HE interaction, much more needs to be done. Kuroda and Passarelli (2009) and Nguyen (2009) each agree that at the very least, some questions need to be addressed:

- How much and what kind of regional cooperation with respect to HE is already present in the region?
- What kind of governing principles and policies already exist that encourage or discourage ROs and HE harmonization?
- What does an examination of existing frameworks and organizations currently involved in ROs, such as ASEAN + 3, the Association of

Pacific Rim Universities (APRU), and the many others, referred to above reveal?
- What would a study of the actors involved, not only countries but also HEIs, tell us?
- What can we learn from a comparative study of other examples in Europe and North America?

For her part, Nguyen (2009) has concluded that comparisons with other world regions show that the efforts at developing a harmonized HE regime in Asia fall far behind. Of particular interest to Asians, in her opinion, are Bologna-like issues such as readable, comparable degrees; a three-cycle degree system; a credit transfer system; student/staff mobility; and a region-wide marketing mechanism. Furthermore, given that the recent assessments of EU progress toward a HE harmonization process and the list of features and capacities above are less than enthusiastic (Musselin 2006; Scot 2011), questions regarding the scale, scope, progress, and indeed the feasibility of a harmonized HE regime developing in Asia are naturally raised.

Centrifugal Forces

While much has been said about the common interests of the Asian region, and the rational reasons behind promoting some sort of a harmonization process, a number of centrifugal forces, some of which were already discussed above, present formidable obstacles to the realization of such a policy (Satow and Li 2005). Several writers cite, echoing the Scalapino and Rozman arguments, the vast and diverse nature of the region, its ethnicities, cultures, languages, religious traditions and beliefs, political economies, and diverse HE histories as being factors that work against such ROs and HE cooperative arrangements (Supachai and Nopraenue 2008; Nguyen 2009, among others). Although student and faculty mobility in the region is one area of progress, overall, this has remained limited when one considers percentages of these cohorts represented in any given national HEI. When compared with other world regions, Nguyen (2009) notes: "Asia is lagging far behind other regions of the world in promoting even the most basic level of policy harmonization to achieve common objectives and interests in the area of higher education" (p. 79).

To illustrate this point, Nguyen (2009) conducted a comparative study of three major Asian ROs: UMAP, AUN, and SEAMEO's RIHED. In summary, she found that one of UMAP's major contributions to the formation of a harmonized regional approach to HE in the Asia region was the development of the University Credit Transfer System (UCTS), a mechanism to satisfy one of the key concerns of most proponents of a regional approach to HE (mobility for students seeking transfer of credits within the region). She found that although 34 countries and over 350 HEIs had joined UMAP and that UMAP had been around for over 20 years, very few institutions have utilized UCTS if indeed they know what it is at all. (In Japan, a major proponent of receiving students from Asia, only 6 percent of their HEIs are utilizing UCTS as a tool.) She notes that the program has a lack of identity in the region and financial support.

Somewhat more successful in terms of usage is the AUN designed in 1995 to support student mobility in the region. While open to all HEIs in the region, in fact, it has become primarily an elite program, as "elites prefer to cooperate with elites" (Nguyen 2009, 80). Therefore, it is somewhat self-limiting and, as of 2011, had about 26 members. More interesting was the subregional networking on QA practices, which seeks to establish some common standards for the region. AUN-QA reaches out to all institutions in the region that wish to get the AUN-QA label.

Finally, SEAMEO's RIHED is another program designed to promote regional cooperation in HE in the region, established in 1959, and more directly interested in governance as a key component to regional HE harmonization. This organization focuses on areas such as HE management, QA benchmarking, IT applications, learning and teaching methodology, R&D capacity, alignment with the private sector, and developing linkages with other ROs.

Of particular interest is RIHED's recent workshop on the topic of harmonization, ROs, and HE in Asia at which it was concluded that the future of this movement would consist primarily of a series of small steps rather than the establishment of a Bologna-type overarching mechanism that "invites doubts and suspicions among Asian countries" (Nguyen 2009, 81). Furthermore, this study and others have concluded that a major goal of the current crop of ROs in the region is to raise awareness in the region about the value of regionalization. UCTS and other such efforts are small steps in the right direction. It is likely that this "small step" approach is the most appropriate for Asia. In summary, the centrifugal forces seem to far outweigh the centripetal forces and include among others:

- Diversity and disparity of countries and HEIs in the region;
- Historical and cultural tensions among the top three East Asian nations (China, Japan, and Korea);
- Variety of languages and ethnicities;
- Differences in credit systems, curricula, and grading systems;

- Lack of uniform QA standards;
- Lack of financial resources and capacity for ROs to promote and market cooperation;
- Lack of commitment at both national and institutional levels;
- Risky "step by step" approach, no guarantee or record that there will be any spill over to the other levels;
- Weak approach by AUN and other such organizations to play an aggressive role in building some sort of cohesive community; and
- ROs do play an important role but at the end of the day, it is the nations and the individual HEIs who are the deciding actors who will determine the progress of this idea of harmonization in the region.

Conclusion

Any regional integration hypothesis must necessarily include two components: one is the interplay between centrifugal and centripetal forces as discussed above; the other is an appreciation of how the various forces of globalization are coming to define and redefine what HE is at virtually every level of analysis. The complexity and diversity of such factors are being developed and attenuated at rates of change and with implications that complicate all such efforts to effectively sort through regional dynamics in a definitive manner. This does not imply, however, that the effort is sterile or without value. Rather, it suggests the necessity of acknowledging the complex dynamics of an increasingly interdependent and interactive world within which the roles that HE are meant to play are themselves in a state of constant flux.

Examples of these global forces for educational change include ongoing changing characteristics of learners and how to measure the quality of these new characteristics. Related to this are emerging new trends that impact the learning process, much of which is diverse, dispersed, and decentralized. This is a more participatory learning process that includes self-learning, peer to peer, networking, collaborative learning to name just a few. Organizationally, education has been transformed as well including issues related to degrees and certificates as well as changes in credentialing (New Media Consortium 2011).

The purpose of noting some of these change attributes of contemporary HE is to underscore both how dynamic this environment is under pressure from the many forces of globalization and increasing interdependence, and how unpredictable the interplay between centrifugal and centripetal forces operating in these environments may be. As we struggle to gain conceptual clarification about regionalization and regionalism, and look into the many implications for HE structures, outputs, and governance relationships, it is necessary to hold sufficient respect for just how rapidly these environments of HE may be changing. One can make arguments that each of these changes or "shifts" has potential for either centripetal or centrifugal consequences – the "proof" will be in seeing how institutions and systems of national education respond to them.

What is very clear, however, is the conviction that all of these shifts derive in some ways from the larger paradigm shift that is occurring within HE in "the region" of Asia-Pacific and throughout the world. The implications for institutions are very wide reaching especially as institutions struggle to meet the challenges of changing faculty roles, issues of how curricula are constructed and delivered, and how to adapt to new "players" in HE markets proffering new versions of existing programs and riding the crest of a wave of innovation and novelty that they may be better equipped to offer simply because they are not required to carry the "burden" of cultural tradition that has been the hallmark of traditional institutions of HE. HE and educational policy makers will have to attempt to strike a balance between these forces if any true "harmonization" is to occur in Asian HE. Important "small" steps are being taken in this direction as evidenced by the recent (2011) announcement by Tokyo University that they will change their academic calendar so that it is more aligned with that of the rest of the world (other HEIs in Japan will likely follow suit) (Koh 2011). These unilateral but symbolic steps will likely accumulate to create a more regional approach to HE short of the establishment of a major new RO.

Note

1. However, note that throughout the region, the proliferation of bilateral trade agreements has undercut both regional and global trade dynamics. Cf. Naya and Plummer 2005 and Aggarwal and Shujiro, eds. 2006.

References

Aggarwal, Vinrod D., and Urata Shujiro. 2006. *Bilateral Trade Agreements in the Asia-Pacific: Origins, Evolutions, and Implications.* New York: Routledge.

De Witt, Hans. 1995. "Education and Globalization in Europe: An Overview of Its Development." Paper presented at CIES Conference in Boston, 1995.
Forest, J. F. 1995. "Regionalism in Higher Education: An International Look at National and Institutional Interdependence." In *Boston College Center for International Education*. Boston: BCIHE.
Kerr, C. 1990. "The Internationalization of Learning and the Nationalization of the Purposes of Higher Education: Two Laws of Motion in Conflict." *The European Journal of Education* 25 (1): 5–22.
Koh Y. 2011. "Japan's Harvard Mulls Radical Calendar Change." *The Wall Street Journal – Japan*. Available at: http://blogs.wsj.com/japanrealtime/2012/01/20/japans-harvard-mulls-radical-calendar-change/. Accessed March 8, 2012.
Kuroda, Kazuo, and D. Passarelli, eds. 2009. *Higher Education and Asian Regional Integration Symposium Report*. Global Institute for Asian Regional Integration, Waseda University, Tokyo, Japan.
Musselin C. 2006. "The Side Effects of the Bologna Process on National Institutional Settings; The Case of France." Paper presented at the Douro Seminar, Portugal.
Naya, Seiji F., and Michael G. Plummer. 2005. *The Economic of the Enterprise for ASEAN Initiative*. Singapore: Institute for Southeast Asia Studies.
Neubauer, D., and J. Hawkins. 2009. "Higher Education and Quality in the Knowledge Society." Concept paper presented to the East-West Center Senior Seminar, Kuala Lumpur, Malaysia, October 21–24.
New Media Consortium. 2011. *The 2011 Horizon Report*. Available at: http://net.educause.edu/ir/library/pdf/HR2011.pdf. Accessed March 8, 2012.
Nguyen, A. T. 2009. "The Role of Regional Organizations in East Asian Regional Cooperation and Integration in the Field of Higher Education." *Asian Regional Integration Review*, Waseda University I: 69–82.
Robertson, S. L. 2007. "Regionalism, 'Europe/Asia' and higher education." *Higher Education*. Available at: www.issi.org.pk. Accessed March 8, 2012.
Rozman, G. 2005. "Regionalization in Northeast Asia." In *The Possibility of an East Asian Community: Rethinking the Sino-Japanese Relationship*, ed. T. Satow and E. Li. Tokyo: Ochanomizu Shobo.
Satow T., and E. Li. 2005. *The Possibility of an East Asian Community: Rethinking the Sino-Japanese Relationship*. Tokyo: Ochanomizu Shobo.
Scot, M. 2011. *Studying the Social Sciences in France*, unpublished manuscript. Paris, France.
Shameel, A. 2003. "The New Asian Realism: Economics and Politics of the Asia Cooperation Dialogue." Available at: www.issi.org.pk/old-site/ss_Detail.php?dataId=273. Accessed March 9, 2011.
Steger, Manfred. 2009. *Globalization: A Very Short Introduction*. Oxford: Oxford University Press.
Supachai, and Nopraenue S. Dhirathiti. 2008. *Harmonisation of Higher Education: Lessons Learned from the Bologna Process*. Bangkok: Seameo Rihed.
Terada, T. 2003. "Constructing an 'East Asian' Concept and Growing Regional Identity: From EAEC to ASEAN+3." *The Pacific Review* 16 (2): 251–277.

Vogel, E. 2010. "Regionalism in Asia: Why We Should Stick with Existing Structures?" for East Asia Forum, Japan Institute of International Affairs Conference on the East Asian Community Idea in Tokyo, on March 17, 2010.

Wesley, M. 2003. *The Regional Organizations of the Asia-Pacific: Exploring Institutional Change.* New York: Palgrave MacMillan.

Yepes, C. P. 2006. "World Regionalization of Higher Education: Policy Proposals for International Organizations." *Higher Education Policy* 19 (1): 111–128.

Chapter 12

The Dynamics of Regionalization in Contemporary Asia-Pacific Higher Education

John N. Hawkins, Ka Ho Mok, and Deane E. Neubauer

In this concluding chapter, we seek to articulate and tie together some of the dominant themes articulated in the preceding chapters. The first part frames these in terms of three "fundamental" observations about the context(s) within which regionalization is taking place in the Asia-Pacific region. In the two subsequent parts, we weave these observations through various other themes established in earlier chapters.

Part One

Observation One: Regionalization is Not a Linear Process: It Ebbs and Flows in Concert with the Nature of Exogenous Events

This view of higher education (HE) may appear self-evident and unexceptional, but on closer inspection represents an important and powerful input to and constraint on the policy process. In a recent work on the interface between the processes of contemporary globalization and those of HE, especially in the Asia-Pacific region, Peter Hershock has emphasized various aspects of contemporary globalization as it becomes manifest as a *complex system* (Hershock 2011). In employing this term, he seeks to move beyond the mere statement of analogy that would compare these HE and related social processes to the formulations that physics and other environmental sciences would employ in seeking to stipulate, frame, and analyze complex systems. His intention is to induce us to view many aspects of contemporary globalization and their related subcomponents as literally portions of a complexity invested upon the world by the whole of the activities of the past four or five decades. While this is not the place to reprise this development, it is useful to note in this context that by positing globalization as a complex system comprised of many highly interactive feedforward and feedback mechanisms, Hershock and others seek to underscore the degree to which such systems give rise, with some regularity (ironically), to unpredictable outcomes and behaviors.[1]

Operating with such a massive, complex system as that of contemporary globalization creates entirely new sets of "problems" for all sorts of actors including in this context institutions of HE, their presumptive regulators and assurers of quality, those who attend them seeking to gain all the features of "an education," and others. In short, in the contemporary world of this recursive complexity, at some level, virtually everything that actors do is contingent on other parts of a complex system, only a portion of which is even visible to them, or capable of being acted upon. The result – for all – is a very high level of uncertainty in terms of what actors seek to do and the probability that their actions will lead to success, but simultaneously (the other side of the dilemma created by this situation) the absolute necessity to *do something*. However one might summarize this situation (which describes us all), it is clear that the nature of our developmental actions is not, cannot be, linear – thereby robbing us of the comforts that most of us seek as institutional actors (whether in the public or private sector) of effective predictability. It is this environment of endemic predictive uncertainty – of fundamental contingency – that leads Hershock in his writing to see these confrontations not as "problems to be solved" but rather as "predicaments" to be faced, addressed, or "dealt" with, but not solved in the conventional manner in which we understand that most problems have identifiable "solutions" if only we have enough information, will, and resources to seek them out. (It is also this dynamic that leads John Hawkins in Chapter 11 to emphasize the simultaneous tensions of centripetal and centrifugal forces operating in virtually all societies and certainly acting as key dynamics within all regionalization equations.)

Within HE, as has often been indicated, this "situation" is perhaps best illustrated by the familiar "alignment" issue, which is replete in the literature and which seemingly enters policy discussions sooner or later in most conversations concerning the value, worth, or productive capacities of HE. The predicament is simple if compelling: HE institutions both historically and in the current era are complex, much given to tradition and traditional organization, and slow to change. Historically, by which we could mean over the past two centuries or so, their primary social function has been something other than an explicit and primary focus on "training/educating" people for a contemporary workforce. And indeed they have not. However, in the current era, driven by the dynamics of contemporary globalization to which we have eluded above, this has increasingly come to be *a* if not *the* primary responsibility of HE as viewed by many of its social constituencies: policy makers and funders, parents, and students themselves. However, first and foremost, it has become the view of the "business community" wherever it exists and within whatever context. In this view, *the* primary responsibility of HE is to train people for the contemporary workforce. Even if this were to be accepted within the complex and often contrary history and presumptions of HE's other roles (e.g., cultural preservation, knowledge creation, etc.), it would still remain only a problem were it not for the absence of linkage (alignment) between the demand function (represented by the labor market place) and its articulators (businesses). As we are increasingly aware, the very authors of these labor capability demands – business enterprises – are themselves uncertain as to what their needs are to be in the short, medium, and long run to succeed in the ever-changing global economy. Misalignment is built into the system by virtue of the uncertainty that exists within the labor market place itself, let alone in the capacity of HE institutions to perform such activities within their own structural limitations.

Alignment is a dilemma throughout HE, and one can find vibrant critiques of it within the policy structures of any advanced economic country and society documenting the shortcomings of HE in meeting the workplace needs of the modern economy. Part of the dilemma arises from the dynamics imparted to labor markets by innovation, automation, the global circulation of employment (see Regina Ordonez's Chapter 8 in this volume), and in fact, all of what we have customarily termed "the factors of production" that have been drawn into global circuits of exchange. That which is experienced as a given labor demand in a particular economy increasingly has its origins somewhere outside that economy. Yet, an additional aspect of this misalignment issue lies in how and where discourse originates and is articulated about such issues within global time and space, a situation in which "the local" remains the "place" where political authority meets local capacity, even while local authority is – in this global marketplace – often significantly unable to deal effectively with the various "causes" of the dislocation, which are situated further afar. Thus, Stiglitz in his analysis of the US role in the 2007–2009 global recession (which was perilously close to becoming a global depression) points out that even as the recession savaged the US job market (which has been very slow to recover and which in fact has heightened the tensions between the HE and political communities over the role US HEIs are playing in "preparing" graduates for the workforce), the dynamics of global trade and the parallel collapse of American consumption caused something in the neighborhood of 20 million unemployed workers in China, despite the efforts of its government to engage a vigorous stimulus program (Stiglitz 2010). These examples can be repeated with variation throughout the global economy.

The burden of these remarks about the complex nature of contemporary globalization for regionalization in Asia is both to underscore our primary point – that regionalization is not a linear process – and to indicate that because of this and all of the contingent uncertainties that come with that fact, regionalization is also a *messy* process. Overall, despite the myriad activities detailed in this volume just primarily in the area of HE, what we might term the "forward thrust" of regionalization tends to lack coherence. Thus, the pathways toward regionalization such as those described by Knight, Mok, Sugimura, and others in this volume have the character of being "actions in the direction" of regionalization (or in Mok's frame "regulatory regionalization"), but they also reflect in large part the continuous dynamics of global uncertainty that permeates this activity.

Observation Two: Demographic Differentiation within the Asia-Pacific Region is a Critical Parameter for Higher Education Regionalization

If, as we contend, it is an error of considerable proportions to attempt a projective assessment of HE regionalization in the Asia Pacific without situating it firmly within the conflicting dynamics of contemporary globalization, it would be one of equal proportions not to factor into this equation the profound and dramatic demographic circumstances of the region. Asian demographics are unique in the world, are affecting change in these societies on a daily basis, and in a fundamental way impact HE at every turn.

They color and affect the particular kind of regionalization taking place in the Asia Pacific. Based on the United Nations Education, Scientific, and Cultural Organization (UNESCO) projections of global population, the import is clear. Global population growth is adding approximately a billion new inhabitants every 13+ years up to the point in approximately 2050 when world population growth will reach 9+ billion people. The vast majority of this growth will occur within Asian societies, even as has been discussed in multiple chapters in this volume, some of those societies are simultaneously faced with declining populations overall and specifically within traditional HE age cohorts.

This differentiated demography cuts athwart the policy dynamics that frame HE throughout the region, leading some countries to focus most of their energies on seeking to develop critical capacity for rapidly expanding populations (Indonesia, India, Malaysia, Vietnam, and Philippines) even as others scale back existing capacity in the face of declining enrollments (Japan, Korea, and Taiwan) – all while seeking to gain competitive HE quality to compete within global markets for educated workers and to gain or sustain advantage in the effort to link HE capacity to national innovation capabilities. The familiarity of this observation does nothing to lessen the complications that these demographic facts interject into the many efforts toward a more comprehensive and effective realization of HE regionalization. As Mok's Chapter 9 foregrounds, the potential for success in these many regionalization efforts, including that toward regulatory regionalization (to which we shall turn again shortly), will ultimately depend both on the way that the broader dynamics of globalization linkage impact individual national economies and subregional economies and on how these differentiated demographic realities shape and constrain the range of national political options in dealing with making appropriate resources available for HE as a national policy endeavor that can be leveraged into regional contexts.

In this regard, the struggles taking place within Europe as this is being written to staunch the fiscal bleeding that continues to flow from the 2007 global recession through powerful restrictions on national budgets that target education at all levels along with other "social services" stand as a cautionary tale of the potent combination of demographic transformation, global fiscal vulnerability, and the persistent alignment dilemma (note that at the core of most European "social problems" is the persistent issue of the unemployability of recent HE graduates). This combination of "variables" will, it would seem, continue to define the essential parameters of how HE regionalism will develop in the Asia Pacific.

Observation Three: Migration in and of Itself Is a Sufficiently Significant Variable to Plot as a Regionalization Force

An attendant aspect of these demographic variables so much in play in this attenuated globalization context lies within the facts of migration themselves. From one perspective, much of what has driven the growth and development of national HE within Asia Pacific countries has been a direct consequence of migrational dynamics. The most typical of these has been within-country migration from the countryside to cities, creating throughout the region both mega-cities and never-before-seen urban concentrations (conurbations). Some observers hold, for example, that the rural to urban migration taking place in China from the mid-1980s through the end of the 1990s may have constituted the largest identifiable migration in human history. Without question, these rapid urban concentrations have fueled the explosive growth of HE throughout the region, while simultaneously being at the center of that which Mok and others in this volume have noted as the creation of strong subnational regions that are often anchored by HE concentrations.

However, in line with other arguments found throughout this volume, the migratory forces in the Asia Pacific have featured significant amounts of out-migration as well as in-country migration making important contributions to the kinds of regional flows Neubauer identifies as circuits of exchange (in Chapter 1) and Knight as essential cross-border flows (in Chapter 2). In yet another variation, as Ordonez makes clear (in Chapter 8), the migratory flows out from the Philippines into global labor markets not only has come to constitute a significant contribution to national GDP, but has also flowed "up stream" as it were, creating distorting signals throughout Philippine HE as HEIs have rushed to both stimulate and satisfy demand for those seeking global labor placement. The result is yet a quite different form of regionalization – an exemplar of a kind of "new regionalism" that can exist relatively independent of the former proximities of spatial and interactive currency typical of older forms.

What to make of these migrational alerts as they are likely to affect regionalization in the various ways discussed in this volume? Without attempting to answer this question in its entirety, we would, nevertheless, offer the view that given the "remainder" of the powerful demographic "surge" to take place before global population growth begins to significantly slow toward the middle of the century – another two billion persons on the planet – that migration of all three types noted here – in-country, cross-border, and temporary global labor market specific – will powerfully affect HE and perhaps more than any other single factor color the nature of HE regionalization. This greater population growth will strain ecological, social, and economic resources throughout the globe. Within the Asia-Pacific region, the effects of population disparities coupled with continued rapid growth are likely to revalue the whole of HE as a resource and outcome of increasing global interdependence. As such, it can only act as a major and perhaps the primary driver of the dynamics that underlie regionalization.

Part Two

The Emergence of Regulatory Regionalism

Realizing the importance of HE and the potential of the education market not only for generating additional national incomes but also for asserting soft power in the highly competitive world, the governments of Malaysia, Hong Kong, and Singapore have put forward serious efforts in their quest to gain regional education hub status; while China has tried to engage overseas partners to diversify transnational HE programs catering to citizens' pressing education demand. In the last decade or so, we have witnessed the rise of transnational HE and a growing trend in the mobility of students traditionally and historically coming from Asian countries to developed economies in the West, particularly studying in the United Kingdom, the United States, and Australia, to admitting students from other parts of the world to study in Asia (see Mok and Lee's Chapters 9 and 10, respectively, in this volume).

The rise of different forms of transnational education in Asia suggests various forms of regional frameworks emerging. The proliferation of providers in education has challenged the conventional mode of governance, especially creating pressure on those countries that have long been adopting a "centralized model" in governing education through government ministries. The diversification of providers and funding sources has inevitably resulted in different forms of governance structures with more involvement of private–public partnerships, market-oriented regulatory mechanisms, and international/global professional organizations in assuring the quality of education (Mok 2008a). New regulatory regimes may emerge with growing influence from multinational corporations (MNCs) instead of universities. It is against this context that we have to revisit whether the model of centralized educational ministries is sufficient in this new environment. Future research should focus more on the emerging forms of regulatory regimes, especially when regionalism and subregionalism are information that has both homogenizing and differentiating aspects.

Analyzing Regionalism and Subregionalism

Having an examination of the recent HE transformations and the rise of transnational HE in Asia, we could analyze such changes as part of the wider contemporary trend to "reinvent the state" or to enhance the "competition state" projects in the globalizing world (Mok 2008b). Yet another contemporary inclination, as we can see in the accelerated integration of the European Union (EU), is regionalism within the wider context of globalization. Thus, accordingly, is there any sign of the emergence of regulatory regionalism in terms of East Asian HE? Admittedly, in addition to developments in East Asia, European HE as a whole has also been dwarfed by its American counterpart since the end of World War II. The successful American model, particularly in regard to research universities, has increasingly posed a challenge to relatively stagnant and conservative European institutions based largely on their heritage from the eighteenth and nineteenth centuries. In the face of these pressures, one of the recent responses from the EU is its attempts at regulatory regionalism that try to synergize the competitive edge of European universities (Dale and Robertson 2002).

The quest for world-class universities is particularly relevant in this regard, and the first effort set to improve the research quality of European universities could be found in the "Lisbon Strategy" initiated by the European Council in Lisbon in March 2000 (Deem et al. 2008).[2] The 1999 Bologna Declaration[3] and its subsequent "Bologna Process"[4] could be regarded as the second effort concerning university learning and teaching, as well as the creation of a common HE market and research area. Academic degree structures of EU universities have henceforth been increasingly harmonized to enable learner and worker mobility, facilitate credit transfers, and ensure quality assurance (QA) (Robertson 2008, 2009). More importantly, the Bologna Declaration, with its goal of achieving a "European Higher Education Area" by 2010, has for the first time created a common ground for the EU to promote its HE to a global market, particularly to Asia. Since Russia and Southeast Europe are now also part of the European Higher Education Area, it thus extends far beyond the EU as a constitutional entity (Robertson 2009, 8).

In comparison, to date, mechanisms to promote East Asian integration in HE have not yet been developed. However, signs of regulatory regionalism could be traced in related collaborations via certain regional organizations, or in the institutional interactions undertaken within a wider framework of the Association of South East Asian Nations (ASEAN) + 1 or ASEAN + 3. For example, the formation of the ASEAN as a regional collaborative framework is a case in point (see Mok's Chapter 9 in this volume). When examining elements of "governance" that enter into regulatory regulation, we must ask the following questions: Are there ways to articulate the dynamic tensions that exist such that some forms of homogenization occur simultaneously with differentiation? Our present volume clearly indicates that when analyzing regional cooperation or competition among Asian universities in general and governmental cooperation in particular, we must not treat such processes as mutually exclusive. The regional platforms that Asian governments have been involved with like ASEAN and other regional cooperative frameworks closely interact with the regional cooperation venues spontaneously emerging from academic and research organizations such as different forms of academic and research associations, societies, or consortium. We would conceptualize government-driven regional cooperation like ASEAN and Asia Pacific Economic Cooperation (APEC) as a "hard approach," while the regional collaborations initiating from individuals and universities or other kinds of research/academic organizations as "soft approach" of regional cooperation.

The central feature of the hard approach is a top-down orientation, normally driven by the nation state and a governance style that is much more "centralized." Unlike the hard approach, the soft approach is far more bottom up, normally driven by local forces and organic in nature, with emphasis on network governance. We may argue that the hard approach would shape national policy directly; however, the soft approach would also influence national strategy and policy since governmentally driven cooperation and the nongovernmentally driven variety are not entirely exclusive but complementary to each other. Deepening regional cooperation in the context of an increasingly competitive environment would certainly require that both the structural and soft approaches interact to maximize the "political capital" generated from the governmentally driven cooperation frameworks and the "network capital" generated from organically formed regional cooperation platforms. Empirical evidence can be found in support of the interactional relationship between hard and soft approaches when analyzing regional cooperation in Asia. Taiwan, for instance, finding difficulty in asserting its national status because of the "One China" issue, has sought different ways to assert its influence through engagement in a variety of regional/international cooperation venues such as academic/research consortia, associations, and societies; while mainland China has also taken more active approach in asserting its regional and global leadership through participating in different forms of regional organizations spontaneously evolving from local/regional communities (Chen 2011).

More importantly, another major observation that needs to be highlighted here is that when analyzing regional cooperation, we must note that regionalism is not a single phenomenon but a set of complex and complicated processes showing subregionalism emerging from regionalism, which requires us to closely examine different forms and natures of regional cooperative frameworks. In addition, we must also note that interregionalism does happen when education delivery and provision are no longer confined to a single geographical location. The rise of transnational education and the adoption of advanced technology in delivering education has made interactions between different "educational territories" more frequent. The growing popularity of joint programs or dual degrees has made conventional a QA system bounded by national borders inappropriate and accordingly more flexibility and innovative measures have been developed to foster deep cooperation between institutions and to accommodate regional collaboration. However, the drive for more regional cooperation also generates tensions in the foreign-policy mix of education, trade, and development. Most important of all, we should also note that the interregional structures themselves also carry their own politics, which in turn shape the terrain of education (Robertson 2008).

Redefining the State–Market–Civil Society and Professional Organization Relationship

The rise of transnational education, together with the increase of regional cooperation, has unquestionably challenged the conventional arrangements for education governance, especially for those countries that have heavily relied on the "centralized governance model." In particular, the proliferation of education providers in Asia has created pressure for governments to rethink their governance model by involving other non-state actors such as the market, civil society, MNCs, and international professional and accreditation organizations in education governance. This leads to the observation that often when societies adopt market rhetoric and practices, events are structured so that the market decides and the state frequently does not provide services when this shift happens. The regulation responsibility does not get carried out as it should. In some public-sector HE institutions that have been privatized, the pressure to diversify income leads to the creation of shadow courses whose primary purpose (some would say: sole purpose) is to generate income. The public sector in all too many instances is now not well regulated, while the private sector is even less so, and the transnationals least well. In this connection, the state, as the ultimate agent responsible for the public interest, cannot really "let go" of the quality issue in education, but various trends are emerging in regulatory arrangements like "deregulatory regulation," "regulated deregulation," "centralized decentralization," and "decentralized centralization" to promote new QA mechanisms in the effort to uphold quality. It is in this context that we anticipate more involvement of international and transitional professional and accreditation organizations and that the role of civil society (in representing consumer interest) will become far more significant in education governance (Mok 2008a).

Part Three

The Variety of "Asias"

It has been argued that the "Asia" region is a highly complex set of nations and subregions and that there are forces and factors that are both conducive to "regional harmonization" and those that are unfavorable to such formations – for example, centripetal and centrifugal forces and factors (see and Knight's and Hawkins's chapters (2 and 11, respectively) in this volume). Put differently, the validity of the notion of regionalization assumes, to some degree, that there are "center" forces that take the leadership and "periphery" locations that follow this leadership. Historically, for East Asia, the center may be said to have been China as Chinese thought and institutions prevailed and formed a kind of regionalization in what has since become known as "Greater China." In that same region, later in the mid-twentieth century, Japan for a period sought to become the center economically and militarily. Much the same historical model occurred in South Asia with India playing the centrist role culturally and to some degree economically. These two large subregions of Asia became known by some cultural geographers as Sinified Asia and Indianized Asia.

It is far more arguable now to say that in fact the region is constituted out of multiple centers, reflecting variable social indicators. At any one time one might identify an economic center that has moved from China to Japan, and now back to China in the case of East Asia, and from the newly emerging Southeast Asian nations of Singapore and Malaysia to formations such as ASEAN seeking, among other things, to provide some competition to the larger East Asian and South Asian economies. Another center might be focused on media and technology, yet another on high-quality education, and so on. This multiplicity of "centers" with their corresponding "peripheries" is just one way to look at the shifting nature of regionalization in Asia. In this sense, centers and peripheries consist of nation states and/or regional bodies (such ASEAN) and presuppose some degree of cohesion whether cultural (as in Greater China and ASEAN) or economic (as in Japan's earlier leadership).

However, it can also be argued that the forces that work against regionalization are equally powerful. While nations may cluster around a particular country or association at any one time, there is ample evidence that very significant barriers to regionalization present themselves in the context of historical and cultural rivalries, strategic concerns, and scale and scope. These barriers have proved to be formidable and are likely with respect to

HE to present obstacles to regionalization efforts in East, Southeast, and South Asia. There is, for example, considerable concern over China's rise in the region, prompting some nations to welcome the current US administration's own version of "look east" as President Obama announced at the recent APEC meetings in Honolulu (November 2011). Thus, there is a complex constellation of "regional" interests that flow out of the multiple circuits of exchange that are present in student and faculty mobility and migration, and shared interests that emerge around globalization (as discussed by Mok 2010). These forces come up against the barriers discussed above to form a kind of ebb tide of regionalization efforts and institutions and associations in the region.

Related to this notion of multiple centers or vectors in the context of the "region" of Asia is the emergence of differential, often national specific HE management and governance regimes over the past decade. Four principal reasons for shifting patterns of governance and management might be cited:

- Growing demand for HE, limited resources = more competition;
- Change in public management governance;
- Rise of the knowledge economy; and
- Massification of HE and quality control.

This shift came on the heels of a parallel shift in what might be called "belief" systems of the purposes of HE: Does such an entity exist primarily as a cultural institution or as a public service institution (including in many cases the promotion of research and innovation)? In the Asia region, the shift seems to be clearly toward HE as a service institution, which in turn helped bring about the idea of managerialism, and a movement toward a contractual model and away from a more democratic egalitarian model. This form of public management is a mix of procedural freedom and responsibilities, utilitarian goals, state guidance of research and development (R&D), and continued state oversight. In the Asian region, the new management model has been primarily a modernization device for state action – a means to strengthen market mechanisms, decentralize decision-making powers, and privatize public enterprises, all of which lead to the "supervisory state." Universities need to have a corporate identity in order to operate in this mode.

In addition, HE systems in the region have become increasingly differentiated as access has expanded. Another factor in changing governance has been the globalization of research, which has brought with it a more managerial approach to funding and accountability. On the one hand, formerly centralized systems have decentralized bringing a degree of institutional autonomy and at the same time (ironically) more regulation often referred to as "steering" from the central authorities. Two important terms in the complex relations between governments and universities are (as several of our contributors point out) "autonomy" and "accountability" – the former meaning the freedom and power to govern without undue outside controls, and the latter requiring the demonstration of responsible actions. These relations are, however, more complicated, and when one adds academic freedom, you get three concepts: academic freedom – freedom of the individual scholar to pursue research wherever it leads without fear of sanction; substantive autonomy – the power of the university in its corporate form to determine its own goals and programs; and procedural autonomy – the power of the university to determine the means of achieving its goals. All these have implications for accountability. If the state intervenes in procedural autonomy, it might be a bother but can be understood. If it intervenes in substantive matters, then it is infringing on the heart of the academy.

This phenomenon and its complexity for regional development have been illuminated best by Cummings et al. (2011). They document empirically how the academic profession has reacted to the external drivers that have pressed for a more privatized approach to HE and research with a parallel reliance on technology and maximization of efficiency measures. The academic profession's belief that this represents a departure from more traditional academic belief systems and cultures and has generally been imposed from above corresponds to a more general departure from national specific governance and management processes toward more regional meta-standards. This has set up a tension between academics, more inclined to joint consultation if not shared governance, and external drivers associated with privatization and marketization. These are forces that are of course not restricted to Asia but occur throughout both mature systems and emerging systems (Japan, Korea, and Hong Kong are represented in the study with respect to the East Asia regionalization focus).

In this volume, Lee (Chapter 10) makes the more specific case for those institutions in the Asian region most affected by these external drivers, especially restructured universities, involved in corporatization and institutional autonomy. While there may be more autonomy as a result of these broader, region-wide forces, a decline in faculty governance and collegial academic decision making has also occurred. What does this mean for governance and management for the region as a whole? What are the implications for the concept of regionalization and what it means for HE in general? There are obvious examples of these linkages in the observable rise of region-wide QA values and beliefs, as well as more specific policies such as accreditation.

To just focus on one of these trends, in a recent survey of 20 APEC nations by A. Stella to assess QA trends in the region, it was found that five such trends were predominant (Stella 2011). First, among educational policy makers in such diverse settings as Vietnam and Japan, it was found that there has been an ever-increasing interest and attention paid to the concept of QA. Second, there is a parallel increasingly shared understanding of what quality and QA means among QA professionals. Third, there is increasing interest in the recent rise of various QA networks that cut across the region. Fourth, this has been translated into a desire for deeper co-operation among countries and their QA agencies. Finally, policy makers in the region favorably view the search for common codes and guidelines of what constitute good practices in education. These five trends, she suggests, provide a basis to argue that in this one area, of QA, the Asian region is positioned for a regional QA strategy.

What are the implications of such regional strategies for the future development of HE in Asia? The discussion above shows that there are a number of implications for the proper role of the state vis-à-vis the private sector, and regionalization in these forms as well as others has a very real impact on the quality of academic life and behavior. Whether this impact will prove to benefit the research and teaching missions of the academy remains to be seen.

Notes

1. The literature on these aspects of contemporary globalization has become vast. See by way of example Harvey 1989, 2011; Steger and Roy 2010; Stiglitz 2010.
2. The Lisbon Strategy aims at making the EU the world's "most dynamic and competitive economy," and in respect of higher education, it has particularly focused on the challenges of knowledge economy and the necessity of innovation.
3. In 1999, the education ministers of 29 European countries and European university heads met to discuss the future development of European higher education, and subsequently issued the Bologna Declaration.
4. "Convinced that the establishment of the European area of higher education required constant support, supervision and adaptation to the continuously evolving needs" (Bologna Declaration 1999), the European education ministers decided to meet regularly to assess progress, thus transforming this commitment into an ongoing policy process.

References

Chen, S. J. 2011. "The Quest for World Class Status: The Reposition of Universities in East Asian Region." Paper presented at the Symposium of *Managing the Global Pressure for University Ranking: Responses from East Asian Region* at the Annual Conference of the Comparative Education Society of Hong Kong 2011, The Hong Kong Institute of Education, Hong Kong, February 19, 2011.

Dale, R., and S. Robertson. 2002. "The Varying Effects of Regional Organizations as Subjects of Globalization of Education." *Comparative Education Review* 46 (1): 10–36.

Deem, R., K. H. Mok, and L. Lucas. 2008. "Transforming Higher Education in Whose Image? Exploring the Concept of the 'World-Class' University in Europe and Asia." *Higher Education Policy* 21 (1): 83–97.

Harvey, D. 1989. *The Condition of Postmodernity*. Oxford: Oxford University Press.

Harvey, D. 2011. The Enigma of Capital: And the Crises of Capitalism. Oxford: Oxford University Press.

Hershock, P. 2011. "Information and Innovation in a Global Knowledge Society: Implications for Higher Education." In *The Emergent Knowledge Society and the Future of Higher Education: Asian Perspectives*, ed. Deane E. Neubauer. New York and London: Routledge.

Locke, William, William K. Cummings, and Donald Fisher, eds. 2011. *The Changing Academy – The Changing Academic Profession in International Comparative Perspective*, vol. 1 and 2. 1st ed., XVII, 390 p. 40 illus.

Mok, K. H. 2008a. "Varieties of Regulatory Regimes in Asia: The Liberalization of the Higher Education Market and Changing Governance in Hong Kong, Singapore and Malaysia." *The Pacific Review* 21 (2): 147–170.

Mok, K. H. 2008b. "Positioning as Regional Hub of Higher Education: Changing Governance and Regulatory Reforms in Singapore and Malaysia." *International Journal of Educational Reform* 17 (3): 230–250.

Mok, K. H. 2010. *The Search for New Governance of Higher Education in Asia*. New York: Palgrave MacMillan.

Robertson, S. L. 2008. " 'Europe/Asia' Regionalism, Higher Education and the Production of World Order." *Policy Futures in Education* 6 (6): 718–728.

Robertson, S. L. 2009. "The EU, 'Regulatory State Regionalism' and New Modes of Higher Education Governance." Paper presented to the panel on *Constituting the Knowledge Economy: Governing the New Regional Spaces of Higher Education*, International Studies Association Conference. New York.

Steger, Manfred, and Ravi K. Roy. 2010. *Neoliberalism – A Very Brief Introduction*. Oxford: Oxford University Press.

Stiglitz, Joseph E. 2010. *Freefall: America, Free Markets, and the Sinking of the World Economy*. New York: W.W. Norton and Company.

Stella, A. 2011. "Trends in Quality Assurance in the Broader Asia-Pacific Region: Potential for a Regional Strategy?" Quality in Higher Education: Identifying, Developing and Sustaining Best Practices in the APEC Region. Honolulu, Hawai'i, USA, August 4–6, 2011.

Index

Note: References to illustrations are printed in bold

3 Campus Comparative East Asian Studies, 53, 149

Academic Consortium 21 (AC21), 53
Academic Cooperation Europe South East Asia Support (ACESS), 40
academic freedom, 163, 203
Academic Ranking of World Universities (ARWU), 68, 73
accreditation, 8, 12, 21, 23, 40, 58, 61, 100, 105, 124–5, **125–6**, 129, 131, 141, 143, 148, 166, 168–9, 171–3, 200, 204
Afghanistan, 59
Africa, 20–1, 33, 43, 48, 81, **120**, 127
   African Quality Rating Mechanism, 21
   African Union, 21
   AfriQAN, 21
   Arusha Convention on the Recognition of Qualifications, 21
   Francophone Africa, 20
   Nyerere African Scholarship scheme, 21
   Open Education Africa project, 21
   Pan-African University, 21
   Sub-Saharan Africa, 20
alignment, 19, 21, 23, **26**, 27, 29, **31**, 32, 81, 178, 185, 192–3, 195
   misalignment, 193
Arab States, 20, 25, 98, **101**

Asia Cooperation Dialogue (ACD), 7
Asia Europe Meeting (ASEM), 7, 39
Asia Link Program, 181
Asia Pacific Association of International Education (APAIE), 41, 53
Asia Pacific Economic Cooperation (APEC), 7, **31**, 32, 39–40, 45, 49, 74, 97, 152, 154, 179, 199, 202, 204
Asia Pacific Quality Network (APQN), 8–9, 21–2, **31**, 42, 49, 56, 57
Asia Pacific Regional Bureau for Education, **31**, 50, 181
Asian Association of Open Universities (AAOU), 41
Asian Barometer, 32–3
Asian Development Bank, **31**, 45, 93, 182
Asian Education and Development Studies, 149–50
Asian Free Trade Area (AFTA), 147
Asian University Federation (AUF), 41
Association of East Asian Research Universities (AEARU), **31**, 53, 88, 148
Association of Pacific Rim Universities (APRU), **31**, 41, 49, 53, 80, 88, 91, 184
   APRU World Institute (AWI), 53

Association of Quality Assurance Agencies of the Islamic World (AQAAIW), 58
Association of Southeast Asian Institutions of Higher Learning (ASAIHL), 31, 41, 53, 148
Association of South East Asian Nations (ASEAN), 4, 7, 11, 22, **31**, 32, 39, 43, 45, 48–54, 57, 60–2, 73–5, 79–80, 82, **84**, 86–7, 89, 91–2, 95, 97, 103–4, 109–10, 130, 144, 146–9, 151–5, 157, 178–9, 181–3, 198–9, 201
  ASEAN economic community (AEC), 146–7
  ASEAN EU University Network Program (AUNP), 53, 181
  ASEAN Higher Education Clusters, 22
  ASEAN India Academic Exchanges, 53
  ASEAN Quality Assurance Network (AQAN), 22, 39, 43, 49, 57, 75, 148
  ASEAN Regional Credit Transfer System, 22, **31**, 97, 182
  ASEAN Regional Forum (ARF), 152
  ASEAN regional groupings, 7, 22–3, **31**, 32, 39, 50, 74, 86, 146, 151, 179, 182–3, 198
  ASEAN Regional Research Citation Index, 22, **31**, 39
  ASEAN security community (ASC), 146
  ASEAN socio-cultural community (ASCC), 146–7
  ASEAN Student Exchange Program, 51
  ASEAN University Network (AUN), 22, **31**, 39, 49, 51–2, 61–2, 147, 181; AUN-Quality Assurance (AUN-QA), 57
  ASEAN Vision 2020, 51, 146
  Bali Concord II, 147
  Hanoi Plan of Action, 147
  Vientiane Action Program 2004–2010 (VAP), 147
  AUN/Southeast Asia Engineering Education Development Network (AUN/SEED-Net), **31**, 49, 51
Australia, 22, 39, 41, 56, 58, 68, 70, 84, 92–4, 103, 140, 144, 149, 152, 180, 183, 197
  James Cook University, 144
  Australian Universities Quality Agency, 58

Bangladesh, 59, **101**, 141
BESETOHA forum, 53, 88–9
Bhutan, 59
bilateral trade agreements, 7, 178, 187
Bologna Process, 7, 9, 12, 17, 21, 24, 33, 39, 56, 97, 145, 149, 156–7, 180–2, 184–5, 198, 204
Botswana, **101**
Brisbane Communiqué, **31**, 56
Buddhism, 93–4, 102
Burma, *see* Myanmar

Cambodia, **33**, 89, 102, 149, 151, 169
  Accreditation Committee of Cambodia, 169
  Public Administrative Institutions (PAI), 169
  Royal Decree on the Legal Status of Public Administrative Institutions, 169
Campus Asia, 9, 22, **31**, 32, 60–2, 69, 74–7, 80
Canada, 39
  Canadian International Development Agency, 39
  International Development Research Centre, 39
  University of British Columbia, 39; Community-based Watershed Management, 39; Localized

Poverty Reduction in Vietnam Project, 39
Caribbean, 23, 178
centers of excellence, 21, 30, 71
Central Asia, 32
centrifugal forces, 14, 178–9, 183–7, 192, 201
centripetal forces, 14, 178, 183, 185–7, 192, 201
Chiba Principles, **31**, 57
China, 6–9, 22, **31**, 32, **33**, 38–9, 46, 48, 52, 56, 59–60, 63, 68–70, 72–6, 79–89, 92, 100–4, 109–10, 138, 141, 144, 148–54, 157, 170, 172, 179, 181–3, 185, 194, 196–7, 199, 201–2
   211 project, 138
   985 project, 138
   Beijing, 53, 59, 88, 102, 182
   Beijing Olympics, 80, 88
   Directorate of Private Higher Education, 105
   dynasties, 102–3
   Fudan University School of Management, 52
   Hong Kong, 10, 14, 41, 53, 56, 68, 73, 75–6, 119, 148–51, 155, 157, 197, 203
   National Accreditation Committee, 105
   Nottingham University, 38
   Office of the Chinese Language Council International, 59
   People's Republic of China, 74, 81
   University of Hong Kong, 53, 149
   university structural reorganization, 170–1
   yayasans (foundations), 105–6, 140
China Civil Aviation Management Institute, 81
China Free Trade Area, 79
China Social Science Citation Index (CSSCI), 150

China's National Plan for Medium and Long-term Education Reform and Development (2010–2020), 87
Chinese Academy of Sciences, 81
Christianity, 93–4, 151
circuits of exchange, 6, 14, 181, 193, 196, 202
citizenship, 13, 34, 88
Confucius Institutes, 59, 80, 104, 148
Copenhagen process, 56
credit transfer, 22, **31**, 38–9, 74, 97, 145, 169, 180, 182, 184–5, 198
cross-border programs, 30, 46, 48, 59
   see also transnational programs
currency, 5, 9, 25, 95, 196

degree, 21, 26, 38, 42–3, 48, 53, 59, 75, 83–5, 88, 99, 117–19, 121, 123–4, 130, 141, 143, 145, 150, 156–7, 159, 165, 182, 184, 186, 198, 200
   Doctorate (PhD), 26, 124
   Masters (MA), 26, 98
   undergraduate (BA), 26
Deutsch, Karl, 5
Dubai, 156
   S. P. Jain Center of Management, 143, 156
Dutch Maritime Institute, 141

East Asia Four Universities Forum, 53
East Asia Vision Group (EAVG), 181–2
East Asian Summit (EAS), **31**, 39, 51, 60, 152
East–West Center, 3
East Timor, 151
Egypt, 98, 140
   Al Azhar, 98, 101
English, 23, 25, 48, 54, 59, 70, 73, 80, 119, 133, 149
engineering, **31**, 49, 52, 80, 85, **86**, 96, 123, 129–30, 140, 143–4

ENLACES, 23
Erasmus Process, 7, 61, 180–1
Europe, 5, 7, 9, 13, 18, 20–1, 24, **31**, 33, 39–40, 43, 48, 52, 56, 61, 73, 81–4, 87–8, 91–2, 100, 119, **120**, 137, 145–6, 149, 154, 156–7, 164, 178–80, 183–4, 195, 198, 204
Eastern Europe, 20
European Commission, 39
European Council, 145, 198
European Higher Education Area, 145–6, 157, 180, 198, 204
European Union, 13, 39, 52, 84, 91, 145, 178, 198

Foreign Trade Agreements (FTAs), 183
France, 181
funding, 30, 37, 71, 109, 140, 162–3, 166–7, 173, 178–9, 182, 197, 202

General Agreement on Trade and Services (GATS), 7, 118, 133
general education, 127, 172
Germany, 81
global citizenship, 34, 88
global financial crisis, 74, 80, 93
Global Initiative on Quality Assurance Capacity (GIQAC), 8
global knowledge system, 91–2, 106
global recession, 194–5
globalization, 3–5, 7, 9, 40, 50, 58, 81, 145, 151, 178–9, 191–5, 198, 202, 204
graduate program, **31**, 50, 60, 70–2, 84–5, 98, 140, 142–3
gross domestic product (GDP), 67–8, 81, 87, 93, 110, 122, 144, 182, 196

human resources, 49, 53, 55, 57, 61, 69–70, 72, 142, 147, 156, 170
hybrid regionalism, 46–7

IESALC, 23
see also UNESCO
immigration, 54, 61, 128, 144

India, 22, 39, 53, 59–60, 63, 69, 76, 144, 150–2, 172, 181, 195, 201
National Assessment and Accreditation Council (NAAC), 172
University Grants Commission, 172
Indonesia, 6, 8, 22, **31**, **33**, 39, 68, 82, **83**, 91–110, 141, 151, 166, 195
Badan Hukum Milik Negera (BHMN), 96, 108
Basic Education Law of 1950, 98
Constitutional Court, 109
Department of Finance, 96
Department of Home Affairs, 96
Department of National Education (DNE), 96
Exploration of a Common Space conference, 97
extension courses, 108–9
Institute of Agriculture Bogor (Institut Pertanian Bogor [IPB]), 166
Institute of Islamic Higher Learning (IAIN), 98–9
Institute of Technology Bandung (ITB), 166
Jakarta, 94, 98–9, 103–4
Jalur Khusus ("Special Passage"), 108–9
Java, 93, 96, 99, 102
Korupsi, Kolusi, dan Nepotisme (KNN), 95, 107
Law 22, 96
Ministry of Education and Culture, 96
Ministry of National Education (MNE), 95a
Ministry of Religious Affairs (MORA), 92, 95–7, 99, 106–7, 109
supervised universities, 99
Office of Private Higher Education, 108
religious groups, 93–4
Res Publica University, 103–4
Sumatra, 94, 99, 102

Index

Taman Siswa (Pupils' Garden), 99
Universitas Gadjah Mada in Yogyakarta (UGM), 166
Universitas Indonesia (UI), 166
Indonesian Islamic University, 98
Information and Computing Technology (ICT), 21
Institut Européen d'Administration des Affaires (INSEAD), 143
institutional autonomy, 88, 161–74
   financial autonomy, 164, 166–7
   interventional autonomy, 164
   organizational autonomy, 164
   policy autonomy, 164
   procedural autonomy, 163, 203
   substantive autonomy, 87, 163, 203
International Alliance of Research Universities (IARU), 53
International Association of Universities (IAU), 53
International Forum for Education 2020 (IFE 2020), 3
International Forum of Public Universities (IFPU), 53
International Monetary Fund (IMF), 93
International Network for Quality Assurance Agencies in Higher Education (INQAAHE), 56–7
internationalization, 19, 21, 29, 34, 42, 47, 49, 52, 69–72, 76, 80, 83–4, 88, 128–9, 137, 139, 148, 167, 178
Iran, 101
Islam, 58, 92, 94, 98–102, 107, 109
   Federation of the Universities of the Islamic World, 100
   fundamentalist organizations, 94
   International Islamic University of Malaysia (IIUM), 100
   Muhammadijah (The Way of Muhammad), 99
   Nahdatul 'Ulaama [NU] (Awakening of Islamic Scholars), 99
   Organization of the Islamic Conference (OIC), 100
   see also Muslim

Japan, 8–9, 22, 25, **31**, 32, **33**, 35, 39, 41, 46, 48, 52, 59–60, 67–77, 79, 81–3, **83**, **84**, 86, 100, 104, 119, 148–9, 151–2, 154, 171–3, 179, 181–3, 185, 187, 195, 201, 203–4
   21st Century Centers for Excellence (COE21s), 71
   Democratic Party of Japan (DPJ), 69
   Funding Program for World-Leading Innovative R&D on Science and Technology, 71
   Global Centers of Excellence, 71
   Hiroshima University, 70
   Keio University, 52–3, 149
   Kobe University, 70
   Liberal Democratic Party (LDP), 74
   Ministry of Economics, Trade and Industry, 72
   Ministry of Education, Culture, Sports, Science and Technology (MEXT), 72
   Nagoya University, 68, 70
   National Accreditation System, 171
   Tokai University, 70
   Tokyo, 68, 74, 157, 182, 187–9
   Toyama Plan, 71
   University of Tokyo, 9, 68, 89
   World Premier International Research Center Initiative, 71
Japan–China–Korea Committee for Promoting Exchange and Cooperation, 74
Japan–China–Republic of Korea Trilateral Summit, 74
Japanese Prime Ministers, 70, 74–5
Japanese university rankings, 68
joint-degree program, 52, 143, 150, 200
Jordan, 140

Kazakhstan, 79
Korea, 8–9, 22, **31**, 32, **33**, 39, 41, 48, 52, 59–60, 68–70, 72–6, 81–3, **83**, **84**, 86, 110, 138, 148–9, 151–2, 157, 159, 171, 179, 181, 185, 195, 203

Korea University, 52
knowledge economy, 18, 137, 144, 156, 202, 204
knowledge society, 4, 60, 162
Kyrgy, 79

language, 5, 22–4, 46, 48, 54, 59, 61, 71, 73, 80, 84–5, **86**, 94, 97, 132, 178, 184–5
see also English
Laos, **33**, 102, 149, 157
Latin America, 20, 23
Latin America and the Caribbean Area for Higher Education, 23
Law on Educational Decentralization, 105
liberalization, 8
Libya, 101
Lisbon Strategy, 145, 156, 198, 204

Malaysia, 10, 22, **31**, **33**, 38–9, 56, 58, 68, 73, 76, 97–101, 103, 138–42, 144, 150, 155–7, 165–6, 195, 197, 201
  Educity in Iskandar Malaysia, 141
  international branch campuses, 100, 139–42
  Klang Valley, 139, 141
  Kuala Lumpur, 139, 141, 148
  Kuala Lumpur Declaration, 148
  Kuala Lumpur Education City (KLEC), 141
  Lembaga Akreditasi Negara (National Accreditation Board), 141
  Ministry of Education (MOE), 139, 141–3, 156;
  Quality Assurance Division, 141
  Ministry of Higher Education (MOHE), 139
  Monash University, 38, 140
  National Higher Education Action Plan, 139
  National Higher Education Strategic Plan 2020, 139
  Nottingham University, 38, 139–40
  Open University Malaysia, 38
  Report by the Committee to Study, Review and Make Recommendations Concerning the Development and Direction of Higher Education in Malaysia (Halatuju Report), 139
  Transformation of Higher Education Document, 139
  Universities and University Colleges Act of 1971, 165
Malaysian Qualifications Agency (MQA), 140–1, 157, 166
Malaysian Qualifications Framework (MQF), 141
Malaysian Qualifications Register (MQR), 140
Maldives, 59
marketization, 72, 203
Middle East, 48, 61, 98–9, 101, 119–20, **120**, 141
migration, 4, 12, 103, 118, 195–6, 202
Ministry of Education, 9, 58, 72–3, 77, 89, 95–6, 100, 139, 141–4, 156, 164, 166, 171–2
MIT (Malaysia, Indonesia, Thailand) Student Mobility Scheme, 22, **31**, 39, 97, 104
multinational corporations (MNCs), 197, 200
Muslim, 93–4, 99–102
see also Islam
Myanmar, **33**, 102, 149, 151

nation states, 5, 12–14, 20, 137, 145, 201
nationalism, 5, 178, 182
neoliberalism, 7–8, 110, 162, 178–9
Nepal, 59
New Zealand, 22, 39, 56, 58, 84, 140, 149, 152
New Zealand Qualifications Authority, 58
Nigeria, 101

nongovernmental organization (NGO), 37–8, 41–3, 47, 148
Northeast Asia (NEA), 32, 73, 75, 183
nursing, 118–19, 121, 123, 126, 129–31

Observatory on Borderless Higher Education, 140
Organization for Economic Development (OECD), 55–6, 58, 76, 84

Pacific Islands Forum (PIF), 43
Pacific Rim, **31**, 32, 40–1, 49, 80, 87, 91, 184
Pakistan, 59
Pan-Asia, 22, 32
Paris
  Institute for Research and Education on Education (IRENE), 144
Philippine Commission on Higher Education (CHED), 117–18, 122, 124, 126, 128–33, 168
Philippine Overseas Employment Administration (POEA), 119–20
Philippine Survey and Research Center, 123
Philippines, **33**, 89, 95, 98, 101, 117–33, 151, 168, 195–6
  Accrediting Agency of Chartered Colleges and Universities in the Philippines (AACUP), 124
  Ateneo University, 129
  Bureau of Immigration and Deportation, 128
  Commission of Higher Education (CHED), 168
  De La Salle University, 129
  Department of Education (DepEd), 127
  Department of Foreign Affairs, 128
  Educational Associations Federation of Accrediting Agencies of the Philippines (FAAP), 124

Filipino domestic helpers (DHs), 119
Higher Education Act of 1994, 168
Memo Order, 128
overseas Filipino workers (OFWs), 118–19, 120, 122
Professional Regulation Commission (PRC), 129
state universities and colleges (SUCs), 122, 131–2
University of Sto, 129
University of the Philippines, 129
population growth, 37, 141, 171, 194–6
population movements, 4
President Obama, 82, 202
privatization, 47, 72, 96, 164, 203
Program for International Student Assessment (PISA), 12
Proliferation Security Initiatives (PSI), 155

quality assurance, 8, 17, 21–3, 25, 30, **31**, 39–40, 42–3, 46, 49, 54–8, 62, 74–5, 100, 107, **125**, 131, 140–1, 145, 148, 156, 166, 169, 173, 178, 198

Raffles Education Corp, 144
Regional Institute for Higher Education Development (RIHED), 22, 39, 52, 97, 179
regional organizations (ROs), 177–81, 183–6
Rozman, Gilbert, 182, 184
Russia, 23, 32, **83**, 146, 181, 198

satellite campuses, 122, 168
Saudi Arabia, **101**
Scalapino, Robert, 183–4
scholarship, 55, 89, 93–4, 98, 109, 128, 138, 143, 150, 155, 181
science, 9–10, 40, 50–1, 56, 60, 70–2, 81, 85, **86**, 98, 100–1, 129, 140–1, 143–4, 147–50, 157, 170–2, 192

Shanghai Cooperation Organization, 86, 155
Shanghai Jiaotong top 500, 100
Singapore, 6, 10, **33**, 52, 58, 68, 73, 76, 87, 103, 110, 119, 138, 141–4, 149–50, 155–6, 166, 173, 197, 201
  Economic Development Board (EDB), 142, 156
  global school project, 138, 142–6
  International Enterprise Singapore, 143
  Nanyang Technological University, 143, 166
  National University of Singapore, 52, 143, 166
  Singapore Management University (SMU), 166
  SPRING Singapore, 143
  Tourism Board, 143
  University Association Quality Assurance Network, 58
  University Endowment Fund, 166
  Wawasan 2020 (Vision 2020), 138–9, 156
Singapore Education, 143
Singapore–MIT (Massachusetts Institute of Technology) Alliance (SMA), 143
socialist countries, 81, 170
Socrates Program, 180–1
soft power, 59, 67, 144, 150–1, 166, 197
software, 5
South Asia, 32
South Asian Association for Regional Cooperation (SAARC), 43, 46, 79–80
South Asian University (SAU), 59–60
South East Asia Engineering Education Development Network (SEAEEDN), 80
South East Asian Credit Transfer system (SEA-CTS), 97
South East Asian Ministers of Education Organization (SEAMEO), 7, 10, 22, **31**, 39, 43, 45, 49, 51–2, 80, 95, 97, 109, 148–9, 157, 179, 181–2, 184–5
South Korea, 39, 41, 48, 52, 59–60, 69–70, 72–3, 75–6, 138, 149, 152, 157, 171–2
  Brain 21 Project, 138
  Korea University Business School, 52
  Seoul, 53, 59, 89, 154, 157
  Yonsei University, 52–3, 149
Southeast Asia (SEA), 6, 10, 20–2, **31**, 32, 39–41, 49, 51, 53, 70, 76, 80, 91–110, 138, 146, 148–9, 150, 157, 179, 183, 201–2
Soviet model of higher education, 170
Sri Lanka, 59
student mobility schemes, 21–2, 30
Sudan, **101**

Taiwan, 6, 32, **33**, 41, 68, 70, 75, 84, 89, 110, 138, 148–51, 153, 157, 195, 199
  National Taiwan University, 150
  Taiwan Social Science Citation Index (TSSCI), 150
Tajikistan, 79
Thailand, 6, 8, 22, **31**, **33**, 39, 41, 58, 68, 82, **83**, 89, 97–9, 100–2, 151, 167, 173, 181
  Bangkok, 50, 75, 97
  Chulalongkorn University, 181
  Higher Education Long Range Plan (1990–2004), 167
  National Education Standards and Quality Assessment, 58
  Ninth Higher Education Development Plan (2002–2006), 167
  Office of the National Education Standards and Quality Assessment (ONESQA), 167
  Second 15-year Long Term Plan for Higher Education (2008–2022), 167

transnational higher education (TNHE), 137–9, 141–5, 150–1
transnational programs, 48–9, 55, 58–9, 62, 139–44, 156, 197, 200
  3 program types, 49
  see also cross-border programs
transnationalization, 12, 137
Tri-lateral Summit, 22, **31**
twinning programs, 38, 128, 139–40

undergraduate programs, 50, 53, 71, 98, 118, 140, 142, 156
United Board for Christian Higher Education, 151
United Kingdom, 56, 70, 72, 141, 197
  Marlborough College, 141
  Newcastle University, 141
  Nottingham University, 38, 139–40
United Nations Charter, 146
United Nations Education, Scientific, and Cultural Organization (UNESCO), 8, 21, 23, **31**, 38–40, 42, 45, 49, 55–6, 181–2, 194
  2009 UNESCO World Conference of Higher Education, 38
  Asia Pacific Education Research Association (APERA), 40
  Association of Universities in Asia-Pacific (AUAP), 40
  Global University Network for Innovation (GUNI), 40
  Massachusetts Institute of Technology (MIT), 143
  Regional Convention on the Recognition of Studies, Diplomas and Degrees in Higher Education in Asia and the Pacific, 42
  UNESCO Institute for Higher Education in Latin America and the Caribbean, 23
  University Network and Twinning Programme (UNITWIN)/ UNESCO Chairs, 40

United Nations General Assembly, 154
United States, 9, 22, 32, 48, 52, 54, 56, 59, 70, 72–6, 79, 82–3, 114, 118–19, 121, 140, 154–5, 180, 182, 197
  DigiPen Institute of Technology, 143
  New York University's Tisch School of the Arts, 143
  University of California, 178
  University of Chicago, 142–3
  US Department of Education, 73
Universitas 21, 38, 53
Universities, see country of origin
University Mobility in Asia Pacific (UMAP), 22, **31**, 41, 49, 181
University Credit Transfer System (UCTS), 185
university rankings, 73
  see also ARWU
Uzbekistan, 59, 79

Vietnam, **33**, 38–9, 53, 81–2, **83**, 87, 89, 102, 149, 151, 168–9, 195, 204
  Hanoi, 53, 147, 169
  Ho Chi Min City, 169
  Localized Poverty Reduction in Vietnam Project, 39
  RMIT University, 38
  see also Canada
visa, 54, 121–2

West Asia, 32
World Bank, 8, 42, 93, 95, 107, 121, 182
World Trade Organization (WTO), 7, 80–1, 178, 182
World Trade Economic Forum, 154
World University Federation, 41
World War II, 118, 145, 198
world-class universities, 68, 71, 73, 145, 151, 198

Yemen, 101